Estimates of different prices of Building &c.

Lime Work either Houses or [...] being laid down Vizt.

Parks or Garden walls Not exceeding
Six feet high 20/ per Rood

Do. Nine or ten feet high 25/ per rood

Office houses or other houses Nine or ten
feet high side Walls 30/ —

Houses two story high Eighteen or twenty
feet in the side Walls 35/ —

Estimates of building dry stone dykes
Six years to the sale

Two feet high 8d Three feet 1/ — four feet 1/[...]
five feet 1/8d

Dry stone Sunk fences to be built four feet
and a half high at 1/ pr. fale the earthen
fence being cleared by the Employer

PRESENTED TO THE LIBRARY OF

in memory of the author

**Freda Ramsay
(1905-1991)**

by her friend
Sandy A. Mactaggart
of Ardmore
Chancellor of the University of Alberta
Edmonton, Canada

THE DAY BOOK OF DANIEL CAMPBELL
OF SHAWFIELD

Also by Freda Ramsay

JOHN RAMSAY OF KILDALTON
Being an Account of his Life in Islay and including
the Diary of his trip to Canada in 1870
Freda Ramsay

AUP Titles of Related Interest

CROMARTIE
Highland Life 1650–1914
Eric Richards and Monica Clough

THE ELGINS 1766–1917
A tale of aristocrats, proconsuls and their wives
Sydney Checkland

AN ALBUM OF SCOTTISH FAMILIES 1694–96
George Home's diary
K&H Kelsall

EMIGRATION FROM NORTH-EAST SCOTLAND
Volume 1: Willing Exiles
Volume 2: Beyond the Broad Atlantic
Margery Harper

The
DAY BOOK
of
DANIEL CAMPBELL
of
SHAWFIELD
1767

with relevant papers concerning the
Estate of Islay

edited and annotated by
FREDA RAMSAY

ABERDEEN UNIVERSITY PRESS
Member of Maxwell Macmillan Publishing Corporation

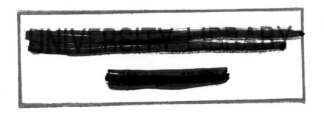

First published 1991
Aberdeen University Press

British Library Cataloguing in Publication Data

The Day book of Daniel Campbell of Shawfield 1767:
with relevant papers concerning the estate of Islay.
 1. Scotland.   Strathclyde Region.   Islay, history
 I. Ramsay, Freda   II. Book of Islay
 941.423

ISBN 0-08-040933-4

Typeset by Macmillan (India) Limited
Printed by Bell and Bain Limited

Q.

²Slip 16. Bir Waheida, was
Bir Waheidi.

A.

Why not? All one place.

An answer from T. E. Lawrence to the Proof-reader of
Revolt in the Desert

*The Day Book of Daniel Campbell
of Shawfield*

is dedicated to the memory of

my father-in-law, Captain Iain Ramsay of Kildalton, whose comprehensive knowledge of Islay History, factual and fictitious, was second to none. Through many difficult times he succeeded in preserving the papers in the Kildalton Charter Chest, from which many of the documents in this book are drawn. To his tutelage I am greatly indebted for such knowledge as I have.

F.R.

Sadly, Freda Ramsay died on 11th September 1991, while this book was in the final stages of production. Although very ill and often in pain during the previous Spring and Summer, she had seen the corrected proofs of the text and the illustrations and could imagine how the book would look in its dust jacket. This work, therefore, stands as a tribute to the memory of both Captain Iain Ramsay of Kildalton and his daughter-in-law, Freda Ramsay.

Foreword

Islay holds a special place in the history of the West Highlands and Islands of Scotland from medieval times to the present and it has been fortunate in receiving the attention of scholars with interests in many aspects of its people's story through the centuries. In the interplay of evidence from written documents, oral tradition and the landscape itself, with its marks of human activity in the form of buildings, dykes, field systems and plantings, a picture emerges of a community with local and particular features as well as characteristics which accord with the history of society in the wider geographical area.

Continuity and change are the twin themes running through the history of the West Highlands and Islands and in no period was this more the case than in the eighteenth century. And while considerable attention has been paid by historians of the Highlands to the political events of the time and their impact on the culture and social relationships of the people, less has been given to the ways in which the principles of agricultural improvement and other estate policies were introduced and implemented.

Without access to the details of eighteenth century estate management and the evidence original documents provide for the effects these had on the lives of all sectors of society – subtenants, tenants, tacksmen – a full understanding of this phase of Scottish history cannot be achieved. The pioneering work of the late Eric R. Cregeen in combining evidence drawn not only from the extensive records of the Argyll Estate (one which acted as a model for others in the area) but also from the rich vein of oral testimony in the form of family and township history and other forms of oral tradition has shown how vital this comparative process can be and how valuable it is to have the raw material provided in documentary sources available in published form for the widest possible use.

The Day Book of Daniel Campbell and the other documents relevant to the history of Islay contained in this volume provide an insight into the community in a period of great change. Here is a rich source of the kind of detail which opens it to investigation: individuals identified by name and often additional information, their townships and occupations their economic resources and their milieu. Communications, both within the island and beyond, are highlighted as are the changing responsibilities of lairds to those linked to them in social and economic terms as older values and traditions of land tenure gave way to new relationships. This interface of continuity and change is an ever-present motif in this volume, and a simple entry such as the payment of salaries to a piper, a schoolmaster and a surgeon serves as a reminder of it.

Of particular interest to many will be the fact that the Islay community represented here is that of the diaspora as well as that at home. The families who left for the New York Colony and the lands known there as the Argyle Patent were the forerunners of a stream of emigrants who have ensured that there are men and women who identify with Islay living in all parts of the world today. There is no doubt in these family histories much to augment the references in this volume, and it will serve as an invaluable sourcebook for all who can claim Islay ancestry.

The history of the Scottish Highlands and Islands, and their emigrant offshoots elsewhere, has often been ill-served by generalisations. But without studies of individual communities, their histories and traditions, the particular details are lacking which can make interpretations truly meaningful and enable them to embrace the variety of experience which characterises Highland society. In this process those with records in their possession have a special responsibility and privilege and that is to ensure that these are available in ways which can make a contribution to the widest possible understanding of the people and their lives and times. For the people of Islay—wherever they are—and for all with an interest in the island and its history, this volume will prove an invaluable resource and will be welcomed with gratitude.

Margaret A. Mackay
School of Scottish Studies
University of Edinburgh

Contents

List of Black & White Illustrations

Endpapers

Front: pp 1 an 2 of Day Book
Back: pp 7 and 8 of Day Book

List of Colour Illustrations

Editor's Note

The Book of Islay, Published in 1895, had at first been compiled from the 17th Century papers in the possession of the Campbells of Shawfield, which fell into the possession of John Ramsay of Kildalton, as Trustee with John Francis Campbell, on the estates of Islay and Woodhall. John Ramsay was a busy man, Distiller, owner of a large Estate and a Member of Parliament, and found that to make as complete a history of Islay as possible, it was necessary to go beyond the papers in his possession. He accomplished a certain amount but had not time before his death in 1892, to do all the necessary research. His widow and his Trustee, James Badenoch Nicholson of Glenbervie, decided to give Gregory Smith, an historian in Edinburgh, the task of collecting as many relevant papers as could be found. The result was a very comprehensive history which covers a period from earliest times to the sale of Islay by the Campbells of Cawdor. The first two Rentals of the Shawfield period were included, leading into the 18th Century.

About half of the original publications, 250 copies, and the documents from the Kildalton Charter Chest, were destroyed by fire when stored, with all the furniture of Kildalton house, in Glasgow during the Great War. To make a complete view of the 18th Century and the gradual modernisation of the Island, these two Rentals are included in the present volume. They help, in some cases, to place the Emigrants to New York State in 1738/39/40. The following papers are a selection of those in the possession of the Islay Estates (John Ramsay having handed over the papers relating to that side of the Island), and those still in the Kildalton Collection, which mercifully had not been stored in Glasgow. They have already proved invaluable for Genealogical research: the great problem always is the incredible repetition of names, but sometimes it is possible with the help of the Baptismal Register to track families. Unfortunately, most present day descendants do not know the Parish, let alone the farm, from which their forbears came.

Please note that, in the eighteenth century, the spellings of all names, for places and people, were by no means standard. Names were spelled phonetically by Scots clerks listening to the slightly varying pronunciations of the different Gaelic-speakers. For example, 'Martin McAlpin, Killinave' (p. 109), 'Martin M'Alpine, Kilneave' (p. 188), 'Martin McAlpine, Kilnave' (p. 209), are all references to the same individual, at the same farm. Even within one document, the spellings can vary. See page 214, 'Storgaig, Storgag, Storkaig', to quote T. E. Lawrence 'all one place'. Likewise, on page 216, 'Neil McCheckeran, Neil McEauchirn, and Neil MacEachern' are all one person.

F. R.

Acknowledgements

I am indebted to the following people and organisations for assistance in the production of this work:

The late Captain Iain Ramsay of Kildalton.
The late Dr. W. D. Lamont and Mrs. Lamont.
The late Professor W. Croft Dickinson.
Lord Margadale of Islay.
The Hon. Mary Morrison of Islay, D.B.E.
Mr. Sandy Mactaggart.
Dr. Henry Best and Mrs. Janna Ramsay Best.
Mr. Bruce Ramsay Best.
Colonel O. B. Clapham and Mrs. Eila Ramsay Clapham.
Dr. Margaret A. Mackay.
Mrs. Averil Gilmore, Blamire
The National Library of Scotland.
The Register House, Edinburgh.
The British Museum.
The Royal Commission on the Ancient and Historical Monuments of Scotland.
The Mitchell Library, Glasgow.
Mr. Fraser MacArthur.
Mrs. Isobel MacNiven.
Mr. Neil Wilson.
Mrs. Kay Whitelaw.
Mr. Allan Wright.
Mr. David Boyd.

Incoming of Campbells of Shawfield
to Islay

'The Day Book of Daniel Campbell of Shawfield 1767':

Such is the title on a small volume, half-bound in calf, in the Library of Ramsay of Kildalton. It contains some memoranda by Daniel (II) but more by his brother and successor, Walter, as well as a few notes regarding measures, in other handwritings, some recognisable as those of a lawyer or clerk. Eighteen pages have been cut out: this, however, must have been done by Walter himself as some of them lie between pages thirteen and fourteen, but the narrative runs smoothly from one page to the other in Walter's handwriting. The period covered is from 1767 to 1785.

These two brothers were the eldest and the youngest of the three sons of John Campbell (a Comissioner of H. M. Customs in Scotland) and Lady Henneret Cunninghame, daughter of William, Earl of Glencairn, and grandsons of that Daniel (I) who was a Signatory to the Act of Union, 1707, and Member for the City of Glasgow in the first United Kingdom Parliament. Daniel (I), the second of the ten children of the Captain of Skipness (and a descendant of Archibald, 2nd Earl of Argyle, who was slain at Flodden) had gone, with three of his brothers, into trade during the closing years of the Seventeenth Century. The Union of the Crown had brought no material benefits to Scotland and the country suffered from dire poverty: her Merchants were greatly handicapped by the English Navigation Act, which prohibited their trading with the American Colonies. However, Daniel (I), having been first apprenticed to a Glasgow merchant was then sent to a cousin, Duncan Campbell, in Boston, Massachussets, from whence he returned in 1694 to become, in 1695, a Burgess of Glasgow. The year 1701 saw him collector of the New Port, Glasgow, and in 1705 he was Tacksman of the Revenue and also a Burgess of Edinburgh, where his brother, John, was Provost. His ingenuity enabled him to bring rich cargoes into the Clyde, in spite of the English Navigation Act. It was with the main intention of breaking this embargo on Scottish Trade that he supported the Act of Union in 1707, which opened up the American market to Scotland. By 1706 he had acquired the estate of Shawfield in Lanarkshire. Subsequently, he added Woodhall (for which he paid £4,384) at Holytown and other properties in the vicinity. Later still, he supported the activities of the Company of Undertakers for raising Thames-water in York Buildings to the tune of £10,000. For the interest on this sum he retained the Tack-duties from the Forfeited Estate of Kilsyth, which was to cause a long and expensive law suit in the days of his grandson.

Daniel married, first, Margaret the daughter of John Leckie of Newlands, one of Glasgow's leading Burgesses and, secondly, Lady Katherine Erskine, sister of the Earl of Buchan.

After several years of negotiation, Sir John Campbell of Cawdor granted him a Wadset, for £6000, of lands lying within the islands of Islay and Jura, dated 3 August and 7 October, 1723. For the right of reversion of sundry lands wadset by the Cawdors to their Tacksmen, Daniel bound himself to pay a further £6000. This became possible in 1725 when an infuriated mob, holding him responsible, as Member of Parliament, for the imposition of the Malt Tax, sacked the splendid mansion he had built for himself in Glasgow; he forthwith claimed and received from the city, damages amounting to £6080. Thus, for £12,000, Daniel became Laird of Islay, in his native Argyll. Two years later, on the marriage of his son John to Lady Margaret Campbell, daughter of Hugh, Earl of Loudon, he entailed his Estates. She died childless in 1733, and three years later, on John's second marriage to Lady Henneret Cunninghame, daughter of the Earl of Glencairn, the Estates were re-entailed.

In Islay, Daniel found the Calder Tacksmen well entrenched, many of them holding Wadsets of the lands they occupied.

The Wadset was a type of mortgage whereby the tenant paid an agreed sum of money, on which he received interest from the Laird, and thereafter held his land free of rent, paying only the Crown Rent and Public dues. As the Cawdors did not look as if they would ever be able to redeem these Wadsets, the Tacksmen came to look upon the Tacks as their own possession and very much resented Shawfield having purchased the right of redemption.

The land was not worked by the Tacksmen, but by their subtenants, who paid their rent in silver and kind. From this source the Tacksman made sure he had a sufficiency out of which he could pay the laird his rent (also in silver and kind). But now Shawfield was anxious to have *every* tenant pay rent direct to him and the Tacksmen to *employ* labour to work their lands. Needless to say, this was not a popular innovation and many of the Wadsetters foresaw that they would return to the status of ordinary Tenants.

1 The Shawfield Mansion, north side of Trongate, Glasgow. **1712:** Built by Daniel Campbell, Esq., M.P. for Glasgow in the first Union Parliament. **1724:** Sacked by the Glasgow Anti–Malt Tax Mob. **1745:** Prince Charles Edward Stuart made his Headquarters there from Christmas Day till 3 January 1746. **1792:** Removed to make way for Glassford Street, named after the last owner of the Mansion. *Courtesy of the Mitchell Library.*

2 Glassford House, 'The Shawfield Mansion'. Watercolour by Thomas Fairbairn. *Courtesy of the Mitchell Library.*

No leases, if there were any, have survived from the seventeenth century. Shawfield, as Wadsetter of Islay, granted a lease in 1724 to Archibald Campbell in Laggan of the lands of Ardimersie, and others in the neighbourhood, and made him his Baillie for the Parish of Kildalton: similarly, Coll MacAllister was appointed Baillie for the North of the Island. This earliest lease was to last for eight years (later they were to be for a longer period) at a rent of £360.11s.6d. Scots money (the Scots pound equalled 1/12th of the English pound) and Teind Duty (Church Tithes). Another important Clause in these troublous times was the discouragement of vagrants who swarmed all over the country as a result of the years of civil strife which had rent Scotland for so long and provided one of the great headaches for the administration. This particular Lease was probably modelled on those of the seventeenth century, as it contains a clause for the payment of Herezald, a feudal term – that is, that if a tenant died within the period of the Lease, his estate was bound to pay the Laird the best animal on the farm. This clause was dropped in the Leases that followed.

Tack
Betwixt
Shawfield
&
Archibald Campbell
of the Lands of
Ardimersie &
Ballinawghten & C
1724

(The original is among the Kildalton Papers and is written on three pages of a double foolscap; signed at the bottom of each page by Daniel and Archibald Campbell: the latter also signs the lower half of the margin of the first page on either side an insertion.)

ATT KILAROW the Twentyninth day of June Jajvyc & twenty four years It is Contracted & agreed betwixt Daniel Campbell of Shawfield Esqr Wadsetter of Ilay comform to an Contract of Wadset past betwixt him & John Campbell of Calder Esqr dated the third day of August & seventh day of October last by past on ye one part & Archibald Campbell in Laggan on ye oyr part as after follows;

THAT IS TO SAY the said Daniel Campbell has Sett & herby for ye mails & duty underwryn Setts in Tack & assidation lets to the said Archibald Campbell his heirs and successors secluding assigneys. Except wt ye said Daniel Campbells Consent All & haill ye Quarter land of Ardimersie & all & haill the just & equall half of all & haill ye the mark land of Solam & the Leorhas land Lergibrack & Arinabeast ye Quarter land of Ballinnawchtanmore & Ballinnawchtanbeg wt howses biggings yards parts pendicles & pertinents yrof Lying with ye parish of Kildalton Ile of Ilay & Sherriffdom of Argyle & yt for all ye days/years and space of eight years a& Cropt next. Immediatly following his Entry yrto which Entry is herby declared to be & beginn to ye hawses grass & pasturage of the sd lands at ye term of Whitt next & to ye Arable & manured lands immediatly after ye Separation of ye Cropt from ye ground ye sd year & thencforth to be La-boured/Injoyed poset by him & his forsaids his own Stock Cattle & Servts dureing ye sd Space Secluding Subtennents which Tack ye said Daniel Campbell oblidges him his heirs & Successors to Warrand at ALL Hands and agst all deadly FOR THE WHICH CAWSES ye said Archibald Campbell binds and obliges him his heirs & Successors & Introrors wt his lands rents goods & geir qtsomever thankfully to Content & pay to ye said Daniel Campbell his heirs or assigneys Or his factor & Chamberlainds in his name ALL & HAILL ye sum of three hundred & sixty pounds Eleven Shillings Six pennies Scots Money of Silver and Tenyd duty at ye term of Martymas yearly beginning the first years payt yrof at ye term of Martimas Jajvyc & twenty-five years & Sua furth yearly dureing this present tack wt Sixty pounds Scots money of Liquidat Expenses for each terms failzie toties quoties as also two sufficient merchantable Stots of twenty four pound Scots as ye value yrof & four bolls multer whereof ye one half meall & ye oyr half bear of Six pounds Scots moy for each boll yrof in ye option of ye said Daniel Campbell at ye term of Martymas yearly beginning the first years payt yrof at ye term of Martymas Jajvyc & twenty five years & so forth yrafter dureing the sd space TOGETHER ALSO wt three pressant weddars four sheep four lambs eight gees eight hens & eight dozen of eggs at ye terms of payt used & wont dureing ye sd Space AS ALSO to bring the Grindable Corns of ye Do teynds to ye miln of or any oyr miln ye sd Daniel Campbell shall apoynt whether already built or to be built & pay ye usuall Multer & knaveship yrfore LIKEAS ye said Archibald Campbell binds and oblidges him & his forsds to make Paytt & Satisfaction of an Equal proportion wt the rest of ye tennents of Ilay of ye Schoolmrs & Cherur-geon ffees and of the whole public dues Cesses/burdens & Impositions qtsomever Imposed or to be imposed on Do lands & ye Service of Arage & Cairage & oyr Services used & wont proportionally wt ye oyr Tacksmen & tennents of Ilay and for Reparation of ye Sucken miln & common Smiddy as use is & sicklike the said Archibald Campbell oblidges him & his forsds to Compear before ye Baily Courts of Ilay qn Called yrto & to observe & obtemper ye haill acts of the sd Courts under ye pains & fyns imposed or to be imposed for transgressing yrof & he Likewise oblidges him and his forsds to pay the Court miall dwes to the Baily of Ilay conform to use & wont & yt ye Weavers dwes (if any be living wtin ye sd lands) shall be punctually payed to ye said Baily yearly & it is hereby declared yt it shall be in ye option of the said Daniel Campbell & his forsds to reicieve paytt of ye Casualitys Carwins in specie of ye value yrof in Moy at ye

common & usual prices for ye Like goods in ye Country & in caice the sd
Archibald Campbell & his foresaids failzie in thankfull paytt of ye sd mails
& dutys at ye rexive terms of paytt yrof then & in yt caice it shall be Leisom
& lawll to ye sd Daniel & his forsds to poynd & Distrenzie ye goods & geir on ye
ground of ye sd lands for paytt yrof & yt fowr penny down of the prices yt ye
same shall be comprised at wtout further processes of Law & ye sd Archibald
Campbell binds & obliges him his heirs & successors to pay to the sd Archibald
[clerical Error in original document; should read Daniel Campbell] Campbell an
herezald if the same shall happen to fall dureing this Tack & further it is herby
expressly provided & Agreed to by both parties yt in a Second unpaid yt in caice
one years Rent shall run in a Second unpaid yt then this present tack shall be void
& null on ye part of the sd Daniel Campbell & it shall be lawll to him to set use
& dispone upon ye sd lands wtout Declarator of any oyr process of law aa if thir
prntts had never been granted & it is Likewise herby Expressly provided & agreed
to by both partys yt in caice ye sd Archibald Campbell shall resett harbour
Encourage or in any ways Countenance theives vagabonds or oyr Idle Vagrant
persons of a bad Character who are convicted to be such that by his so doing this
present tack shall become void & null & he shall loose all benefit yrby & in Like
manner the said Archibald Campbell binds & obliges him & his forsds to uphold
& maintain ye haill houses & biggings on ye grounds of yr sd lands dureing this
present tack & to putt & leave ye Same in an Sufficient habitable Condition at ye
Expiration herof but prejudice to him at his Removal to Claim paytt from ye
Intrant tennent for ye timber yrof according to the ancient Custom of the
Country & ye sd Archibald Campbell is herby oblidged to allow any of ye
tennents of Ilay to cary off sands from ye sd lands they always paying to ye said
Archibald Campbell ye Dammadges his grass or Corne may sustain yrby at yee
Sight of two Sworn Birlymen and the sd Archibald Campbell binds & oblidges
him & his forsds to flitt & Remove from ye sd lands at ye Expiration herof wtout
any Process of Removing or oyr order of Law to be used for yt Effect & both
partys oblidge them to perform their part of the premises HINC INDE to oys
under ye penalty of fowrty pounds Scots to be paid by ye party failzier to ye
party observer or Willing to oberve ye premises ATTOUR PERFORMANCE
Consenting to ye Registration herof in ye books of Council & Session oyrs
Competent to have ye strenth of an Dectt Interponed yr to yt Lers of Horning on
Six days & oyrs needfull may pass yron & CONSTITUTES THEIR PRORS IN
witness whereof they have Subscbd thir prntts (written on this & ye two
preceeding pages by Archibald McAlester Servitor to Allexr McMillan Wryr in
Edinburgh) Day month plane & year of God Cawrin before these Witnesses of
Alexander McMillan Writer in Edinburgh & Colin Campbell Younger of
Skipnes inserter of the date & witnesses and writer & witness to the marginal note.

(signed) COLIN CAMPBELL witness   DANIEL CAMPBELL
          ALLEXR McMILLAN witness   ARCH: CAMPBELL

3 Extract from Tack between Daniel Campbell of Shawfield and Archibald Campbell, 1724, the earliest extant showing the mediaeval term 'Herezeld' in the third line. This term is dropped in all future Tacks. Kildalton Papers. *Photograph by Fraser MacArthur.*

First Rental 1733

The first Rental of Islay in Daniel's period, is dated Whitsunday 1733. It is of particular interest because it gives the Extent of each holding in the age old valuation of the land, based originally on the number of cattle that could be supported on any one piece of land. Later there are complications when the rental was converted from a beast to its money value. The system is not always easy to follow, but it has been very thoroughly discussed by Dr. W. D. Lamont in "Old Land Denominations and 'Old Extent' in Islay", and also in "Islay: 500–1615 A.D." which he completed just before his death and is now on microfilm in the National Library of Scotland, Edinburgh. This Rental also shows the proposed increased Rent in Scots money and its equivalent in Sterling. Gressum, or Grassum, was the fee payable on the renewal of a Lease.

Rent Roll of the Parish of Kildaltan in Isla, Commencing at Whitsunday, 1733

Extent	Names of the Lands	Possessor's Names	Old Rent Scotch	Gressum Sterling	Stotts at 20 mks	New Rent Scotch	New Rent Sterling
18 pt. land	Proaig	Charles McAlister of Tarbert	123. 2. 0.	10. 0. 0.	½	135. 2. 0.	11. 5. 2.
1 qr. „	Ardtalla	Malcolm McNeil of Tarbert	167.10. 8.	....	1	185.10. 8.	15. 9. 2⅔
1 leorhace	Surnage, Barr, and Cragnagore						
18 pt. land	Clagnagaroch	„　　„　　Donald and Hugh Carmichael each a horsegang and John Carmichael and Finlay McPhadan a horse-gang,	58. 11. 2.	23. 0. 0.	¼	70. 11. 2.	5. 17. 7⅙
18 pt. „	Trudernish	John and Dougald McVourish	97.15. 4.	10.10. 0.	½	118.15. 4.	9. 17. 11⅓
18 pt. „	Craigfin	Neil Campbell 6', Archibald and Dougald McKenzie 4', Margaret Brown 2', Duncan Carmichael 4',......	76. 8. 8.	17. 0. 0.	½	103. 8. 8.	8. 12. 4⅔
11	Stoin	Baillie Coll McAlister	89.15. 4.	10. 0. 0.	½	110.15. 4.	9. 4. 7⅓
31	Arras & Keantour	Marion Thomson and Archibald Campbell 4', James and George Campbell 6', Patrick McMillan 4', John Campbell 4', Angus McNivin 3', and James Stewart, millar, 3'	36. 4. 4.	5. 0. 0.	¼	42. 4. 4.	3. 10. 4⅓
	Miln of Keantour	James Stewart	139. 6. 4.	10. 0. 0.	¾	160. 6. 4.	13. 7. 2¼
	Changehouse of Keantour	James McIlchonel, with a bolls sowing and two cows grass,	29. 13. 4.	6. 0. 0.	...	59. 13. 4.	4. 19. 5⅓
18 pt.	Ardmainoch	Alexr. Campbell in Ardmore.	....	....	...	18. 0. 0.	1. 10. 0
18 pt. „	Ardmore	„　„　„　„	121.15. 4.	12. 0. 0.	½	149.19. 4.	12. 9. 11⅓
18 pt. „	Kildalton	„　„　„　„	149.15. 4.	15.15. 0.	½	176.15. 4.	14. 14. 7⅓
1 qr. 18 pt.	Knock and Ardelister		117.15. 4.	15.15. 0.	½	144.15. 4.	12. 1. 3⅓
18 pt.	Ardimissy	Neil Oig McNeil	265.10. 8.	30. 0. 0.	1	313.10. 8.	26. 2. 6⅔
18 pt.	Ardnabist	Archd. Campbell, Chamberlain	167.10. 8.	....	1	185. 10½. 8.	15. 9. 2⅔
18 pt.	Ballynachtanmore	„　„　„	107. 0. 0.	....	½	131. 0. 0.	10. 18. 4.
18 pt.	Ballynachtan beg	„　„　„	101.15. 4.	46.15. 0.	½	117.15. 4.	9. 16. 3⅓
½ mk.	½ of Soalam	„　„　„	44. 0. 0.	....	...	55. 0. 0.	4. 11. 8.

Extent	Names of the Lands	Possessor's Names	Old Rent Scotch	Gressum Sterling	Stotts at 20 mks Scotch	New Rent Scotch	New Rent Sterling
4'	4' of Largy	″ ″	10. 0. 0.	…	…	13. 0. 0.	1. 1. 8.
½ mk.	½ of Soalam	Donald Campbell	44. 0. 0	…	…	55. 1. 10	4. 11. 9.
2'	2' of Largybrecht	″ ″	5. 0. 0	5. 8. 0.		6. 18. 2	0. 11. 6
2'	2' of Largybrecht	John Campbell, son of Archibald Campbell,	5. 0. 0.	0. 12. 0.		6. 18. 2.	00. 11. 6⅙
18 pt.	Kilcolmkill	John Campbell	110. 8. 8.	10. 10. 0.	¾	113. 8. 8.	9. 9. 0⅔
11	½ Largybrecht	″ ″	20. 0. 0.			26. 0. 0.	2. 3. 4.
20'	Upper Dunuvig	Colin Campbell 5', Andrew McNabb, Alexr. McLachlan, Duncan McNabb, Donald Carmichael, Dun. McNokard, Alexr. McDougald, each 2½'	113. 14. 2.	10. 0. 0.		137. 14. 2.	11. 9. 6
20'	Nether Dunuvig	Duncan McDougald 5', with a house 15' to Duncan, Alexr, Patrick, Dugald Campbell, John Cameron, John Orr, and John McLachlan – each a seventh	42. 2. 4.			58. 0. 0.	4. 16. 8⅔
20'	Miln of Dunuvig	Colin Campbell	141. 5. 6.			233. 6. 8.	19. 8. 10⅔
20'	Kilbryde	Angus McKinnish 12½', Margaret and Angus McDougald 2½', Malcolm McKinnish 2½', and John McNabb 2½'	67. 0. 0.	8. 8. 0.		100. 0. 0.	8. 6. 8.
10'	Ardinistell		88. 8. 8.	10. 0. 0.	½	112. 8. 8.	9. 7. 4⅖
		The Rev. Mr. John McVicar	71. 3. 8.	24. 3. 0.		84. 3. 8.	7. 0. 3⅔
1 qr.	Torodale	Charles McAlister of Tarbert	170. 4. 0.	20. 0. 0.	1	196. 4. 0.	16. 7. 0.
1 qr. 1 cowland	Balyneil and Arvolhalm	Rond. and Alexr. McDonald	154. 4. 0.	15. 0. 0.	1	178. 4. 0.	14. 17. 0.
1 qr.	Tycarmagan	Lachlan Campbell	130. 4. 0.		1	154. 4. 0.	12. 17. 0.
11	Upper Lewrin	″ ″	49. 11. 0.	6. 0. 0.		65. 11. 0.	5. 9. 3.
18 pt.	Nether Lewrin	Hugh and Ann Sutherland 12', Duncan McDougald 4'	84. 8. 8.	12. 0. 0.		116. 8. 8.	9. 14. 0⅖
18 pt.	Tyndrom	″ ″	67. 15. 4.	10. 10. 0.	½	83. 7. 4.	6. 18. 11⅓
31	Balyvicar	Archd. Graham 12', James and Alexr. Graham 12'	110. 13. 0.	17. 0. 0.	¾	143. 13. 0.	11. 19. 5.

	Place	Tenants					
20'	Cornabus and Kilnachtan	Malcolm McNeil 4 cowlands, Donald Carmichael 1 cd. John Campbell ½ cd. and Torquil McNeil ½ cd	78. 12. 8.	10. 00. 0.	½	100. 4. 8.	8. 7. 0⅔
	Changehouse of Kilnachtan	Neil Clark, with a bolls sowing and 2 xcows grass	...	...	...	24. 0. 0.	2. 0. 0.
	Changehouse of Lyrabolls	Lachlan Campbell, with 2 bolls sowing and 3 cows grass	...	...	...	18. 12. 0.	1. 11. 0.
1 qr.	Lyrabolls	John, Archd., Robert and Cuthbert Campbell, John McKerrel, Archd. McKerrel, Alex. Graham, and William Calder, each 4'.	166. 4. 0.	18. 0. 0.	1	190. 4. 0.	15. 17. 0.
1 qr.	Balychatrican	Archd. and Alexr. Graham 8', Alex. McNabb 4', Dun. McDugald 4', Donald Calder 4', Kat. Sutherland 4'. And. McGibbon and Margr. McIlbryde 4', John McGilchrist 4'	158. 4. 0.	20. 0. 0.	1	206. 4. 0.	17. 3. 8.
1 qr.	Stromnishmore	Patrick McArthur 6', John McMath 6', Jas. Calder 4', Mal. McVorin 4', Mal. Smith 4', Dond. McAlister 4', Neil McMath 2', Mal. McLintock 2'	179. 10. 8.	20. 0. 0.	1	215. 10. 8.	17. 19. 2⅔
1 mk.	Stromnishbeg	Dun. and Gilbert McArthur, 3 cowlands and 1 cowland to Alex. McDougald, ...	72. 12. 10.	10. 0. 0.	½	96. 12. 10.	8. 1. 0.
51	Killean	Duncan More Campbell	160. 8. 4.	24. 0. 0.	1¼	187. 8. 4.	15. 12. 4⅓
	Miln of Killean	" "	45. 0. 0.	15. 0. 0.		66. 0. 0.	5. 10. –
	Changehouse of Killean	...	...	...	...	16. 0. 0.	1. 6. 8.
31	Gill	Dun. McIlbryde 4', Archd. Smith 4', Gilbert McIlroy 4', Edmund McCowig 4', Duncan McIntaggart Hugh and Duncan Campbell 8'	132. 13. 0.	18. 0. 0.	¾	177. 13. 0.	14. 16. 1.
10'	Nether Glenastell	John McCowig and John McNabb each a ½	52. 11. 0.	7. 0. 0.		82. 11. 0.	6. 17. 7.
1 mk	Upper Glenastell	Dond. McCowig 2 cowlands, and 2 to John McCowig and Mary Graham	42. 10. 2.	9. 0. 0.		72. 10. 2.	6. 10. 10.
1 qr.	Cragabolls	Angus, Henry, William, Donald Duncan McCowig and Duncan Carmichael, each a horse-gang	124. 17. 4.	18. 0. 0.	1	151. 17. 4.	12. 13. 1⅓
18 pt.	Keantra	Donald McNeil of Knocknahall,	136. 10. 8.	25. 0. 0.	1¼	166. 10. 8.	13. 17. 6⅔
31	Grastell	" "					

Extent	Names of the Lands	Possessor's Names	Old Rent Scotch	Gressum Sterling	Stotts at 20 mks	New Rent Scotch	New Rent Sterling
11	Tokomiln	Ferquhard Campbell	41. 11. 0.	4. 0. 0.	¼	47. 11. 0.	3. 19. 3.
30'	Machrie	Mary McIlbowie and Alexr. McGilchrist 6', Mary McCowig and Neil McGilchrist 5', Ronald McGilchrist 6', Allan McDougald 4', Essy McAlpine and Dond. McCowig 5', Angus McGilchrist 4'.	100. 13. 4.	12. 0. 0.	1	115. 13. 4.	9. 12. 9¼
1 qr.	Glenegedale	Alexander and Duncan McGilchrist, senior, Duncan McGilchrist, junior, and Angus Sutherland 8', Lachlan Hunter 4', Duncan McIntyre 4', Ann McKay, Duncan McArthur 4' each.	174. 4. 0.	21. 0. 0.	1	204. 4. 0.	17. 0. 4.
1 qr.	Duoch	James Campbell	144. 17. 4.	20. 0. 0.	1	168. 17. 4.	14. 1. 5⅓
3 qr. 18 pt.	Lagan & Torro	Ferquhard Campbell	206. 4. 0.	21. 0. 0.	1	236. 4. 0.	19. 13. 8.
18 pt.	Island	Patrick McCowig 12' and John Graham 4'	63. 16. 0.	10. 0. 0.	½	87. 16. 0.	7. 6. 4.
31	Correry	Donald Carmichael, Donald McNokard and Kat. Oconocher, each 8'	69. 8. 0.	10. 10. 0.	½	90. 8. 8.	7. 10. 8⅔
11	Curaloch	Donald Campbell in Kilcherin	20. 0. 0.	3. 5. 0.	¼	23. 0. 0.	1. 18. 4.
11	Island Taxel	John Campbell in Scanlaston	42. 0. 0.	5. 0. 0.	…	66. 0. 0.	5. 10. 0.
	Lowdown Ferry to Ireland	Alexr. McDonald	12. 0. 0.	…	…	12. 0. 0.	1. 10. 0.
	2 Cottages near Lagavulin	Neil Schaw and Donald McLardy, each 4'	…	…	…	8. 0. 0.	0. 13. 4.
			4603. 1. 2.	662. 11. 0.	28	6994. 18. 10.	582. 18. 2⅚

Rent Roll of the Parishes of Killarow and Kilmenie, Commencing at Whitsunday, 1733.

Extent	Names of the Lands	Possessors' Names	Old Rent Scotch	Gressum Sterling	Stotts at 20 mks	New Rent Scotch	New Rent Sterling
1 qr. 2 cow-lands	Ardlaroch	John Campbell of Laganlochen and John McKay	143. 4. 0.	18. 0. 0.	1	161. 4. 0.	13. 8. 8.
31	Grobels	John Simpson	97. 19. 8.	10. 0. 0.	$\frac{3}{4}$	103. 19. 8.	8. 13. $3\frac{2}{3}$
31	Gartlosk	Mary Brown, Roger Brown and William Cameron, each 8'	100. 6. 6.	12. 0. 0.	$\frac{3}{4}$	115. 6. 6.	9. 12. $2\frac{1}{2}$
30'	Upper Garthossen	Charles Frazer	106. 6. 4.	10. 0. 0.	1	94. 6. 0.	7. 17. 2.
10'	Nether Garthossen	William Smith	33. 8. 8.	. . .	. . .	33. 8. 8.	2. 15. $8\frac{2}{3}$
31	Delouach	Malm. McEwan, 12', Neil McEwan 8', Archd. McMillan 4'	82. 0. 0.	18. 0. 0.	$\frac{3}{4}$	100. 0. 0.	8. 6. 8.
1 qr.	Balytarsin	Dond. and John Spence 16', Moses and Alex. McNaught 8', Dun. McCormig, and Alexr. McIntyre	125. 6. 8.	12. 10. 0.	1	140. 6. 8.	11. 13. $10\frac{2}{3}$
1 qr.	Nerebie	Archd. McLachlan 8', Duncan McPhie 8', Alex. McPhie 8', Florence McKay and Archd. McPhie 4' John McIlergan 4'	112. 17. 6.	15. 0. 0.	1	130. 17. 6.	10. 18. $1\frac{1}{2}$
1	Moulindra	John and Archd. Campbell 20', Duncan McIntyre 10', and Donald Carmichael 10'	144. 17. 4.	18. 0. 0.	1	165. 17. 4.	13. 16. $5\frac{1}{3}$
18 pt.	Rosequernn	Patrick McNabb and Margaret Carmichael, each $\frac{1}{2}$	58. 8. 8.	10. 0. 0.	$\frac{1}{2}$	70. 8. 8.	5. 17. $4\frac{2}{3}$
1 qr.	Noseberg	Dond. McNabb 8', Neil Smith 8, Alex. McDougald and Ann McPhie 6', Charles Campbell 4',	144. 0. 0.	18. 0. 0.	1	162. 4. 0.	13. 10. 4

Extent	Names of the Lands	Possessors' Names	Old Rent Scotch	Gressum Sterling	Stotts at 20 mks	New Rent Scotch	New Rent Sterling
26'	Talent	James Campbell 6'					
26' 18 pt.	Averlusse	Alexr. Campbell . . . . Duncan McVicar 4', Neil McNokard 4', Donald McLugish, 5½, and Duncan McIntyre 2⅔.	97. 19. 8.	9. 0. 0.	$\tfrac{3}{4}$	118. 19. 8.	9. 18. 3$\tfrac{2}{3}$
18 pt.	Nether Killenan	The Rev. Mr. John Campbell	45. 0. 0.	10. 0. 0.	$\tfrac{1}{2}$	60. 0. 0.	5. 0. 0.
18 pt.	Upper Killenan	,, ,, ,,	79. 2. 0.	9. 0. 0.	$\tfrac{1}{2}$	91. 2. 0.	7. 11. 10.
1 qr.	Kinegary	Dond. McMillan 8', Angus McPhaiden 4', Neil McEwan 4', Margt. Carmichael 4', Angus McMillan 4', Donald McIlbra, Neil and John Roy McMillan 8'	66. 4. 4. 172. 17. 4.	9. 0. 0. 20. 0. 0.	$\tfrac{1}{2}$ 1	78. 4. 4. 196. 17. 4.	6. 10. 4$\tfrac{1}{3}$ 16. 8. 1$\tfrac{2}{3}$
18 pt.	Cattadill	Donald and Angus McNokard & Allan McDougald, each $\tfrac{1}{3}$	55. 15. 4.	10. 0. 0.	$\tfrac{1}{2}$	73. 15. 4.	6. 2. 11$\tfrac{1}{3}$
1 qr.	Barr	Angus Campbell 8', Dugald Tayler and Arch. Ban McDougald 8', Hugh McDougald 8', Archd. McVourish and Archd. McDougald 8'	118. 4. 4.	18. 0. 0.	1	136. 4. 4.	11. 7. 0$\tfrac{1}{3}$
18 pt.	Storgag	Charles McAlister of Tarbert	50. 0. 0.	8. 0. 0.	$\tfrac{1}{2}$	59. 0. 0.	4. 18. 4.
18 pt.	Ariguary	Duncan Livingstone Archd. Galbraith, Donald and Neil McNeil, each 4' . . .	69. 16. 0.	10. 0. 0.	$\tfrac{1}{2}$	81. 16. 0.	6. 16. 4.
1 qr.	Ardochy	Malcolm Campbell 8', Angus Campbell, 8', Alexr. Campbell 4', John McCowig 4', in tack, and Robt. Frazer 8' annual	91. 10. 8.	10. 10. 0.	1	106. 10. 8.	8. 17. 6$\tfrac{2}{3}$
1 qr.	Knockcroch,	Alexr., McPhie, Neil McQueen, John McNabb, and John McArthur, each 8'	116. 17. 4.	12. 0. 0.	1	128. 17. 4.	10. 14. 9$\tfrac{1}{3}$
18 pt.	Balygrand	Archd. McEwan	54. 8. 8.	10. 0. 0.	$\tfrac{1}{2}$	78. 8. 8.	6. 10. 8$\tfrac{2}{3}$
	Miln of Balygrand	,, ,,	97. 0. 0.	10. 0. 0.	. . . .	134. 16. 0.	11. 4. 8.
	Changehouse of Balygrand	,, ,,	. . . .	. . . .	. . . .	6. 0. 0.	0. 10. 0.

Denom.	Place	Tenants	£. s. d.	£. s. d.		£. s. d.	£. s. d.
3 qr.	Scanlaston	John Campbell	300. 0. 0.	30. 0. 0.	⋮	336. 0. 0.	28. 0. 0.
18 pt.	Carnbeg	Finlay McKecheren	65. 2. 0.	8. 0. 0.		77. 2. 0.	6. 8. 6.
31	Kilrolmkill	John Campbell 12', Dond. and Archd. McNeil, each 6'	104. 0. 0.	10. 0. 0.	$\frac{1}{2}$	119. 0. 0.	9. 18. 4.
31	Persabolls	Angus Schaw 12', Archd. Campbell 4', Patrick Campbell 2', Alexr. Adaire 2', John Schaw 4'	106. 13. 4.	13. 0. 0.	$\frac{3}{4}$	118. 13. 4.	9. 17. $9\frac{1}{3}$
2 cowlands	Port Ascock and Changehouse. Ferry	Angus Schaw 4'	20. 0. 0.		$\frac{3}{4}$	20. 0. 0.	1. 13. 4.
		Archd. Campbell, with 3 bolls sowing and 4 cows grass	18. 0. 0.		⋮	18. 0. 0.	1. 10. 0.
	Maltkiln and Changehouse of Balochroy		24. 0. 0.		⋮	36. 0. 0.	3. 0. 0.
31	Balychillen	Duncan Campbell 8', Angus Campbell 4', Lachlan McLachlan 6', Charles McAlister 6', John Campbell 4', John McIndore 4'	127. 10. 8.	18. 0. 0.	1	145. 10. 8.	12. 2. $6\frac{2}{3}$
1 qr.	Baluive	Archd. McLauchlan	128. 17. 4.	20. 0. 0.	1	149. 17. 4.	12. 9. $9\frac{1}{3}$
18 pt.	Nether Stoinsha	Neil McClean 4', Malm. McPhie 8', Dugald Campbell 4'	80. 8. 9.	10. 0. 0.	$\frac{1}{2}$	96. 0. 0.	8. 0. $0\frac{3}{4}$
18 pt.	Upper Stoinsha	Archd. Campbell	77. 15. 4.	9. 10. 0.	$\frac{1}{2}$	93. 7. 4.	7. 15. $7\frac{1}{3}$
18 pt.	Milrish	John Campbell, son to Archd. Campbell	54. 8. 8.	9. 0. 0.	$\frac{1}{2}$	66. 8. 8.	5. 10. $8\frac{2}{3}$
1 qr. and 3 cowlands	Portnellan	Baillie Coll McAlister	177. 1. 8.	22. 0. 0.	$1\frac{1}{4}$	210. 1. 8.	17. 10. $1\frac{1}{3}$
1 qr.	Shingart	Neil McLean	108. 17. 4.	18. 0. 0.	1	120. 17. 4.	10. 1. $5\frac{1}{3}$
1 qr. 18 pt.	Keppolsmore	Neil McQuary 6', John McMurchy, 6', Dun, McIchan 6', Dond. Campbell 6', Malm. McEwen 6', Adam McVourich 6', Archd. Ochiltree 6', Alex. Stewart 6'	190. 19. 5.	20. 0. 0.	$1\frac{1}{2}$	208. 19. 5.	17. 8. 3.
1 qr.	Esknish	John and Duncan Campbell 8', Neil and John Smith 8', Archd. Smith 4', Donald Ferguson 4', Allan McDougald 8'	158. 0. 0.	20. 0. 0.	1	182. 0. 0	15. 3. 4.
61	Eorobols	Archd. Campbell 24', John Campbell 16', Archd. Baan Campbell	149. 10. 8.	18. 0. 0.	$1\frac{2}{3}$	161. 10. 8.	13. 9. $2\frac{2}{3}$
31	Balymertin	Duncan McLachlan	109. 19. 8.	16. 0. 0.	$\frac{3}{4}$	130. 19. 8.	10. 18. $3\frac{1}{3}$
18 pt.	Duisker	" "	71. 6. 2.	10. 0. 0.	$\frac{1}{2}$	90. 6. 2.	7. 10. $6\frac{1}{6}$
1 qr.	Balycharvie	Margt. & Alexr. Campbell	140. 17. 4.	15. 0. 0.	1	152. 17. 4.	12. 14. $9\frac{1}{3}$

Extent	Names of the Lands	Possessors' Names	Old Rent Scotch	Gressum Sterling	Stotts at 20 mks	New Rent Scotch	New Rent Sterling
1 qr. 18 pt.	Balol & Leek	Duncan Campbell	205. 6. 0.	30. 0. 0.	$1\frac{1}{2}$	241. 6. 0.	20. 2. 2.
1 qr.	Scarabolls	Archd. Campbell	120. 17. 4.	18. 0. 0.	1	142. 9. 4.	11. 17. $5\frac{1}{4}$
11	Tynaknock	Mathew Hunter	34. 17. 8.	5. 5. 0.	$\frac{1}{4}$	49. 17. 8.	4. 3. $1\frac{1}{2}$
1 qr. 18 pt.	Octovulin	Archd. Campbell 8', Colin Campbell 8', John McIntyre 4', Malm. McIntyre 4', Dugd. McPhie 6', John McIlvivorie 6', Alex. McKay 6', Alex. Montgomery 6'	189. 12. 8.	20. 0. 0.	$1\frac{1}{2}$	219. 12. 8.	18. 6. $0\frac{2}{3}$
1 qr. 2 cowlands	Skerrols and Avinogy	Coll McAlister	111. 10. 8.	15. 0. 0.	1	129. 10. 8.	10. 15. $10\frac{2}{3}$
	Tuckmiln	Jas. Cargill, with 4 cow grass	40. 0. 0.	2. 0. 0.	...	52. 0. 0.	4. 6. 8.
	Killarow Miln	1 horse grass, and gleib	109. 0. 0.	15. 0. 0.	...	181. 0. 0.	15. 1. 8.
2 horsegangs	Eolobolls	Baillie Coll McAlister	42. 6. 0.	...	...	42. 6. 0.	3. 10. 6.
18 pt.	Knochans	Alexr., Robertson, $\frac{1}{4}$ therof being	24. 0. 0.	...	...	24. 0. 0.	2. 0. 0.
4 horsegangs	Kenabolls	deducted for a park			...		
	New park	Thomas Chrichton	60. 0. 0.	...	...	60. 0. 0.	5. 0. 0.
31	Carabolls	Angus Campbell 8', Duncan and Alexr. McDougald 8', Margaret Ker and Archd. Hyndman 4', Archd. McPherson 4'	22. 12. 0.	...	...	133. 6. 8.	11. 2. $2\frac{2}{3}$
18 pt.	Culabolls	Alexr. Symson and Isobell McNeil	102. 6. 5.	9. 0. 0.	$\frac{3}{4}$	111. 6. 5.	9. 5. $6\frac{5}{12}$
18 pt.	Lyrabolls	Alexr. Symson and Isobell McNeil	75. 2. 0.	8. 0. 0.	$\frac{1}{2}$	84. 2. 0.	7. 0. 2.
18 pt.	Torobolls	McNeil	75. 2. 0.	8. 0. 0.	$\frac{1}{2}$	84. 2. 0.	7. 0. 2.
3 qr.	Dale, Surn & Kilbranan	Fewduty	38. 13. 4.	...	...	38. 13. 4.	3. 4. $5\frac{1}{3}$
		Colin Campbell of Dale	92. 6. 8.	35. 0. 0.	...	164. 6. 8.	13. 13. $10\frac{2}{3}$
6 qr.	Losset & c.	John Campbell, baillie of Muckairn	251. 6. 8.	60. 0. 0.	...	420. 0. 0.	35. 0. 0.
2 qr.	Balichaven & Robolls	John Campbell of Balichavan	110. 0. 0.	30. 0. 0.	...	170. 0. 0.	14. 3. 4.
3 qr.	Kilinalen, Ardnahow, Bolsa Dudil and Cove	Alexr. Campbell of Killinalen	137. 15. 0.	...	...	198. 1. 8.	16. 10. $1\frac{2}{3}$

7 qr. 18 pt.	Rim, Balynis and Gortented Town of Killarow		204. 1. 4.	...		204. 1. 4.	...	17. 0. 1⅓
	Angus Campbell 24', John McInclerie 12', Ann Campbell 3', John McMillan 3', Don. Smith 2', Wm. Cargill 6', Dug. McPhaden 6', Alexr. McChristan 6', Dond. Arnot 4', Dun. Ferguson 4', Hugh McCristan 6', John McKay 3', Dun. McLachlan 8', Archd. McLachlan 10', Archd. McLean 15', Mary Brown, 10', Alexrs. Stewart 12', John Simpson 6', Thos. Crichton house and Gorten. (Note: T.C. pays for Gorten) 20', Dun. McIndore 6', Archd. McMurchy 4', Janet Stewart 2', David Catch	174. 0. 0.	...		174. 0. 0.	...	14. 10. 0.
			0. 2. 0.	...		...	...

Rent Roll of the Parish of Kilhomen, Commencing at Whitsunday, 1733.

Extent	Names of the Lands	Possessors' Names	Old Rent Scotch	Gressum Sterling	Stotts at 20 mks	New Rent Scotch	New Rent Sterling
1 qr. 37⅓'	Koningsby ⅓ Octomore, changehouse & malt kiln, malt kiln at Glassens, miln of Skiba and Gartahar	Archd. McLean	168. 17. 4.	25. 0. 0.	1	204. 17. 4.	17. 1. 5⅓
84'	⅔ Octomore, Grimsa, Dudil & Goaline	George Campbell of Octomore	252. 13. 4.	...	...	508. 13. 4.	42. 7. 9⅓
			136. 0. 0.				
1 qr.	Glassans	George Dallas 20', Alexr. Dallas 12'	167. 10. 8.	18. 0. 0.	1	197. 10. 8.	16. 9. 2⅔

B

Extent	Names of the Lands	Possessors' Names	Old Rent Scotch	Gressum Sterling	Slots at 20 mks	New Rent Scotch	New Rent Sterling
18 pt.	Carnglassans	Widow McMillan and Donald McMillan	54. 8. 8	8. 0. 0	$\frac{1}{2}$	66. 8. 8	5. 10. $8\frac{2}{3}$
18 pt.	Toronich	Alexr. Stewart	65. 2. 0	8. 0. 0	$\frac{1}{2}$	77. 2. 0	6. 8. 6.
18 pt.	Craigfad	Archd. McEwan 8', Nicholl McCalman, 4', Dond. McCurrie 4'	73. 15. 4	9. 0. 0	$\frac{1}{2}$	88. 15. 4	7. 7. $11\frac{1}{3}$
18 pt.	Almond	Alexr. Gillis	54. 8. 8	5. 0. 0	$\frac{2}{3}$	66. 8. 8	5. 10. $8\frac{1}{3}$
1 qr.	Nerebolls	Patrick, Neil and Hugh McEwen each 8', John Sutherland 4'	154. 5. 0	18. 0. 0	$\frac{1}{2}$	172. 5. 0	14. 7. 1.
	Octofad	Duncan McIlchonil 4'	140. 17. 4	12. 0. 0	1	158. 17. 4	13. 4. $9\frac{2}{3}$
1 qr.	Miln of do.	Duncan McVicar	31. 0. 0	6. 0. 0	1	56. 4. 0	4. 13. 8.
1 qr.	Wester Ellister	George Campbell of Ellister few duty	170. 13. 4	25. 0. 0	···	266. 13. 4	22. 4. $5\frac{1}{3}$
1 qrt	Balygalie	George Campbell of Ellister	60. 8. 8	25. 0. 0	$\frac{1}{2}$	72. 8. 8	6. 0. $8\frac{2}{3}$
18 pt.	½ of East Elister	William Campbell	115. 19. 8	9. 0. 0	$\frac{2}{3}$	145. 19. 8	12. 3. $3\frac{2}{3}$
31	Arihaloch	Archd. Campbell	160. 17. 4	14. 0. 0	$\frac{3}{4}$	184. 17. 4	15. 8. $1\frac{1}{3}$
1 qr.	Kelso	"	160. 17. 4	14. 0. 0	1	184. 17. 4	15. 8. $2\frac{1}{3}$
1 qr.	Lossett	"	60. 8. 8	14. 0. 0	1	72. 8. 8	6. 0. $8\frac{2}{3}$
18 pt.	½ of East Elister	John Campbell	48. 0. 0	8. 0. 0	$\frac{1}{2}$	84. 0. 0	7. 0. 0.
1 qr.	Cultoun and Calumsary		75. 0. 0	25. 0. 0	···	93. 0. 0	7. 15. 0.
18 pt.	Olista	Robert Montgomery	148. 18. 0	9. 0. 0	$\frac{1}{2}$	175. 18. 0	14. 13. 2
1 qr.	Gerrich	Kenneth Clark 4', Alexr. McMath 4', Donald McNokard 4', John McPhie 4', Archd. McKecheran 4', Angus McIlvoil 4', Donald Smith 4', Duncan McIntyre 4'	160. 0. 0	20. 0. 0	1	187. 0. 0	15. 11. 8.
1 qr.	Tormistell	Duncan and John McInturner 12' Dond. McIntyre 8', Donald McLergan 4', Jas. Odocherty 5' Wm. Odocherty 3'	95. 4. 0	11. 15. 0	$\frac{3}{4}$	104. 4. 0	8. 13. 8.
31	Braid	Donald Campbell	213. 8. 10	30. 0. 0	$1\frac{3}{4}$	240. 8. 10	28. 0. 8.
1 qr. 31	Kilcherin	"	218. 0. 0	32. 10. 0	$1\frac{7}{8}$	249. 10. 0	20. 15. 10.
711 k	½ of Kilhomen	The Reverend Mr. John Campbell	15. 10. 0	3. 0. 0	···	20. 0. 0	1. 13. 4.
	½ Miln of Kilhomen	The Reverend Mr. John Campbell					

71 1 k	$\frac{1}{2}$ of Kilhomen	Duncan Campbell of Sunderland	218. 0. 0.	32. 10. 0.	$1\frac{7}{8}$	249. 10. 0.	20. 15. 10.
	$\frac{1}{2}$ Miln of Kilhomen	Duncan Campbell of Sunderland	15. 10. 0.	3. 0. 0.	. . .	20. 0. 0.	1. 13. 4.
7 cowlands	Small	Alexr. Campbell of Kilinalen $\frac{2}{3}$, and Alex. Campbell $\frac{1}{3}$	108. 18. 6.	14. 0. 0.	$\frac{1}{2}$	126. 18. 6.	10. 11. $6\frac{1}{2}$
1 qr.	Migrim	Alexr. Campbell of Kilinalen $\frac{2}{3}$, and Alex. Campbell $\frac{1}{3}$	127. 10. 8.	21. 0. 0.	1	151. 10. 8.	12. 12. $6\frac{2}{3}$
1 mk	Crulin and Ardtornish	Alexr. Campbell of Kilinalen $\frac{2}{3}$, and Alex. Campbell $\frac{1}{3}$	16. 18. 6.	7. 0. 0.	$\frac{1}{2}$	22. 18. 6.	1. 18. $2\frac{1}{2}$
1 qr. 18 pt.	Sanaigmore	John Campbell	154. 4. 0.	20. 0. 0.	$1\frac{1}{2}$	172. 4. 0.	14. 7. 0.
1 qr.	Keandrochead	" "	107. 19. 6.	20. 0. 0.	1	134. 19. 6.	11. 4. $11\frac{1}{2}$
	Mergadill	Alexr. Campbell of Kilinalen					
	Ardnave		163. 7. 4.	. . .	1	163. 7. 4.	13. 12. $3\frac{1}{3}$
2 qr. 11	Mergadill	Alexr. Campbell of Kilinalen	26. 13. 4.	. . .	. . .	26. 13. 4.	2. 4. $5\frac{1}{3}$
	Brecachie		166. 4. 0.	. . .	1	166. 4. 0.	13. 17. 0.
1 qr.	Kilnave	John and Rond. Johnston 16′, John McArthur 8′, Angus McIleur 4′, and Archd. McMillan 4′	136. 17. 4.	18. 0. 0.	1	160. 17. 4.	13. 8. $1\frac{1}{3}$
31	Leckgrunart	{ Malm. McFarlane 8′, John McLellan 6′, Archd. McNabb 6′, Archd. McDermed 4′	106. 13. 4.	16. 0. 0.	$\frac{3}{4}$	130. 13. 4.	10. 17. $9\frac{1}{3}$
	Miln of Balenabie	James Campbell of Balenabie	36. 0. 0.	. . .	. . .	36. 0. 0.	3. 0. 0.
4 qr. 11	Sunderland	feu duties	182. 0. 0.	. . .	. . .	182. 0. 0.	15. 13. 4.
3 qr. 18 pt.	Balenabie	wadsett and tiends	211. 6. 8.	60. 0. 0.	. . .	355. 6. 8.	29. 12. $2\frac{2}{3}$
		Total Rent-roll of Kilhomen	4780. 7. 4.	580. 15. 0.	$26\frac{3}{4}$	5777. 11. 4.	481. 9. $2\frac{1}{3}$
		Total Rent-roll of Killarow and Kilmenie	5700. 19. 10.	810. 15. 0.	38	8089. 5. 5.	674. 2. $1\frac{5}{12}$
		Total Rent-roll of Kildaltan	4603. 1. 2.	662. 11. 0	28	6994. 18. 10.	582. 18. 2.
			15084. 8. 4.	2054. 1. 0.	$92\frac{3}{4}$	50861. 15. 7.	1738. 9. $7\frac{5}{12}$
		Stotts at £1.2s.$2\frac{2}{3}$d. each	. . .	. . .	. . .	. . .	103. 0. $6\frac{2}{3}$
						Grand Total	1841. 10. $2\frac{1}{4}$

Rent Roll of Jura, Commencing at Whitsunday, 1733.

Extent	Names of the Lands	Possessors' Names	Old Rent Scotch	Gressum Sterling		New Rent Scotch	New Rent Sterling
	Crackag	Wadsett lands prorogated to Campbell	. . .	84. 0. 0.	. . .	200. 0. 0.	16. 13. 4.
	Kames	John and Archd, Campbell, baillies of Jura.	. . .	21. 0. 0.	. . .	200. 0. 0.	16. 13. 4.
	Tarbert	In my own hands	. . .	. . .	. . .	400. 0. 0.	33. 6. 8.
		TOTAL	. . .	105. 0. 0.	. . .	800. 0. 0.	66. 13. 4.

A State of the Rents in Isla and Jura.

		Sterling
Amount of the Parish of Kildaltan Stotts	28	582. 18. $2\frac{5}{6}$
,, ,, ,, ,, Killarow and Kilmenie Stotts	38	674. 2. $1\frac{5}{13}$
,, ,, ,, ,, Kilhomen Stotts	$26\frac{3}{4}$	481. 9. $3\frac{1}{3}$
The $92\frac{3}{4}$ Stotts at $\pounds1.2s.2\frac{2}{3}d.$ each is	$92\frac{2}{3}$	103. 0. $6\frac{2}{3}$
Amount of the Rents in Jura		66. 13. 4
		$\pounds1908.$ 3. $6\frac{1}{4}$

Deductions

Feu duties payable to the Crown are 500, for which I pay the Earl of Darnly	$\pounds300.$ 0. 0.	
Stipend to Mr. John Campbell	50. 0. 0.	
Stipend to Mr. John McVicar	43. 7. 10	
Salary to Coll McAlister, baillie and chamberlain	33. 6. 8.	
,, to Archibald Campbell, chamberlain of Kildaltan	16. 13. 4.	
,, to schoolmaster, surgeon, pyper and officers	22. 0. 0.	465. 7. 10.
	NETT RENT	$\pounds1442.$ 15. $8\frac{1}{4}$

New York Colony

The dissatisfaction among the Tacksmen and their families finally resulted in a large emigration of the younger men, their families and sometimes their servants, to New York Colony, organised by Captain Lachlan Campbell of Leorin. He had negotiated with the Governor of New York Colony for lands up the Hudson River, whereby each adult would receive 1000 acres and each child 500 acres: Lachlan undertaking to bring out at least eighty families for settlement. Thus, in the years 1738, 39 & 40, ships left for New York Colony carrying 472 passengers. Unfortunately, on their arrival, the Governor reneged on his original agreement and was only prepared to convey the land to Lachlan Campbell, the emigrants to hold their land from him and not direct from the crown. This they flatly refused to do and it was twenty-five years before a settlement was finally made.

Fortunately, the "History of the Somonauk Presbyterian Church" has preserved the full sailing lists, plus a number of other documents, which show what happened to most of the emigrants and the number and size of each lot apportioned to the survivors or their descendants in the lands known as the Argyle Patent.

Excerpted from
History of the Somonauk Presbyterian Church
the
ARGYLE DOCUMENTS
Document VIII

(Endorsement) A List of the Persons Brought from Scotland by Captain Lauchlin Campbell to settle the Kings Lands at the Wood Creek from 1738 to 1740

   89 Familys 358
   Persons 112 Single 112
                                                           470 Persons

Memorandum of Passengers who Came in the years 1738, 1739 & 1740.
A List of Passengers from Islay with Captain Lauchlin Campbell bound for
New York, July 1738. No Claim Ronald Campbell, Dead. John Campbell of
Ballinabie and Anna Campbell his wife. Alexander Montgomery & Anna Suther-
land his wife. Hugh Montgomery, Mary Beaton, Duncan McEuen, Janet
McEuen (son & Daughter to Hugh McEuen). Mary McEuen. Mary McEuen,
Daughter to John McEuen. Janet Ferguson (her son, Alexander McDonald).
Archibald Johnston & Christine Johnston his wife. No claim Mary Graham,
Dead. John McNeil & Eliz: Campbell, his wife & Barbara, Peggie, Catharine,
Betty & Neil, 5 Children. Margaret McNeil, Angus McAlister, Elisbie Thomp-
son of Dunardrie. No Claim, Alexander McLean, Died at Cuba. No claim,
William Campbell, Joiner, Dead family But in Scotland. No Claim William
Campbell Wheelwright, Dead. Alexander Graham, Donald Carmichael & Eliza-
beth McAlister his wife, John, Alexander & Mary his three children. James
Campbell & Anna McDougall his wife. Archibald Lauchlin Eliz. & Janet his
4 Children. Neil McArthur & Mary Campbell his wife & Alexander, John and
Christian his three Children, Donald Shaw & Merrin McInish his Wife, Mary
Campbell, Elisbie Sutherland and her Children, James, Alexander, Duncan
Margaret & Elizabeth Gillies 5 Children. Duncan Taylor & Mary his Wife and
Mary his Daughter. Archibald McEchern & Jean McDonald his wife & Catharine
his Daughter. Donald McMillan & Mary McEachern his wife. Donald McCloud
& Cath Graham his Wife, John & Duncan his 2 sons. Ronald McDougall & Bettie
McDougall his Wife, John & Alexander his 2 sons. Allan McDougall & Elizabeth
Graham his Wife, Margaret, Anna & Hannah his 3 Daughters. Archibald
McDougall & Christian McIntyre his Wife, Alexander & John his 2 sons. Hugh
McDougall. Archibald McKellar & Jannet Reed his Wife. Charles McKellar
& Florence McEachern his Wife. Margaret, Catharine & Mary his 3 Daughters,
Catharine Fraser, Alexander McNaught (on) and Mary McDonald his Wife,
John, Moses, Janet & Eleanor his 4 children. John McNiven & Mary McArthur
his Wife, Elizabeth & Mary his 2 Daughters. Merran McNiven. Rachel
McNiven. Patrick McArthur & Mary McDougall his Wife, Charles, Colin
& Janet his 3 children. Duncan McArthur & Anna Mcuin his Wife & Anna,
Mary, Margaret & John 4 Children. Alexander McArthur U Catherine McAr-
thur, his Wife, John, Donald, Duncan, Catharine & Florence his 5 Children.
Donald McEachern & Anna McDonald his Wife, & Catharine his Daughter. Neil
McDonald & Anna McDuffie his Wife, Donald, Archibald & Catharine his
3 children. Duncan Gilchrist & Florence McAlister his Wife & Mary his Daughter. John McKenzie & Mary McVurrich his Wife, Archibald & Florence 2 Children. George McKenzie & Catharine McNiven his Wife, Donald & Colin his
2 sons. Malcolm McDuffie & Rose Docharty his Wife, Margaret & Janet his
2 Daughters. Dudley McDuffie & Margaret Campbell his Wife & Archibald
a son. John McIntagart. Malcolm Martine & Florence Anderson his Wife. Dugald
McAlpine & Mary McPhaden his Wife, Donald & Mary his 2 Children. John
McIntaylor. James Stewart. Donald Campbell & Mary McKay his Wife, Robert,
James, Margaret & Isabel his 4 Children. William McGie, Duncan Smith, James
Livingston. John Gilchrist. Alexander Gilchrist. Lauchlan McVuirich. Alexander

Campbell. Allen Thompson. Donald McIntyre. Murdoch Hammel. Donald McIntaylor. John McColl. John McLean. Christain Paterson. Catharine Lessly. Mary Ross. Jean Ross. Merran Hameel.

33 Familys, 42 Passengers, 177 Persons.

Passengers from Islay, June 1739.

Robert Fraser & Mary McLean his Wife, Charles, Coline, Sarah, Catharine, Mary & Isabel 6 Children. Archibald McEuen & Janet McDougall his Wife. Malcom McEuen, James Nutt & Rebecca Creighton his Wife, Robert, John & Elizabeth his 3 Children. Neil Campbell. Peter Green. John Caldwell & Mary Nutt his Wife, Alexander & James his 2 sons. Neil McPhaden & Mary McDearmid his Wife, Dirvorgill & Margaret his 2 Daughters. Angus McIntosh. Alexander McChristen. Catharine Campbell. Jean Cargill. Florence McVurich. Archibald McVurich & Merran Shaw his Wife. Neil Shaw. Catherine Shaw. John McQuary & Anna Quarry his wife. Patric McEachern & Mary McQuarrie his Wife. Donald McPhaden. Duguald Thomson & Margaret McDuffie his Wife. Archibald, Duncan & Christie & his Brothers Daughter 4 Children. Patrick Anderson & Catharine McLean his Wife. Duncan Campbell & Sarah Fraser his Wife. Charles McAlister & Catharine McInnish his Wife, John & Margaret his 2 Children. Duncan McAlister & Effie Keith his Wife. Donald Ferguson & Flory Shaw his Wife with One Child of his Own & Catharine & Anna Ferguson his Brothers Children. William Clark his Wife & one son John. Donald Livingston & Isabel McCuarg his Wife. John & Duncan his 2 Children. John McEuen & Anna Johnston his Wife & his son Malcolm. Lauchilin McVurich. John McDonald. James Cameron. Mary Thomson. Murdo McInnish & Merran McKay his Wife, Catharine, Archibald, Neil, Anna & Florence his 5 Children. Archibald McDuffie & Catharine Campbell his Wife, John and Duncan his 2 sons. Neil McInnish & Catharine McDonald his Wife. Duncan Reid & Mary Semple his Wife, Alexander, Nicholas, Angus & Jennie his 4 Children. Neil Shaw & Florence McLachlin his Wife. John Shaw & Mary McNeil his Wife, Neil & Duncan his 2 sons. Gustavus Shaw. Archibald McGown with his 3 Children, Duncan, John and Margaret. Malcolm McGown with Patrick alias Hector his 2 children. John McGown & Anna McCuarg his Wife, Malcolm & Angus his 2 sons. Donald McMillan & Janet Gillies his Wife & Alexander his son. Alexander McDuffies Widow. Anna Campbell, (he Dieing at sea), Archibald, Duncan, James, Mary & Isabel his 5 Children. Duncan McQuarrie alias Brown & Effie McIpheder his Wife, Donald, John, Gilbert & Christian his 4 Children. Archibald McIlpheder. Catharine McIlpheder. Donald Lindsay & Mary McQuarrie his Wife, Richard, Duncan, Effie & Christian his 4 Children. Neil Gillaspie & Mary McIlpheder his Wife, Gilbert and Angus his 2 Sons. John Reid & Margaret Hyman his Wife and His son Donald. Roger Reid. Dugald Carmichael & Catharine McEuen his Wife, Janet, Mary, Neil & Catharine his 4 Children. Merran McEuen with her Daughter. Christain McAulla, Patrick Robertson. Duncan McDougall & Janet Calder, his Wife, John, Alexander, Ronald, Dugald,

& Margaret his 5 Children. Dugald, Gilbert, Flory & Margaret his 3 Children. Archibald McCollum & Merran McLean his wife & Donald, John, Margaret, Mary & Allan, his 5 Children. James Torry & Florence McKay his Wife & his Children Mary & Catharine. Nicholas McIntyre & Margaret Peterson his Wife & John his son & Catharine. George Torry. Cornelius Collins. Angus McDougall. Alexander Hunter & Anna Anderson his wife, his Children, William, Alexander & Janet. Alexander McArthur & Catharine Gillies his Wife, Duncan & Flora his 2 Children. Angus Campbell with his son John. John McPhail & Christy Clark his Wife. McIntyre.

42 Families, 24 Single Passengers, 193 Persons.

Passengers from Islay, November 1740.

Neil Campbell. Edward Graham & Jean Fraser His Wife. John McEuen. William Adair. Malcolm Campbell. Alexander Campbell & Margaret Campbell his Wife & One Daughter Merran. Duncan Campbell of ye family of Duntroon. Alexander Campbell of ye family of Landie. Duncan Campbell & Anna Campbell his Wife (Lenos) and one Daughter Catarine. Robert McAlpine. Duncan Campbell of Lochnel. William Campbell. Archibald Campbell of Ardenton. Anna Campbell. Duncan Campbell of ye family of Dunn. Duncan McCollum. John McIntyre. John Christy & Isabel McArthur his Wife, Hannah & Mary his 2 Daughters. John McArthur & his son, Neil, daughter Christian. Angus Clark & Mary McCollum, his Wife & Catharine & Mary his 2 Daughters. Anne McNeil Widow to Hugh McEuen, with her son Alexander and Mary, her 2 Children. Elizabeth Cargill. James Cargill. John, David & Margaret Cargill. Ann McArthur. Jean Widrow. Merran McIndeora. James McEuen. John Shaw & Merran (Sarah) Brown his Wife. Donald Mary & one Infant Margaret (born at sea). Christian Brown. John McGibbon. Archibald Graham. Roger Thomson. John Campbell. Duncan McKinven & Marian McCollum his Wife and Donald & Mary his 2 Children. John McGilvrey & Catharine McDonald his Wife, Hugh, Donald, Bridget and Mary his 4 Children. Anthony Murphy. Duncan McKay. Dudley McDuffie & Margaret McDougall his Wife, Dugald & Mary his 2 Children. Duncan McPhadden & Flory McCollum his Wife, John and Duncan His 2 Children. Archibald McCollum & Flory McEacheon his Wife, Hugh & Duncan his 2 sons. Archibald Hammel. Mary Hammel. Catharine Graham. Margaret McArthur Wife to Archibald McCollum at New York & Anna & Mary his 2 Daughters. Mary Anderson. Widow with her 2 Children. Duncan Leech & Mary Leech. Margaret McAlister. Effie McIlvrey. Lauchlin McLean. Angus Graham. Roger McNeil. John Reid. Ann McArthur.

DOCUMENT IX

List of Persons brought from Scotland and by Capt. Laughlin Campbell in 1738–40. This list was probably prepared in 1763.

Heads of Families Imported in 1738

1. Ronald Campbell Dead. No family with him.
2. John Campbell Dead, brought a Wife with him who is Dead and they have left no Children, but he has a sister called Ann, who is married in the Highlands[1] & has 5 Childn. married Duncan Campbell who is in this list hereafter.
3. Alexander Montgomery, now living, has a wife and no Children. . . .200
4. Archibald Johnston he is Dead. His Wife Kerstain Johnston is living as also two Sons and three Daughters. She is married to Daniel McAlpine. Malcolm Johnston for himself one Bror. & three Sisters 250
5. John McNeil, he is Dead, his Widow is living and four Daughters in this Province and one in England. N.B. one of the Daughters Named Jane came over in 1740 four Daughters 200
6. Donald Caemichael, he is Dead, has Children, but hath none in this Province.
7. James Campbell, he is Dead, his Wife Anna McDougall and one Son Archibald and two Daughters are living. Widow (100), Archibald the Son (50), Isabel (50) 200
8. Neil McArthur Dead, His Widow and five Children Living 300
9. Donald Shaw Dead Son and Daughter living 200
10. Elizabeth Sutherland She is living and four Children 400
11. Duncan Taylor living, and has a Wife and Eight Children three of them married 500
12. Archibald McEachern brought a Family Consisting of a Wife and Daughter
13. Donald McMillan living, has a Wife and five Children two of whom are Married 400
14. Donald McCloud is Dead, & Has one Daughter living 150
15. Cormick McCoy Dead his Widow living and a Son and Daughter who are Married 200
16. Ronald McDougall living, with a Wife and two Children who are both Married. John one of his sons is Dead & hath left two Children 300
17. Allan McDougall Dead the Widow, one son and four Daughters living 300
18. Archibald McDougall Living, has a Wife and five Children three of whom are Married 350
19. Archibald McKellar Dead hath left a Widow & 8 Children one Married 450
20. Chas. McKellar Dead hath left a Widow and Seven Children. one of whom is Married. The Mother of these two McKellars Came over with them but is Dead 400
21. Alexander McNaught (on) Living, has a Wife and four Children three of whom are Married, he has 8 Grand Children. 500
22. John McNiven Dead One Son and four Daughters living three of whom are Married 250

---

[1] Highlands – The mountainous area of the Hudson in the vicinity of West Point

23. Malcolm Martine Dead his Wife alive not Known
24. Patrick McArthur living, has a Wife two sons and one Daughter 250
25. Duncan McArthur Dead, his Widow and two sons and two Daughters living, three of whom are Married 250
26. Alexander McArthur Dead, two sons and four Daughters four are Married. John the Eldest son Dead and has left a Widow and two Children . . .350
27. Donald McEachern Dead his Widow and three sons and three Daughters living, two Married 350
28. Neil McDonald living, has a Wife and Six Children living, one Married 400
29. Duncan Gilchrist himself, Wife, and Six Children living, one Married 400
30. John McKinzie Dead. One Daughter left 100
31. Cormick McCoy before (see No. 15)
32. George McKenzie living with his Wife and four Children two of them Married. Lives in New Jersy 300
33. Malcolm McDuffie & Wife, living with three sons and four Daughters one married 450
34. Dudley McDuffie Dead Married and (had) a son & a Daughter the Daughter Married 150
35. Dugald McAlpine and Wife and two Children, who are both Married 200
36. Donald Campbell Dead. his Wife and four Children living, one of whom is Married 250

Heads of Families Imported in 1739

1. Robert Fraser Dead, three Daughters living and William Fraser the son of Charles who was the Eldest son of Robert & two Sisters 250
2. Archibald McEuen, Dead, two Children living a Son & Daughter . . .150
3. James Nutt living, and one son who is Married 200
4. John Caldwell doubtfull whether living or not, but has Daughter living in N. York, who is Married & two sons which he took to Pensilvania.
5. Neil McPhadon and Mary his Wife and one Daughter Called Margaret who is Married & hath 2 Children are now alive 200
6. Archibald McVarick Dead, his Widow living, who hath two Children living by another Marriage.
7. John Quary and his Wife and four Children, one Married 300
8. Patrick McEachern Dead, his Widow living 100
9. Dugald Thomson and his Wife, three sons, two sons Married 300
10. Patrick Anderson, Dead, his Widow & two Daughters by him, &c Many Children by another Marriage 200
11. Duncan Campbell Dead, his Widow & three sons and a Daughter living, the Daughter married 250
12. Charles McAlister Dead, left two sons, three Children of the Eldest son living, & the youngest son 200

13. Duncan McAlister, Dead, One Son and two Daughters living 200
14. Donald Ferguson, Dead, one Daughter living and a Daughter of his Brother whom he brought over 150
15. William Clark his Wife and two Children, a Son and Daughter 250
16. Donald Livingston Dead, his Widow and Daughters living 150
17. John McEwen living, and his Wife and five Sons 400
18. Murdoch McInnish Dead, three Grandchildren by the Widow of his son Neil by another Marriage, and three by his Daughter Florence 200
19. Archibald McDuffie Dead, One son Duncan & two Children & two Children half Blood 150
20. Neil McInnish the son of Murdock above mentioned Widow Married to Allen McDonald 100
21. Duncan Reid Living brot. over his Wife and 8 Children all Dead . . .500
22. Neil Shaw Dead. Five Grand Children living Neil the Eldest to Youngest 200
    Neil the Eldest 200
23. John Shaw Dead, Neil and two other Children living, two Married, provided for above . . . .
24. Archibald McGown Dead. A Grandson living Named Archibald and a Daughter who hath 4 sons 200
25. Malcolm McGown, hath one son living who is Married & hath Children150
26. John McGown, & Wife both alive 200
27. Donald McMillan, alive, five Children 3 Sons & 2 Daughters 350
28. Alexander McDuffie, Died at Sea, his Widow and two Daughters, his son Duncan Duffie who is dead hath left one Daughter called Anne 250
29. Duncan McQuore & Wife and Five Children four Sons & One Daughter are living, the four Sons are married 400
30. Donald Lindsay living One Son & two Daughters living one son & One Daughter Married 250
31. Neil Gillaspie living as also his Wife & one Daughter 350
32. John Reid living as also his Wife and five Children, three Boys and One Girl the Daughter Married 350
33. Dugall Carmichael Dead One son living Named John brought over a Numerous family 200
34. Merrian McEuen Dead the above named John the son of Dugall is Her Nephew.
35. Duncan McDougall Alive as also his Wife & six Children three Sons & two (three) Daughters two sons & a daughter Married the Daughter a Widow & 4 Children 400
36. Dugald Campbell, Dead. Archibald Campbell of N. York his Heir . .150
37. John McPhail Dead, his Widow a son and a Daughter living 200
38. Archibald McCollum living, with two sons and One Daughter one son & the Daughter Married 250
39. Nicholas McIntire Dead his Widow two sons and two Daughters living 250
40. James Torry Dead, two sons and two Daughters living, Daughters Married 200

41. Alexander Hunter Dead, son & Daughter living who are both Married and have children 200
42. Alexander McArthur Dead his Widow & one Son living brought over a large family 200
43. John Campbell & Mary his Mother Dead. Archibald the Nephew of John Living, provided for

Heads of Families Imported in 1740

1. Edward Graham Dead One Daughter living, provided for
2. Alexander Campbell Dead, two Daughters living 150
3. Duncan Campbell living as also his Wife, with her three Sons and two Daughters 350
4. John Christy Dead his Widow One Son & three Daughters living, two Daughters Married 250
5. John McArthur Dead a Son and Daughter living, both Married 150
6. Angus Clark Dead, two sons & One Daughter living. Daniel the Eldest son Dead, leaving a Son & Daughter 250
7. Anne McNeil said to be living at Basking Ridge in New Jersey with her Children.
8. John Shaw Dead, his Widow and four Children living 2 Sons & 2 Daughters, a son and (two) Daughters Married 250
9. Merrian McCollum the Parties know nothing of this Person at present she having moved to N. York.
10. John McElvrey Dead One son living at Amboy 100
11. Dudley McDuffie Dead, his Widow & two sons and two Daughters living. One Daughter Married 250
12. Duncan McPhaden Dead One son John the Eldest Dead Leaving 4 children & One son Duncan living 200
13. Archibald McCollum living with a son and a Daughter several Grand Children 250
14. Archibald McColeman Dead Widow and one son and two Daughters living 200
15. Mary Anderson living, with two Daughters both married, who have sons grown up 200
16. Duncan McKinven Living and one son & three Daughters, one Daughter Married New York 250

Single Persons Imported in 1738

1. Hugh Montgomery living in N.Y. & is Married and has two Children 200
2. Mary Beaton living, is a Widow and has a son Married 200
3. Duncan McEuen ⎫
4. Jennet McEuen ⎬ living in the Jerseys and are Married there.
5. Mary McEuen ⎭

6. Mary McEuen lives in or about the same place & is Married there
7. Jennet Ferguson Dead, One son living in N.Y 150
8. Mary Graham Dead, has Children living in the Manor of Livingston .200
9. Margaret McNeil Living in the Highlands . . . .
10. Angus McAlister Said to be living in Carolina.
11. Alexander Graham Died, has left two sons both in N.Y 200
12. Hugh McDougall lives in Livingston Manor 200
13. *Merran McNiven 200
14. *Rachel McNiven
            *both live in New York and have Children.
15. James Livingston Dead, his Widow and Children live in Trenton in Jersey.
16. *John   Gilchrist 200
17. *Alexander   Gilchrist 200
            *both living, and are Married in the Highlands of this Province.
18. Alexander Campbell, is Married & has a family in Amboy.
19. Donald McIntire Lives in New York, one son & a Wife who likewise came
    over with Capt. Campbell as p. List 250
20. Murdoch Hammel lives in the Island of Jamaica.
21. John McLean Has a Relation in Town.
22. *Lauchlin   McLean . . . .
23. *Mary Ross married after their arrival 200
            *Died leaving one Child named Catharine Who is now in Albany.

Single Persons Imported in 1739

1. Malcolm McEwen is Dead but has left three Children who now live in New
   York 200
2. Neil Campbell lives in the Island of Jamaica.
3. Catharine Campbell lives in the Highlands 150
4. Jane Cargill married in New York to Mr. Van Vleck Merchant 150
5. Florence McVarick, is Married and has Children, in Livingston Manor
  200
6. Catharine Shaw lives in New York is Married and has one Child . . .150
7. Mary Thomson Married and lives in Pennsylvania.
8. *Archibald McIlpheder 200
9. *Catharine McIlpheder 150
            *both Married and live in the Highlands & have Children.
10. Roger Reid Married and lives in the Highlands, & has 3 Children . . .200
11. George Torry Dead, has left one Child in N. York 150
12. Cornelius Collins lives in the Jerseys.
13. Angus McDougall is Married and lives in the Highlands 200
14. David Shaw Dead. Widow living in Tappan 150

Single Persons Imported in 1740

1. John McEuen lives in the Province of Pennsylvania a Doctor.
2. Malcolm Campbell lives in New York, a Merchant 200

3. Alexander Campbell Dead but has one Daughter 1 alive in New York
. 150
4. Robert McAlpine lives in New York, has a family of five sons & 2 Daughters
. 200
5. Duncan Campbell Married in New York and has sevl. Children 200
6. *William Campbell 200
7. *Archibald Campbell 200
   *both Dead, but have left Children who live in the Highlands.
8. Anne Campbell lives in the Highlands & is Married & has a family of
6 Children . . . .
9. John McIntire a Clergyman in Pennsylvania 200
for a place of Worship & School house 500
10. Elizabeth Cargill lives in Tappan and is Married there 150
11. *James Cargill 200
12. *John Cargill 200
13. *David Cargill 200
   *All living in N.Y. and are Married and have Children.
14. Margaret Cargill is a Widow, has Children & lives at New Rochell . .150
15. Anna McArthur. Married in Albany 150
16. Jane Widrow is Married & has a family of 7 Children in the Highlands
. 200
17. James McEuen Said to live in Boston . . . .
18. Roger Thomson Dead, his Widow lives in Amboy & his Children
19. John Campbell Married in New York 200
20. Mary Hammel Dead, but has a Daughter left who lives in the Highlands
. 150
21. Margaret McAlister is Married and lives at the Manor of Livingston . .150
22. Angus Graham lives in New York, has two sons & 3 Daughters.
23. Roger McNeil Living on Long Island 200
24. Anne McArthur Lives in the Highlands & has 5 Children 200
25. Margaret Gilchrist Lives New York 150
26. John Torry Married and living in N. York 200
  (Colonial Manuscripts, Vol. 72, p. 170 New York State Library)

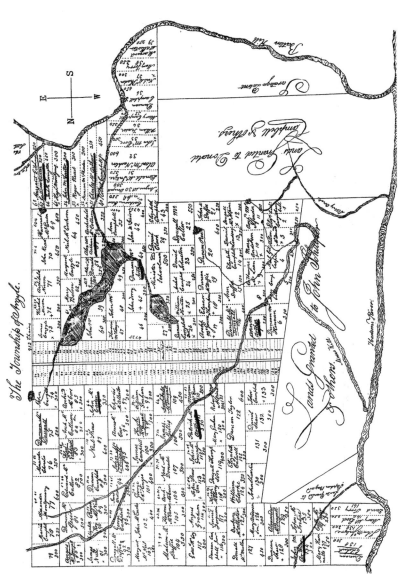

4 The Township of Argyle, New York Colony. Outline Map of Argyle Patent, with names of the Lot Owners, from the original survey made in 1764 by Archibald Campbell and Christopher Yates. (from *The Fort Edward Book* by Robert O Bascom, 1903, Keating, Pub., Fort Edward. N.Y.)

DOCUMENT X

A further Account Delivered by Alexander McNaught (on) and Duncan Reid of Persons who did Emigrate with Captain Campbell in 1738, 1739 and 1740, and who have or their Descendants or persons Impowered, lately appeared and Requested a Proportion of the lands Intended to be Granted . . . . This account was delivered on . . . . the 10th May 1763.

George Campbell of the City or New York Merchant came over in pursuance of a Letter written by Captain Campbells orders to him and dated in 1742. Offering him Incouragement Concerning the lands then promised . . . .

John McCore came over in 1739, he is now Married and lives in the Highlands . . . .

Archibald McCore came over in 1739, is Married and lives in Tappan . . . .

James McNaught (on) dead, came in 1740 but his Brothers son John McNaught (on) who lives in Tappan, prays his proportion and Engages to settle it . . . . provided for before.

Duncan Campbell came in 1740, and his Brothers Daughter Mary Ann Campbell of the City of New York, prays his proportion & will Engage to settle it . . . .

Angus McAlister came in 1738, is now living in South Carolina and his Sisters Daughter who is Married to Jacob Vandle of N.Y. will enter into any Engagements necessary during his Absence . . . .

Peter Robertson came in 1739, is dead – his Cousin John McDonald of the City of New York Carpenter prays his proportion and Engaged to settle it . . . .

Mary Thompson came in 1739, lives in Pensilvania, her Cousin Duncan Reid of N.Y. prays her proportion and Engages to settle it . . . .

Charles McArthur of the City of N. York with his Wife and Family came on Board in 1738, and the Ship being too much Crouded was turned ashore, and as they had sold all their Effects this Obliged them to go to Ireland where he took a Passage and arrived here a fortnight before the ship in which he first Engaged with Captain Campbell . . . .

Donald McMillan came in 1738, he is now dead & Allan McDonald of the City of New York Tavern Keeper his Kinsman Engages to settle his Proportion . . . .

Neil Campbell lives in Jamaica, came in 1739, Alexander Montgomery of Tappan who is Married to his Mother will take a Grant in Trust for him & Enter into the Necessary Engagements.

Ronald Campbell came in 1738. George Campbell of this Province Pedlar, prays his proportion being his nearest Relation . . . .

Donald Campbell now living in Jamaica came in 1738 his Cousin Duncan Campbell of this City appears to act in Trust for him . . . .

Jennet Ferguson is now dead came in 1738 and her son Alexander McDonald a Rope Maker in New York prays a grant of her proportion & Engages to settle it . . . .

William Campbell Joiner now dead, came in 1738 his Cousin Alexander McNaught (on) in Tappan prays a Grant of his share & Engages to settle it . . . .

Catharine Graham came in 1740 died in New York and her Brothers son John Graham of New York prays a Right to her share &c . . . .

John McDonald came in 1739, is now at sea, his Cousin Allan McDonald of N. York will act in his Absence . . . .

John Reid came in 1740 is gone to Virginia, his Uncles Son Peter Reid in Tappan Engages to Act for him . . . .

Duncan McKay came in 1740, went to sea & is dead, his Cousin Mary McKay of the City of New York Widow prays a right to his share which she Engages to settle . . . .

Margaret Gilchrist came in 1740, lives in New York . . . .

Duncan McCollum came in 1740, died here, and Daniel Campbell of this City his Cousin prays a right to his share which he Engages to settle . . . .

William Adair came in 1740, dead, his Cousin Duncan Reid prays a right to his share which he Engages to settle . . . .

John McIntaylor came in 1738 and his Uncles Son Donald Smith of the City of New York Mariner prays a right to his Proportion which he Engages to settle . . . .

Archibald McEachern and his Wife Jean McDonald and one Daughter came in 1738, and his Cousin Finlay McEachern is desirous of Taking their proportion in Trust until they can be found . . . .

Alexander Christy came 1738, is dean and his Cousin Mary Christy who is Married to Duncan Campbell of New York prays a right to his proportion which he will Engage to settle . . . .

William Campbell Wheel wright came in 1738 is dead and his Cousin Mary Mackey of the City of New York prays a grant of his proportion which she will engage to settle . . . .

Donald McIntaylor came in 1738 is dead and his Cousin Alexander Taylor in Tappan prays a Grant of his Prportion which he will Engage to settle . . . .

Jane Ross came in 1738, is Dead, has a Daughter living which is a Minor, and John Torry of N. York prays a grant of her Proportion which he Engages to settle in Trust for the Minor . . . .

Donald McIntyre came in 1738, is Dead leaving Malcolm Grahame of N. York Pruke maker his son . . . .

Malcolm McDuffie came in 1739 is Dead, & his Kinsman Duncan Reid of N. York prays his Proportion which he will settle . . . .

Roger Thomson came in 1740 died in the Provincial Service has left a Widdow

& one Child in Amboy, who hath appointed Archibald Gilchrist of N. York to
act for them . . . .

Catharine Fraser came in 1739, is Dead leaving one Daughter called Elizabeth
who lives in New York, who hath appointed her Cousin Robert Campbell of
N. York to act for her . . . .

Mary Fraser came in 1739 and is married & lives in New York . . . .

Gustavus Shaw came in 1739, is Dead & his Nephew Neal Shaw of the City of
New York Rope maker, in Trust for the Rest of his Heirs prays his proportion
which he Engages to settle . . . .

Catharine Fraser came in 1738 is Dead, and has left two Grand-daughters, one
named Catharine Montgomery & tother Catharine Stevenson who are both
Married & live in New York . . . .

Elizabeth Fraser came in 1739 and is Married & lives in New York . . . .

John McLean came in 1738 is Dead and his Cousin Alexander McLean of the
City of Albany prays his share which he Engages to settle . . . .

Marion Culbreth came in 1739, is dead, & Duncan Reid her next heir Prays her
share which he Engages to settle . . . .

Alexander Campbell came in 1738, lives in Amboy, hath applyed and declares
his willingness to settle such Proportion as shall be granted to him . . . .

John Brady came in 1740, had 5 Children, one of whom named Hugh lives in
Amboy and prays his fathers proportion which he Engages to settle . . . .

Effie McIlevray came in 1740, and lives in New York . . . .

John McDougall came in 1739, died a privateering in the last war, his Brother
Dougal McDougall of New York prays his proportion &c. (Endorsement)

(New York Colonial Manuscripts, Vol. 72. p. 171, in the New York State
Library, Albany, N.Y.)

DOCUMENT XI

On August 12th 1771 Sarah, the widow of John Shaw presented the following:

PETITION OF SARAH SHAW AND OTHERS, 12th AUG. 1771. To the
Honourable William Tyron Esqr. Governor In & Over his Majesties Province of
Newyork & the territories thereon depending in America, Chancellor, And Vice
Admiral of the same.

The Petition of Sarah Shaw Widow & Relict of John Shaw Late of the City of
Newyork Yeoman Deceased, that Neal Shaw William Castle & Mary his Wife
that These are the Children of Margaret McDougall. Daughter of the sd. John
& Sarah Shaw Most humbly Shrweth.

That About the year of One Thousand Seven Hundred & forty Your Peti-
tioner Sarah Shaw together with her husband John Shaw, her Children Danl.
Shaw & Mary Castle then Mary & One Christian Browne Since decd. Enfants
Left there habitation, in the Shire of Arguile in Scotland in the Iland of Great

Britain, & Embarked On board the Ship Happy Return Captain Locklin Campbell, for this Port, being Encouraged by the Assurance Given by the Said Capt. Campbell, that Every head of a family Should on their Arrival in America Should obtain a grant of 1000. Acres of Land & that every Child that was a full Passenger should have 500. Acres Each, That your Petitioner Margt. Shaw was born at Sea in the Voyage so that the sd. John Shaw To. Gether with his Wife Children & the sd. Christian Browne Made up Six Passengers.

That On there Arrival in Newyork they Underwent The Greatest hardships by the Land not being Granted According to the sd. Captain Campbells Assurances & their distress Was very Much, Heightened, As the sd. John Shaw, Nor Any One of his family Could Spake One Word of English. & the sd. John Shaw was Obliged to work at hard Labour During the Rest of his Life for the Maintaince of himself and family & died abt. Eleven years Since Without Obtaining Any Land at all & by his death yr. Petitioner the sd. Sarah Shaw looks Upon herself in Right of her sd. husband to be Entitled to such Quantity of Land as he would have binn Entitled to had he been Living & the Said Christian Browne, Being some time since deceased, the sd. Sarah Shaw as her Sister & hier at law, Looks Upon herself to be Entitled Also To, the sd. Lands of Christian Browne, which were to have bin Granted had the same bin Obtained in the Lifetime of the Said John Shaw, & Christian Browne.

That, your Pertitioners the sd. Neal Shaw Mary Castles & Margt. McDougall, Humbly Presume that they are Entitled to such Quantity of Land Each, as Were Originally Promised To be granted to Children of Passengers who, Came with the Sd. Captn. Campbell Namely 500. Acres to each Child. And more so, as the sd. Danl. Shaw the Eldest Son of the Said John & Sarah Shaw has Already Obtained a Quantity of Land by Virtue of the Right Under Which your Petitioners His Brothers and Sisters Claim.

That, and 8 years Since Aplication was made to your Petitioner Sarah Shaw by One George Campbell Duncan Reade & Alexr. McKnight for money for her & childrens. Proportions of the Exspence of Surveying & Obtaining the Lands in the Argile Patent, Which Several Proportions the sd. Sarah Shaw did then Accordingly Pay.

And has Since Chearfully Contributed to that End as often as she has binn Asked so to doe but Notwithstanding all the Exspence she has pd. Neither your Pertitioner the said Sarah Shaw Nor Any One of your Pertitioners have Obtained Any Land, Tho the Argyle Patent Out of which the said Lands Was to have, been Granted to your Pertitioners has Binn Some time Since divided & the Only Satisfaction your Pertitioners have Binn Offered Upon their Applying to the Trustees is to have so much money repaid to your Pertitioners the sd. Sara Shaw, as she has Contributed On the Behalf of herself & the Rest of your Pertitioners her Children Which your Pertitioner Cannot think to be an adequate Satisfaction for their Writes in the said Lands.

Your Pertitioner therefore humbly Pray your Excellency To take their Case into Consideration, & that your Pertitioners May Obtain as much Land as they are Entitled To in Equal Proportions With the Rest of the Propriators of Land in the Arguile Patent. Or if it should Appear that the whole of the Sd. Patent Should be divided that your Pertitioners May be Allotted So Much Land in some Other

Pleace as may be Equivalent to their Wrights in the Sd. Arguile Patent, and that in that Case the Trustees for the said Arguile Patent may Pay Back to the sd. Sarah Shaw as much Money as she has Already Paid in Respect of Obtaining the Lands in Said Arguile Patent.

And Your Pertitioners Will for Ever Pray.

Newyk. August 12. 1771

(Addressed)   To His Excellency Willm. Tryon Esqr. Present.

(Endorsed)   Petition of Sarah Shaw Widow of John Shaw Recd: 26th August. 1771

1771 August. 28 Read in Council and referred to a Committee.

The lands were granted to the Petitioners Brother. Rejected.

(New York Colonial Manuscripts, 97:73, in the New York State Library, Albany, N.Y.)

Rental 1741

In 1736 Daniel started to convert the gaunt tower house of Kilarow into the charming house that forms the main part of the present Islay House. It was his grandson, the second Daniel, who completed the conversion. Much of the furniture and pictures with which they and their successors embellished it, remained in the house until it and the policies were sold in 1986.

Between the house and the River Sorn was the parish Church of Kilarow and a lochan (believed to have been artificially formed to provide a fish-pond for the mediaeval priests). Across this, stepping-stones led to the village, crushed between it and the river. An entry in the Stent book for 1755: 10/- paid for a "slype to the stepping stones". Here also was the Tolbooth and the Gallows, standing on a slight eminence, where now there is the empty watch tower, built during the Napoleonic period.

The second Rental of 1741 shows the Rents now in Sterling but the Extent of each farm remains the same – indeed, they are referred to in this manner until the 19th Century, although they were also assessed in acres.

The Wadsetters and bigger Tacksmen do not return the names of their sub-tenants in either Rental and the full number of small tenants do not appear until the Standardisation of the Leases in 1799.

Rent Roll of the Parish of Kildaltan in Isla, Commencing at Whitsunday, 1741.

Extent	Names of the Lands	Tenents' Names	Sterling £. s. d.
18 pt.	Proig		
1 qr.	Balimiel	Charles McAlister of Tarbert (Kintyre)	27.15. 7.
1 qr. 11	Arivolhalm		
	Ardtalla		
	Surnag Barr and	Malcolm McNeil of Tarbert (Gigha)	22.16. 0.
18 pt.	Cragnagore		
½ mk.	Clagnagaroch		
12'	½ Solum		
	Largybrecht		
18 pt.	Kilcolmkill		
1 leurace	Island Texell	John Campbell of Askomell	34. 2. 2.
18 pt.	Craigfin		
18 pt.	Trudernish	Alexander Campbell in Ardmoir	18. 0. 0.
1 leurace	Stoin	Baillie Coll McAlister	3.15.11.
3 leurace	Arras and Kaintour	Duncan and John Carmichaels 8', James and John Campbells 8', John Campbell, senior, 4', Patrick and Donald McMillans 4'	14. 4. 0.
	Miln and Changehouse of	Wm. Stewart, with 1 boll sowing and 2 cows grass and 4 cows grass from the town paying the Tenents 6 mk.	4.10. 0.
	Arras and Kaintour		
18 pt.	Ardmoir		
18 pt.	Ardmenisn		
18 pt.	Kildaltan	Alexr. Campbell in Ardmoir	35.19. 0.
1 qr. 18 pt.	Knock & Ardelster	Neil McNeil of Ardna croish	25. 0. 0.
18 pt.	Ardimissy		
18 pt.	Ardnebeist		
18 pt.	Balnachtanmoir		
½ mk.	Balnachtanbeg		
4'	½ Solam		
	Laegybreckt	Archd. Campbell of Arderignish	44. 2. 0.

Extent	Names of the Lands	Tennents' Names	Sterling
20'	Upper Dunuvig Miln		
20'	Nether Dunuvig	Alex. Duncan and Archd. Campbell and John Orr, for whom Baillie McAlister is surty	16. 5. 0.
20'	Kilbride	Angus and John McInnish 10', Malcolm McInnish 5', and John McDougall 5'	16. 6. 0.
10'	Ardmistill		9.10. 0.
1 qr.	Torodell		
1 lourace	½ Tyndrom	The Rev. John McVicar	28. 5. 0.
18 pt.	½ Tycarmagan	William and James Calder and John Campbell	7. 0. 0.
18 pt.	″ ½	Donald McDonald	7. 0. 0.
3 leurace	Upper and Nether Leurin	Alexander Campbell	15. 4. 0.
1 leurace	½ Tyndrom	John McDougall	3.15. 0.
3 leurace	Balivicar	Archd. Alexr. and Charles Grahames	14. 1. 0.
20'	Cornubolls and Kilnachtan	Malcolm McNeil 4 cowlands, Dond. Carmichael, senior and junior, 1 cowland, Kathrin Carmichael 1 cowland	8.19. 0.
	Changehouse of Killnachtan	John McKoulikan, with 1 horse and cows grass and 1 boll sowing	2. 0. 0.
3 leurace	Lyrabolls	John McCuaig 8&, Neil Campbell 4', Robt. Campbell 3' John Campbell, junior, 3', Archd. Campbell 4', Duncan Campbell 2', with ¾ of two bolls sowing and 3 cows grass formerly belonging to the changehouse	13.19. 0.
1 leurace	Koilibolls	Alex. Graham and John McDougall with the other fourth of the above sowing and grass	5. 3. 0.
1 qr.	Balichristan	Duncan McDougall 4', Wm. and Thos. Calder 4', Duncan and Hector McGibbon 4', John Calder 4', John McGilchrist 4'	19.11. 0.
3 qr. l,	Stromnishmore	Gilbert McArthur 8', Malcolm and John McVoren 6', John and Dougall McMath 6', Neil McMath 4'	12.13. 0.
1 leurace	Assibolls	Patrick McCuaig, officer	5. 5. 0.
1 mk.	Stromnishbeg	Patrick McArthur 10th, Duncan Campbell 1 cowland	7.16. 0.
1 qr.	Killean	Alex. McNabb 4', Alex. Gilchrist 4', Finlay McNab 4', Neil McVorem 4', Archd. McTaggart 4', John McIlbride 4', Donald McGowan 8th	13.12. 0.

Measure	Place	Tenants	£ s. d.
1 leurace	Kinnibolls, with Miln and Changehouse	Duncan Campbell	11. 8. 0.
3 leurace	Gill	Duncan, McIlbride 4', Gilbert McIlroy 3', Edmund McCuaig 2', Duncan Carmichael 2', Duncan and Hugh Campbells 6', Duncan McTaggart 3', Hugh McCuaig 4'	15. 0. 0.
10'	Nether Glenastill	John McCuaig and John McNabb	6. 4. 0.
1 mk.	Uper Glenastill	Donald and John McCuaigs	5.16. 0.
1 qr.	Cragebolls	Donald, Henry, and Duncan McCuaig, senior 18', Duncan Carmichael 6', Wm. and Duncan McCuaig, junior, 8'	13. 4. 0.
18 pt.	Kentra	Donald McNeill of Knocknohan	29. 0. 0.
3 leurace	Grastill		
1 leurace	Tockumill	Duncan Gilchrist, senior, 4', Janet McIlchrist 4', Dun. Gilchrist junior 7', Angus Sutherland 4', Lauchlan Hunter 4', Duncan McIntyre 4'	18. 3. 0.
30'	Machrie		
1 qr.	Glenegedill		
1 qr.	Duock	Mary McNeil and the Rev. Mr. John Campbell	19. 3. 0.
1 leurace	Stranabodauchq	Farquhard Campbell	20.16. 0.
3/18 pts.	Laggan and Torra	John Graham 2/3, Ronald Johnstone 1/3	3.19. 0.
1/2 of Island		Donald Carmichael and Donald McNoquard	8. 0. 0.
1 leurace	Corrary	William Campbell, Kilcherran	2. 4. 0.
1/18 pt.	Curoloch		

Total 589. 5. 8.

Cottages, houses in Lagvuline pays, 1. 0. 0.

590. 5. 8.

Of the above rent-roll of Killdaltan parish there is subscribed coppy delivered by Shawfield to me, amounting to five hundred and ninty pounds five shillings eight pence Stg. Dated the 11th February 1742 years.

(Signed) John Campbell

Rent Roll of the Parishes of Killarow and Kilmenie in Isla, Commencing at Whitsunday, 1741.

Extent	Names of the Lands	Tennents' Names	Sterling £. s. d.
1 qr. 2 Cowlands	Ardlaroch and Cruach	John McKay and his son Hugh	14.11. 0.
3 leurace	Groballs	Mary Brown 12', Rory and Donald Brown 12'	9.10. 0.
3 leurace	Gartlosk	Archd., Ochiltree 8'; Donald Smith 8'; and John Stewart	10. 9. 0.
20'	Upper Gartahossen	Charles Frasser*	6. 0. 0.
10'	Upper ,,		
10'	Nether ,,	William Smith, Wm. and James Cameron, each $\frac{1}{3}$	6. 0. 0.
3 leurace	Delouach	Malcolm McEuan 12', Archd. McEuan 12'	9. 4. 0.
1 qr.	Balitarsin	Dond. and John Spence 16', Dun. McCormich 8', Archd. McMillan and Malcolm Campbell 8'	11. 0. 0.
1 qr.	Nerebie	Archd. McLauchlan, James McNabb, Neil McEilmichael and Archd. McNakaird	12. 1. 0.
18 pt.	Rosequeren	Dond. McNakaird 4', Duncan McNabb 4', Angus McNakaird	5.10. 0.
1 qr.	Naseberg	Neil Smith 8', Alexr. McDougald 8'; Hugh McDougald 4' and Patk. McNabb 12'	14.15. 0.
5 leurace	Mulendra	John and Arch. Campbell and Archd. McLugash 20', Donald Carmichael and Dond. McNiven 20'	14.19. 0.
26'	Talent	Duncan McIntyre, Duncan Bean McIntyre, and Duncan McCallum	10.15. 0.
18'	Averlussa	Wm. Campbell in Kilcherran	5.11. 0.
1 qr.	Killcarnenm, Upper & Nether	The Rev. Mr. John Campbell and Duncan Campbell, his son.	13.14. 0.
1 qr.	Kinegarie	Angus Duncan and Neil McMillan and John McVurich, Donald McGilevray, Angus and Finlay McFadzen, John McNakard	17.11. 0.
18 pt.	Catadell	Alexander McLauchlane	6.14. 0.
1 qr.	Barr	Dugall Taylour, Hugh and Archd. Baan McDougall, and Sorlie Smith	11.10. 0.

* In another copy styled "surgeon"

Measure	Place	Tenant	Rent
1 leurace	½ Areguirie	Neil and John McQueen, his son	3. 14. 0.
1 qr.	Ardachie	During pleasure	. . .
18 pt.	Ballegran with Mill and Changehouse	Duncan McLauchlane	39. 12. 0.
3 l	Ballemartin	" "	
1 qr.	Knock Clerock	John McNab 16', Angus Campbell 8', Mallcolm Campbell 8'	11. 17. 0.
56⅓'	Scanlastone	Archd. Campbell of Saneg	28. 0. 0.
18 pt.	Carnbeg	Finlay McKechron	7. 0. 0.
3 leurace	Kilcolmkill	Andrew Adair 12', Angus Campbell 6', John McIntyre 6'	10. 15. 0.
3 leurace	Changehouse in Balochroy	Colin Agey, with 1 horse, 3 cows, 12 sheep and gleb	1. 10. 0.
1 l	Persabolls		
	½ Ariguary		
2 cowlands	Port Askock, changehouse, ferry, malt-kiln, and changehouse of Balochroy	Angus Shaw	19. 12. 0.
18 pt.	½ Ballegillean	Baillie Coll McAlester	25. 10. 1.
5 l	Portnellan	Baillie Coll McAlister	
10'	{ Eolobolls		
	Miln of Killarow	" ", " ", during pleasure	20. 12. 0.
18 pt.	Knockens		
18 pt.	½ Ballegillean	Ronald Campbell	6. 13. 0.
1 qr.	Balulve		
1 l	Nether Stensha ½	Archd. McLauchlane	23. 17. 0.
18 pt. add 1 cowd.	{ ½ Skerrols and Avenvogie		
	Upper Stunsha	Archd. Campbell of Sanaig	22. 0. 0.
18 pt.	Scarabolls		
1 qr.	{ Shingart	Archd. McLean	21. 9. 0.
1 qr.	½ Nether Stunsha		
1 l	Skerrols and Avenvogy	John McMurphy 8', John McGillevorigh 8', John Campbell 8', Donald McCulleam 6', Donald and Charles Campbell 6', Alexe. McGillivrey 6', Duncan McIchan 6'	19. 2. 0.
18 pt. and 1 cowd.	Kepelsmoir		
1 qr. and 18 pt.			

Extent	Names of the Lands	Tennents' Names	Sterling
1 qr.	Esknish	John and Duncan Campbell 8', Archd. Smith senior, 4', Archd. Smith, junior, 4', John Smith 4', Donald Ferguson 6', James Smith 6'	16. 6. 0.
6 1	Eorobolls	Archd. Campbell 3 leurace, Colin Campbell 2 leurace, Archd. Bann Campbell 1 leurace	15. 3. 0
18 pt.	Duisker	Donald Campbell	8. 2. 0.
1 qr.	Ballieharvey	Alexr. Campbell	11.15. 0.
1 qr. and 18 pt.	Ballool and Leek	Duncan Campbell	21.16. 0.
1 leurace	Tynaknock	Mathew Hunter, mason	4. 9. 0.
1 qr. and 18 pt.	Octovulen	Samuell Watson	16.10. 0.
	Tuke Milhn	James Cargill, with 4 cows and 1 horse grass and a gleib	4. 6. 8.
1 horsegang	Kenabolls	Farqbhar Campbell	5. 0. 0.
3 leurace	Carabolls	John McIndore 6⅔', John McDougall 6⅔', Archd. McPherson 6⅔', Archd. and Donald Hyndman	10. 3. 0.
18 pt.	Culabolls	Alexr. Simpson	15. 3. 0.
18 pt.	Lirabolls	Sir Alexander Murray, Bart., few-duty	3. 4. 5⅓
18 pt.	Torobolls	Colin Campbell of Dale, wadsett	13.13.10⅔
3 qr.	Dale, Surn and Kilbranan	Donald Campbell of Lossett, wadsett	35. 0. 0.
6 qr.	Lossett & c.	Ronald Campbell of Ballachlaven, wadsett	14. 3. 4.
2 qr.	Balachlaven and Robulls	Alexr. Campbell of Killinalen, wadsett	11. 7. 1⅓
2 qr. 11	Killinallen, Corsabolls and Bolsa	Alexr. Campbell, Killinalen	17. 0. 0.
3 qr. 18 pts.	Reim, Balinish and Gortented	Colin Campbell of Ardnahow	5. 0. 3⅓
3 1	Ardnahow and Cove	Town of Killarow and inclosures: Mrs. Campbell 2 inclosures, north; Angus Campbell, south, his father's house and middle inclosure; John Simson, his house and 2 south inclosures.	∴ ∴
		William Smith, barber, his house and garden	1.13. 4.
		Daniel Campbell, bleacher, his possession continued gratis	∴ ∴
		John McMillan, weaver, his house, garden, and cows grass	0. 5. 0.
		Mary Smith, her house gratis	∴ ∴
		Hector McLean, his house and garden	0.10. 0.
		Ronald Campbell, the house that Margaret McCrison had.	0.10. 0.
		Total	£ 672. 0. 10⅔

Rent Roll of the Parish of Kilhowman in Isla, Commencing at Whitsunday, 1741.

Extent	Names of the Lands	Tennents' Names	Sterling £. s. d.
1 qr.	Konigsbay	Dougald and Donald McAlpine, Alexr. Campbell, R. Robertson, each 4', Dugald and Archd. McGillespigh 4', Donald McLean 4', and Archd. McCurich 8'	20. 0. 0
1 qr.	Octomore		
1 qr.	Grimsey		
1 qr.	Coultersay & Lergba		
1 1	Dudellmoir		
1 cowd.	Gylyne	Alexr. Campbell of Octomore, Wadsetter	30. 0. 0.
	Changehouse, malt-kiln, and		
	Miln of Skibo		
18 pt.	Gartahar	Alexr. Campbell ,, ,,	8. 7. 0.
1 qr.	Glassany		6. 0. 0.
		George Dallas 12', Maegt. Dallas 8', John Dallas 8', Archd. McDuff 4', with the priviledge of the changehouse allowing the others 5th and 10th yearly	17.12. 0.
1/18 pt.	Carnglassansy	Alan McLean	14. 8. 0.
1/18 pt.	Olista	Alan McLean	7. 0. 0.
1/18 pt.	Torronich	Robert Montgomery	7.19. 0.
1/18 pt.	Craigfad	Archd. McEwan 8th, John McLergan 4th, Dond. McQuary 4th	6. 2. 0.
1/18 pt.	Ammond	Ferquhard Campbell	
1 qr.	Nerebolls	Neil McDonald 12th, Hugh McDonald 8th, Duncan McDonald 4th, Donald McDonald 4th, Charles and John McArthur 4th	
1 qr.	Octofad and Miln of Nerebolls	William Campbell	15.10. 0.
33 2/3 d.	Wester Elister		19. 0. 0.
33 1/3 d	Balygawly		
	Arychally and Island Oversaw	George Campbell of Elister	22. 4. 5 1/3
	Easter Elister		
1 qr.	Kelsoe	William Roy Campbell	29.14. 0.
1 qr.	Aryhallauch	Coline Campbell, Ardnahue	13. 0. 0.
3 1			

Extent	Names of the Lands	Tennents' Names	Sterling
1 qr.	Lossit	Archibald Campbell	16.11. 0.
1 qr.	Coultown	} John Campbell, Coultown	7. 0. 0.
	Calmusary		
1 qr.	Gerrich	Hector McLean 8th, Keneth Clark 6th, Neil McEachern 4th, Dond. McNougard 6th, Finlay McIntyre 4th, Archd. McLergan 4th	
1 qr.	Tormistle	James Campbell of Balinaby	15.16. 0.
	Miln of Breakauchy	" " "	15. 0. 0.
31	Braid		3. 0. 0.
1 qr. 31	Kilcherran	William Campbell	31.10. 0.
711 kerrm	½ Kilchoman		
	½ Miln of Kilchoman		
711 kerrm	½ Kilchoman	Duncan Campbell of Sunderline	22.10. 0.
	½ Miln of Kilchoman		
1 cowland	Smail	The Rev. Mr. John Campbell and Duncan Campbell, his son.	22.10. 0.
1 qr.	Migrim	Alexr. Campbell, Kilinalen	
1 mk.	Crulin and Ardtorinsh	N.B. The five pound added to the above tack lands	
1 qr. 1/18 pt.	Sanaigmore	by mistake should be added to the wadsett lands	
1 qr.	Keandrochead	Archibald Campbell in Sanaig	33. 0. 0.
1 qr.	Ardnave		18. 0. 0.
	Breakauchie		
	Mergidill		
	Killnave		
31	Leekgrunart	} John Campbell in Ardnave Alexr. Campbell of Kilinalen, 10th, Malcolm McFarlane 8th and John McLean 6th	56.12. 0.
		Add for Arieballach above short charged	4.18. 0.
4 qr. 11	Sunderline & c.	Duncan Campbell of Sunderline, feupduty	15. 3. 4.
3 qr. 1/18 pt.	Grunart & c.	James Campbell of Balinaby, wadsett and teinds	23.12. 2⅔
			508.16. 0.
			0. 19. 11
			£ 509.15. 11⅔

After the Jacobite Rebellion

Daniel had successfully kept Islay from involvement in the Jacobite Rebellion of 1745: a token company only, under the Captaincy of Archibald Roy Campbell, being sent out to join the Government troops. They were stationed in Castle Stalker, in Appin, which was used as a supply base.

Shawfield's daughter had married Duncan Campbell of Lochnell, whose Aunt was the mother of the Gentle Lochiel (Donald Cameron). Dr. Archie Cameron, a younger and very devoted brother, organised that, on the retreat of the Jacobite Army from England, Prince Charles, Lochiel and his chief officers should be billeted in Shawfield's Glasgow mansion and, by so doing, saved it from looting by the Highland Army. After their defeat at Culloden, Charles, Lochiel, Dr. Archie and many others escaped to France where Lochiel was given a commission in the French Army. In the years that followed, Dr. Archie came secretly to Lochiel to collect his brother's rents for the support of the fugitives but in March 1753 he was captured by Lord George Beauclerk at Inversnaid and brought to the Tower of London. He stood trial in May, arraigned as a Traitor and executed on Tower Hill on 7 June. He had married, as his second wife, a Belgian lady who was permitted to visit him. Whilst in the Tower he was forbidden to have the means of corresponding with anyone.

However, he seems to have acquired scraps of paper and a pencil and wrote notes to Shawfield asking for his intervention. These were given to his wife for delivery but whether they ever reached the aged and ailing Shawfield, who died shortly afterwards, is doubtful. His son John had died in 1746 and his grandson and heir was a young boy, so nothing was done on Dr. Archie's behalf. These tragic scraps of paper were found among the Gask Papers.

Roads & Bridges

The Act for Repairing Roads & Bridges – 1669 – really applied to the Lowland and East Coast roads which were already in being at this time. It was not until the Jacobite Rebellion of 1715 that the lack of roads in the Highlands was fully appreciated and General Wade then commenced in 1720 his tremendous work of opening up the country with his system of military roads. He met with much opposition from the Northern Chiefs, who felt they were losing their great asset of isolation. However, the General continued his work and the last tendril entered Argyll over the great mountain pass of the Rest and be Thankful and down into Inveraray in 1747, the year before his death. The Lairds and Landowners all over the country had realised that the success of the Government troops during the 1745 Rebellion had owed much to these military roads, and were anxious to improve or make roads through their lands. In Islay, Daniel I, through the Stent Committee, formed in accordance with the above Act, organised the making of roads in July 1747. "The Hyghways are by apoyntment of the above gentlemen to be Eight, ninth and tenth July and there former surveys and surveys". [Stent Book p. 33] The gentlemen referred to were:

Patrick Campbell (Persabolls)
Archd Campbell of Arderignish
(Ardimersie)

Arch. Campbell (Sanaig)
Alexr. Robertson (the Surgeon)
John Campbell (Ardnave)

Duncan Campbell (Balool & Leek)

George Campbell (Elister)

John Campbell (Balaclaven
& Robolls)
John Campbell (Kilchoman)
Ard. Campbell (Lossit)
Coll McAlister (the Bailie
Stoin etc.)

From then on the work on roads, and the quays at Portaskaig and Bowmore, were apportioned among the nearest farms and inspectors were appointed, at the annual meeting of the Stent Committee.

The 1669 Act was largely superceded on the mainland, from 1750 by the Turnpike Acts, but as these did not apply to Islay, the 1669 Act remained in force with the 'Statute Labour' which it instituted. The high cost of this work, with all else that was required, encouraged the second Daniel to apply for a grant in the 1760's. He got half of what he asked for and applied it where most necessary, on the quays at Portaskaig and Bowmore. Later, in the 1780's, his brother Walter also applied for a grant, particularly with regard to the road from Portaskaig to Bridgend, which he wished to extend to Bowmore: It was an important road as most of the imported materials had to come in from Portaskaig. [He did get a grant for improvements, but not specifically for the Road] It came to be known as the "Islay Road", and as such, was inspected in 1827 by Lord Colchester, Chairman of the Board of Parliamentary Roads and Bridges [as opposed to the Military Roads, which by this time had been handed over to the Counties they traversed] from 1803 to 1817, in virtue of his position as Speaker of the House of Commons, and it was during this period that the "branch" roads in Arran, Jura and Islay were officially taken over by the Commissioners, though the basic roads had been laid down by the respective landowners thirty years earlier. The last reference to the Portaskaig road in the Stent Minutes [pp. 201, 202] 1815. "The sum allowed by this Meeting for finishing the New Road from Portaskaig – £20 . . . . . . The Meeting conceiving it to be highly useful that the road from Portaskaig should be rendered complete, do willing stent themselves in the sum stated here".

ACT FOR REPAIRING ROADS & BRIDGES
1669

His Majesty with advise and consent of the Estates of Parliament doth appoint and ordain the Sheriff of the Shire and one of his deputies being always ane heritor therein . . . . . . to conveen at the heid burgh . . . . . . upon the 1st Tuesday of May for ordering of highways bridges and ferries, ... to divide the paroches . . . . . . as they by most evest [nearest] to the several highways to be repaired, and as thay may have the most equal burden: and to appoint such of their members or other overseirs of such parts . . . . . . as are most convenient and nearest to their ordinary residence, ... and are hereby authorized and strictly required to call . . . . . . all Tenants & coatters and their servants, within the bounds appointed . . . . . . to have in readiness horses, carts, sleds, spades, shovells, picks, mattocks and such other instrument as shall be required . . . . . . and to appoint them fit wages for their attendance. Providing that the days they are required to work not exceed the number of sex days for man & horse yeerlie for the first three years and four days yeerlie thereafter and that they be only betwixt the bear seid [Sewing of barley] and haytime or harvest thereafter. With power . . . . . . to poind the readiest goods of the absents for twentie Shillings Scots money for the absence of ilk man dayly and threttie [thirty] Shillings for man & horse . . . . . . which highways shall be twenty foot of measure broad at least and shall be so repaired that horse and carts may travel summer and winter thereupon . . . . . . His Majesty doth hereby authorize and require the whole freeholders and hertors . . . . . . to call for an account . . . . . . of what is needful for reparation of highways and others foresaid, and what charges and expences is requisite . . . . . . and accordingly to stent the heretors . . . . . . not exceidung ten shillings Scots upon each hundreth poun of valued rent in one year.

Instrument of Consignation
Daniel Campbell of
Shawfield
Agt
Colin Campbell of Daill
1749

(The original is among the Kildalton Papers and is written on two sheets of Deed papers which have been stuck together. It is signed in the margin over the join by fferqrd Campbell N.P.)

AT KILLAROW in Islay the fifteenth day of May One thousand Seven hundred and fourty Nine and of his Majesties reign the twenty Second Year.

WHICH DAY In presence of me Notary Publick & Witnesses Subscribing COMPEARED personally within the parish Kirk of Killarow John Campbell of Askomell As provs Constitute Impowered & authorized to the effect aftermtd By Daniel Campbell of Shawfield heretable proprietar & Reversar of the Lands aftermtd Conform to the Letters of Prorys granted to him therenent Dated at Woodhall the fifteenthe day of Frbry last HAVING and in his hands holding Ane Contract & prorogation Enterd into and perfected betwixt the sd Daniel Campbell of Shawfield as having right to the reversion of the lands afrermtd on the one part And Collin Campbell of Daill, Lawful eldest son of Lauchlin Campbell, on the other part dated the thretteenth day of July Jajvyc and twenty four years, WHEREBY (after Narrating a Contract of Wadset past betwixt Sr Hugh Campbell of Calder and the sd deceast Lauchlan Campbell on the one and other parts Dated the twenty sixth Day of November Jajvyc & Eighty five years by which the sd Sr Hugh Campbell (for the soume of ffive thousand merks then payd him) Did wadset for the time, To the said Collin Campbell & his forsaids personally or at their dwelling place In presence of two famous witnesses (and that in place of the premonition of Sixty Days Stipulate by the Original Contract of Wadset @mentd) And in case of absence or refusal to receive the sd soume the Same to be Consignd in the hands of the Baily of Ilay, Or any other responsible man within the sd Island to be made furthcoming on the peril of the Consigner, which prorogation or Coppy therof with a Declaration under the hand of the Baily of Ilay that Intimation was made in maner forsaid Is Declard sufficient for using the sd Order of Redemption And the sd Daniel Campbell is obligd immediately after the redemption to pay the sd Collin Campbell & his forsds the Value of the biggings on the sd Lands, as the samen should be found due on terms of the forsd Contract of Wadset betwixt the sd Sr Hugh & Lauchlan Campbells & his forsds, AS ALSOE HOLDING in his hands Ane other Contract & prorogation dated the third day of August Jajvyc & thretty two years past betwixt the saids Daniel & Collin Campbells, Whereby the said Daniel Campbell (for the

5 The opening of the Instrument of Consignation, 1749, Daniel Campbell of Shawfield and Islay and Colin Campbell, Wadsetter of Dail, later tenant of Carnbeg and finally Laird of Balinaby. Kildalton Papers. Photograph by Fraser MacArthur.

reasons therein (@speit) ffurther PROROGATS and Continows the Redemp-
tion of the Lands & oyrs @speit ffrom the said Collin & Dispone to the said
Lauchlan Campbell & Anne Campbell his Spouse in Lyfrent and their heirs
yrinment in fee ALL and HAILL the towns and three quarters lands of Daill,
Surn, Kilbrandan & Octofreigh wt the houses & pertinents & teinds parsonage
& Viccarage included in the Stock all lying in the parish of Killarow Island of
Islay and Sherriffdome of Argyle, REDEEMABLE by the sd Sr Hugh Campbell
his heirs & assigneysp from the sd Lauchlan his heirs and Succors Upon payment
of the forsaid soume of Five thousand Merks at the term & upon the Premonition
specified in the Clause or reversion contd in the forsaid Wadset right) HE the said
Daniel Campbell of Shawfield (for the causes yrinment) SUPERCEDED DE-
LAY & SUSPENDED the forsaid Reversion and Redemption of the lande teinds
and others mentd from the said Collin Campbell his heirs and Succors ffor the
Space of Eight Yrars from and after the term of Whitsunday then next Jajvyc
& twenty five years, But the said space being Expird, the saids Lands & pertinents
are declared Redeemable by payment to the said Collin Campbell and his forsaids
within the parish Kirk of Killarow, of the above soume ffive thousand merks
Scots mony, Upon Ane Intimation of Sixty Days to be made off before by the sd
Daniel Campbell and his forsds, or by the Baily of Ilay for Campbell & his
@wan, for the Space of other Eight years from and after the term of Whitsunday
Jajvyc & thretty three years, But redeemable alwise by the sd Daniel Campbell
& his forsds at any term of Whitsunday after Expiring of the sd Eight years, upon
payment or consignation of the forsaid Soume of ffive thousand Merks in maner
mentd in the provision of Reversion stipulat by the above first Contract & prorogation expede betwixt them, AND SICKLIKE HOLDING in his hands Letters
of Prory dated the fifteenth of ffebry Last from the sd Daniel Campbell Constituteing and Authoriseing the sd John Campbell his provs to Serve & Execute
the premonition aftermentd in maner afterspet AND IN LIKE MANER having
holding ane Instrument of premonition dated the ffifteenth day of March last,
under the hand & subscription of me Nory Publk subscribing BEARING That
he as Baily ofIlay and prov for & in name & behalf of his Constituent Shawfield
had then made due and Lawful Intimation and premonition To the said Collin
Campear to Compear this day & place and receive from the said Daniel Campbell
or others in his Name the forsd Soume of ffive thousand Merks Scots for the
Lawfull Redemption from him his heirs and Succors of the forsd Lands & Pertinents sput, And to being with him and Deliver to the said Daniel Campbell or his
prov forsd Sufficient Dispositions & Assignations to, OR Discharges Renunci-
ations of the forsaid wadset Right together with the forsd Original Contract of
Wadset & Infeftment yron & prorogations mentd, And that he had Certificatne
to him if he failied to Compear, of Compearing, should refuse to accept & receive
the sd Soume of Five Thousands Merks & deliver up the Writes mentd That then
the same soume would be Consigned in terms of the Clause of Reversion Stipulat
in the prorogations @narrated, And that therupon the said Lands would be
holden & repute as Duely & Lawfully redeemed from him & his @wans in all
time therafter, As the saids two several Contracts & prorogations, Leres prorys
& Instrument in themselves more fully proports AND IN LIKE MANER HE of

new Exhibited & repeated the forsd prory of premonition of ye date @amentd ALSOE Constituteing Authorizing & Impowering him the sd John Campbell as prov To Compear this day & place and to make due and Lawfull Consignation of the forsd Soume of ffive thousand Mks In the hands of James Campbell of Ballinaby, OR any other responsible person within Ilay, ffor redeeming the forsd prorogations past betwixt the sd Daniel & Collen Campbells as the sd prory fully bears, All which writes and papers were at Desire of the sd Prov publickly read & Explained by me sd Nory Pubk AND THAT being done the said John Campbell as prov for & in name & behalf of the said Daniel Campbell Did Number out & tell down the forsaid Soume of ffive thousand Merks Scots mony in Sufficient Gold & Silver of the Currency of Great Britain And oft and Diverse times (after open Calling at the most patent door of the sd Kirk) Desired & Required the said Collin Campbell or others in his Name sufficiently Authorised to Compear & Receive the samen Soume for the Lawfull Redemption of the forsaid Lands of DAILL. SURN Kilbrandan & Octofreign with the teind & pertinents, and thereupon to deliver him as prov forsd for & in name & behalf exprest, The forsdaid Original Contract of Wadset & Infeftment thereon, with the two several Prorogations @speit. Together with a sufficient Disposition & assignation to, on Discharge & Renunciatne of the haill premisses in favours of the sd Daniel Campbell & forsds, to be used at pleasure AND, with us, having Waited & Attended in this Kirk till the Suns setting and the said Collin Campbell absenting & failing to Compear, And noe other Compearing in his Name to the effect @mentd Notwithstanding the premonition formerly servd & Intimations now made by frequent publick Calling at the most patent door of the Kirk. THEREFORE the said JOHN CAMPBELL prov for & in name & behalf forsaid DID CONSIGN the forsaid Soume of FFIVE thousand Merks Scots mony In the hands of the said James Campbell of Ballinaby then & there present & who accordingly received the same to be made furthcoming as accords, And made offer likewise of paying the Value of the timber of the houses of the forsd Wadset Lands Soe far as the said Daniel Campbell his Constituent is bound thereanent, AND PROTESTED THAT thereupon the lands and others amentd Were and might be held & reputes duely & Lawfully Redeemed from the said Daniel Campbell his Constituent In terms of & conform to the provision of Reversion Contd in the two Contracts & prorogations narrated in all pointes, AND FURTHER PROTESTED That the sd Collin Campbell might be liable to the said Daniel Campbell In the expences of a process of Declarator of Redemption to follow yron and for all other cost skaith interest & expences his Constituent should Sustain or incurr by the sd Collin's not Receiving the forsd Wadset Mony now consigne throw his default & not giving up the Wadset Rights & oyr Writes @amentd in terms of the Clause of Reversion aforsd. AND THERUPON & upon the haill premisses the said John Campbell for & in name & behalf forsd asked & took Instruments in the hands of me Nory Pubk subing, THIR THINGS were done in the said Kirk of Killarow & within my seat there betwixt the hours of Eight & Nine in the afternoon of the day Moneth & year of God wam Before & In presence of Duncan Campbell of Shinderland, Lauchlan McNeil of Knocknahae Provost of Campbelltown, Collin Campbell of Ardn-

6 The last paragraph of the Instrument of Consignation, 1749, showing the flamboyant signature of ffergunard Campbell, Public Notary, Tacksman of Laggan, who figured largely in the Public Affairs of Islay. Kildalton Papers. *Photograph by Fraser MacArthur.*

ahow, George Campbell of Elister & Dond Campbell tacksman of Duisker, with diverse & sundry other witnesses specially called & required to the premises.

(signed)
Collin Campbell Witness
George Campbell Witness

Frismissa esse Vera Attestor
fferqrd Campbell N P

WADSETS & FEUS

Kilchoman 1686
To Archibald Campbell
  Ochtomour, Coultorsay, Lorgba, Grymsay, the kow land of Gylin & Dowdil-
  lmor.
    Pays of few dewtie & tynd silver xxxvj^{lib}xiij^{s}iiij^d
To Duncane Campbell
  Ellistererrach, Ellandowrrsay, Balladalie & Corieskallag
    Pays of few dutie & tynd silver j^{c}zlvj^{lib}13^{s}4^d
To Duncane McArthour
  Coultowne & Calmasarie
    Pays of few dutie & tynd dewtie xxiiij^{lib}
To Archibald Campbell
  Coull, Sinderline, Forland, Machirvealin & Cladavell
    Pays of few dutie & Tynd dewtie j^c lxxxij^{lib}
To John Campbell
  Leack, Sannagbeg, Kowland of Keanchyllane in Machoroshinis Grunzard,
  & Corspallane
    Pays of few dutie & tyne dewtie lxvj^{lib}xiij^{s}iiij^d

Herries
To Lachlan Campbell
  Dallochtonafeych [Daill] Kilbranan & Surne
    Pays of silver rent & tynd silver liij^{lib}vj^{s}viij^d
To Alexander Campbell set in few
  Torrobolis & Persobollis
    Pays few maillis & tynd silver lxxxxij^{lib}xij^s
To John Campbell of Ballaclaven
  Keppullis, Robollis, & Ballaclavane
    Pays few dewtie & Tynd silver lxxiiij^{lib}
To airis & relict of wmquhile Alexander Campbell
  Killinalziane, Crosmoir & Aldgarnstill
    Pays of few dutie & tynd silver xiiij^{lib}13^{s}4^d
To Archibald Campbell of Ochtomoir
  Dudilmore [in Rental of the Rhynds]

Kilarow   *1722*   *Kilmeny*

To Collin Campbell of Dail
    Dail, Octonafreich, Kilbrannen & Surn. 5000 mks
        Pays few duties of Silver Tynd 53^{lib}6^{s}8^d
To Donald Campbell by Sir Alexander of Cawdor
    Lossit, Gertontibber, Gortenenles, Kilsleavan, Balluchturk, Balleclach, Kilmenie & Turmagan 10,000 merks
        Pays of few dutie £91.6.8 of Teind Dewtie £64
To Neil Campbell
    Torrobols, Feu
        Pays of feu dewtie & Teind Dewtie £38.13.4.
To John Campbell of Ballieclavan
    Ballieclavan & Robolls 3000 merks
        Pays of Feus & Teind dutie £74.0.0.
To John Campbell by Sir Hugh of Cawdor 2,500 mks
    Killenallein
        Pays of few duties & Teind dewtie £20.0.0.
To Neil Campbell by Sir Alexander of Calder
    Bolsa, Uabernick, & Ardnahow 3,550 mks
        Pays of Few & Teind duties £67.15.0.

Kilchoman

To George Campbell by Sir Hugh of Calder 7,000 mks
    Octamore, Cultorsa, Lorgba, Grimsa, Dudilmore, & Gaylin
        Pays of few & Teind duties £136.0.0.
To Colin Campbell of Ellister 3,500 mks
    Elister Wester, Ballegallie, Anscallaige
        Pays of few & Teind Duties £146.13.4.
To John Campbell by Sir Hugh of Calder £1,000 Scots
    Coultuine,
        Pays of few & Teind dewtie £24.0.0.
To Archibald Campbell of Schinderline [Sunderland]
    trlnds in feu & Pays of few & teind duty £182.0.0.
To Donald Campbell of Ballenabie 7,500 merks
    Leack, Sannaigbeig, Grannard & Caspellan
        Pays of few & Teind duties £100.

Churches Manses and Teinds

In 1732 the Stent Committee had decided that a new Parish Church should be built in the neighbourhood of Lagavuline and the medeaeval Chapel of Kildalton, beside the High Cross, deserted. The new church was built on the quarterland of Ballinaughton More beside the Track that led via Kilbride, Leorin, Arivochalum and Glen Machrie down to the Big Strand, at that time the main road between Kilarrow Parish and Kildalton & Oa. This church was used, also, as the school, but the scholars so vandalized it that another school was built in the village of Lagavuline and the church repaired; it lasted till a second was built on a part of the Surnaig lands in 1825. A manse was not built at this time as Daniel did not care to move the old Tacksman out: his son was given the Tack of the Inn and farm of Gartchahossan at Bridgend and the Minister was allowed £12 "Manse Money" to hire a house in the neighbourhood, though he had full use of the glebe at Surnaig. The "old" Tacksman, Hugh MacDougall, probably then only about sixty, lived to a ripe old age and it was not until 1825 that the Tacksman's house was refurbished as a manse, and the first occupant was the Reverend Archibald Mactavish, who lived in it for 35 years. On his death, the next minister demanded a new and larger manse, the present Surnaig House, built by John Ramsay of Kildalton in 1860. John Ramsay had planned a house similar to an earlier 18th Century one in which his Uncle had lived at Innerpefray & where he had spent many happy holidays. This house had four rooms on the ground floor & five on the first floor – including a small room over the entrance hall. However, the new Minister did not consider this sufficiently large, so the plans were altered, eliminating two of the back rooms, one up and one down, which were converted into passages and a series of cupboards. Another wing to accommodate a kitchen, scullery, and larder, and two bedrooms above, was added on to balance the first wing of four rooms. The result was a charming long house facing South. A third Parish Church was built in 1911 by his son, Captain Iain Ramsay, and closed by the minister in 1971.

Daniel had approached the Synod of Argyll in 1747 saying that he did not consider two ministers, based at Kilarrow and working East and West respectively, over country served only by cattle tracks and strands, to be sufficient for the needs of the Island with a population of over 5000, and he submitted a proposal for a third erection. He offered to provide the necessary Churches, Manses and Glebes, to pay the stipends and Communion money to the three ministers, provided that the Synod would transfer to him the valued Teinds of Islay and the Queen Anne's Bounty (specifically given for the building and repair of churches, education etc.) in view of the considerable outlay in which he would be involved. His offer was accepted unanimously.

It was then discovered that the Royal Bounty had already been allocated to the Rev. John Campbell, Minister of Kilarow, for life. Thus it was not until the reverend gentleman had died and Daniel's young grandson, the second Daniel, had picked up the reins of his inheritance that the matter would be taken up again.

EXTRACT DECREE OF VALUATION
OF THE ISLAND OF ISLAY
Dated 2nd March, 1636

ATT Edinburgh the Second Day of March one thousand Six hundred and thirty-six the Quihilk day in presence of the Commissioners appointed be His Majestie, and Estaites of his heines laite Parliament for surenderis and teindis under written They are to say, John, Archbishop of St Andrew, Chancellor, Thomas, Erle of Hadingtoun, Lord Privy Seal, Patrick Archbishop of Glasgow, George, Erle of Wintoun, William, Erle of Drumfrice. David, Bishop of Edinburgh, Thomas, Bishop of Galloway, George Lord Forester, Sir Robert Spotiswoode of Donypace, Knight, President of the College of Justice, Sir John Hay of Baro, Knight, Clerk of the Register, Sir Thomas Hope of Craighall, Knight, Barounet, His Majestie's Advocate, Sir James Lermont of Balcomie, Knight, Sir Robert Griersone of Lag, Knight, Archibald Tod Edward Edzer and William Gray Burgesses of Edinburgh, and Gabriel Cunninghame, Burges of Glasgow – Anent the Summond is raised at the instance of Neil, Bishop of the Ylles against John Campbell, feire of Calder, Collein Campbell of Finarline, Alexander Campbell of Glasseries, Neil Campbell of Torrobollis, Mr William Campbell of Torrobollis, and Duncan McEwine, Heritors of the lands within the Yle of Isla Making mention that quhair albeit it be his Majestie's gracious will and pleasure that the Teinds parsonage and viccarage throughout the several parochines of this Kingdome be valued to the intent that his Majestie's annuity may be cleirat and the Heritors may have the right of the Teinds of their proper Lands nevertheless thair was no valuation maid of the teinds of the Lands within the Yle of Isla quhairof the said Bishop of the Isles is titular and thairthrow his Majertie wald have been prejudgit of his heines' annuity necessarr theirfor it was that the said Bishop shuld been admittit to lied and deduce before the saidis Commissioneris and lawful probation of the worth of the Teindis of the landis parsonage and viccarage within the said Yle of Ilay and that letters should have been direct for that effect And anent the charge given to the said Defenders to have compeared before the saidis Commissionerie at an certain day bygane to have heard and seen ane just and true valuation maid of the teindis parsonage and viccarage of the lands within the Isla foresaid or else to have shawine and reasonable cause why the samen shuld not have been done with certification to thame if thay failziet The said Commissioners wald admit sie lawfull probation as the said Neill Bishop of the Isles wald use anent the worth of the teindis parsonage and viccarage of the said Isle of Ilay, as in the said Summondis executions and Indorsation thereof at more length is contenit – uhilk being called this day and the said persewer Compearand personallie with John Pitcairn Advocate his procurator quha desirit the Defender's to be halden as confest upon the rentall of the Teinds of the Lands particularlie after mentionat parsonage and viccarage ly and within the said Isle of Islay pertaining to the persons afternamed as the samen extends to twenty-ane hundred merks money And delared that he referred the treuth of the rentall to the

Defenderis' eithes of verity simpiciter and the said John Campbell fiere of Calder compearand personallie with Mr. James Aikenheid his procurator and als the said remanent Defenders compearand by Mr. George Norwell thair procurator quha craved inspection of the said rentall to be restricted to the soume of Nynteen hundred merks and offerit to prove the daids defalcatiois Quhilk being refusit by the saids Commissioners the saidis parties referred the reasones and defalcationes to the saidis Lordes and the saidis Lordis Commissioneris having taken the samen to their consideration They ffand Declaret and Ordaineit and be this presents thay ffind Declair and Ordaine the teinds parsonage and viccarage of the lands underwritten to be worth in constant rent in all time coming the soume of two thousand merkis usual money of this Realm and Ordaines the said soume to be dividet amongst the saidis Defenderis heritoris foresaidis proportionallie ilk ane for their awn parttis conform to the rental given in by the said Neil, bishope of the Yiles suberyveit with his hand according quhearunto the teindis parsonage and viccarage of the defederis' landis within the said Yle of Ilay extends in constant rent in manner following, vizt. The Teindis of the haill landis with in the said Yle of Ilay pertaining to the said John Campbell feire of Calder in propertie to the soume of une thousand seven hundreth and four score four merks in yearlie con-stant rent baith parsonage and viccarage of the Landis within the said Yle of Ilay pertaining to the said Collein Campbell vizt Coull Smarline fforlane Ma-cherunen Lyne and Cladewell in constant rent yearlie of parsonage and viccarage Teinds Thriescoir aught merks and the Teinds baith parsonage and viccarage of the Landis within the said Yle of Ilay pertaining to the said Alexander Campbell vizt Glasseris in constant rent sixtein merks and the Teinds baith parsonage and viccarage of the Landis within the said Yle of Ilay pertaining to the said Neil Campbell vizt Torrobollis and Persebollis in constant rent yeirlie Twenty merkis, and the Teindis parsonage and viccarage of the landis within the Iyle of Ilay pertaining to the said Duncan McEwine and John McEwine his sone vizt Ballehervie and Octocornoch in constant rent yeirlie of parsonage and viccarage teindis haith parsonage and viccarage of the landis within the said Yle of Ilay pertaining to the said Mr. William Campbell vizt Keppoillis mour Keppoillis beg Hayen Torrobollis Kerrebeach, Bailole, Quaskere, and Ballemertene in constant rent yeirlie of parsonage and viccarage teind fourscore sextein merks and quhilkis several soumes of money above the written saidis Commissioneris Decerns and Ordainis to stand as any constant rent and worth of the Teindis of the said Landis rexive above specified baith parsonage and viccarage in all time coming without deduction of his Majestie's ease and without prejudice to the takis set to the said John Campbell fiere of Calder of the Teindis of the foresaid Landis for the yeirs therein continit because the said perswer Compeared as said is produced the said Rentall and craved the saidis defenderis to be holden as confest upon Twa Thousand one hondreth merks money and the differ betwixt the saidis perties being represented to the arbitriement of the saidis Lordis Commissioneris Decerns and Ordainis to stand as any constant rent and worth of the Teindis of the said Landis rexive above specified baith parsonage and viccarage in all time coming without deduction of his Majestie's ease and without prejudice to the takis set to the said John Campbell fiere of Calder of the Teindis of the foresaid Landis for the yeirs therein continit because the said perswer Compeared as said is produced the said Rentall and craved the saidis defenderis to be holden as confest upon Twa Thousand one hundreth merks money and the differ betwixt the saidis parties being represented to the saidis Commissioneris as said in and bath the saidis parties having referit themselves to the arbitriement of the saidis Lordis Commissioneris Thairfore the Saidis Lordis ffand Declaret and Ordainit the teinds parsonage and viccarage of the foresaidis Landis to extend to the quantities of money above specified in all time coming according to the said divisione without deduction of his Majestie's ease and but prejudice of the Takis foresaids set to the said John Campbell for the haill yeirie and terms thairincontenit in manner foresaid

Extractum sic subscibitur   W. HAY

GIFT *of the Revenues of the Bishopricks of Argyll and the Isles to the Synod of Argylle, 14th July 1705*

ANNE, & c. – Forasmuch as we, taking to our Royal consideration the prudent moderation and wise management of the Ministry of the Synod of Argyle and that they do with great care employ the revenue of the vacant stipends which they have by Act of Parliament within their own bounds for educating young men at the Universities, and qualifying them for the Ministry, and thereby have planted almost the haill churches situated in their bounds with sufficient well qualified Ministers, and that thay are very industrious in having erected above 40 schools (whereof 12 are grammer schools) in the Highlands for teaching of the English Language and Latin tongue, and do employ for that purpose and other pious uses the revenue and rents of the two Bishopricks of Argyll and the Isles, and that the said Synod has given a great example of moderation in assuming to their body, of their own accord, a considerable number of the Episcopal Clergy, and are still willing to assume more, and that the late King William and King Charles the First, of ever blessed memory, gave the whole revenues of the said two bishopricks of Argyll and Isles for the pious uses above mentioned: and we, being most willing to omit nothing that may tend to the civilizing of the Highlands and propogation of the Gospel among them, and at the same time to put a distinguishing mark of our Royal favour upon the Synod: Therefore, wit ye us in Prosecution of the former grants made by our said deceased brother and grandfather, with the special consent and advice of John, Duke of Argyll, our Commissioner for the Kingdom of Scotland, James, Earl of Seafield, Lord High Chancellor; William, Marquis of Annadale, and Hugh Earl of Loudonn, principal Secretaries of State, David, Earl of Glasgow, Lord Treasuerer-Depute, and our right trusty Mr Francis Montgomery of Giffen, and Sir John Home of Black-adder, Lords Commissioners of our Treasury and Exchequer, as also with advice and concent of the remanent Lords and other Commissioners thereof within our said Accient Kingdom, to have given, granted and disponed, like as we by the tenor hereof give, grant, and dispone to the said Synod of Argylle, and the factors to be by them nominate for their behoof the haill rents, revenues, casualties and emoluments of the said two Bishopricks of Argyll and Isles, for the crop and year of God 1705, and for all other years and terms preceding and resting-owing, and in time coming, during our pleasure only, or until the same be recalled by writ, under our hand of our Royal successors, and that for settling of schools, repairing of churches, educating and training up of Ministers, supplying such of the

Ministers as have small stipends, and prosecuting the other pious ends and uses above mentioned, as thitherto they have been in use to do, with full power to the Moderator and remanant members of the said Synod and their successors in office to nominate and appoint factors, for whom they shall be answerable, and to meddle and intomit with, uplift and receive from all and sundry heritors, fruuars, liferenters, tacksmen of tithes, tenants, and others liable in payment thereof, the rentall bolls, feu, blench or tack duties, and all other rents, casualties, and emoluments formerly payable to the late Bishops of Argyll and Isles, and their predecessors, and if need be, to call and convene them therefor before whatsoever judge or judges competent, decreets and sentences against them to recover, and the same to due and lawful execution cause be put acquittances and discharge to grant which shall be as calid to the receivers as if we or the general receivers of our rents in our name had subscribed the same, and generally to do all and sundry other things whatsoever necessary anent the premises which we or our receivers might have done before the granting hereof during the space foresaid: Providing always that the said Synod and members thereof shall be accountable to the Lords of our Treasury for their management of the said rents for the Pious uses and ends above mentioned: Providing also that this present gift shall be but prejudice to the allocationa already granted or to be granted by the Commission of Parliament for Plantation of Kirks and Valuation of Teinds, or by the said Lords of our Treasury out of the funds above mentioned in favour of Ministers, whithin the bounds of the said Synod who are not sufficiently provided, and who are no ways to be hereby prejudged. – Given, & c., at our Court at Windsor Castle the 14th of July, and of our reign the fourth year, 1705.

First Surveys of Islay

Daniel I employed a Stephen MacDougall in 1749/50/51 to make a detailed survey of the Island and he produced the first modern map of Islay, showing all the holdings. Unfortunately, only two or three of the detailed maps of this survey have survived, though in the Inventories of Islay House Library in 1776 and 1777 references are made to "The Map Book of Islay" and a "Book of Maps of Islay", but they are not listed in the 1830 catalogue. It is possible that they may have been used by Langland on his compilation of the County of Argyll in 1801, for which Robert [Walter's second son and himself something of a cartographer] was a sponsor. However, the estimates of the capabilities of each farm have survived.

Stephen MacDougall, though from the mainland, was related to the Torrodale MacDougalls, some of whom had emigrated to the American

7 Major General Alexander MacDougall, b. 1732 in Islay, d. 1786 in New York. **1738:** Emigrated with his parents to New York, with Captain Lachlan Campbell of Leorin, from Torodale, Kildalton. **1751:** married (1) Nancy MacDougall (d. 1763). **1756:** Captain of Privateers *Tiger* and *Barrington* in war with France. Major General in Washington's Army. **1767:** married (2) Hannah Bostwick. **1778:** Commanded at West Point.

Colonies in 1739. Alexander, the future General in Washington's Army, made a trip, during his privateering days, across the Atlantic to Islay, where he married his cousin Ann, daughter of Stephen. Their descendants now live in Vermont, U.S.A. and have many interesting papers and letters of the Revolutionary War.

View of Contents
of the Baroney and Estate of Islay
Parish of Kilchoman

	Arable			Green Pasture			Heathy Pasture			TOTAL		
	Acres	R.	P.	Acs.	R.	P.	Acs.	R.	P.	Acs.	R.	P.
1. Isle Noresay (sic)	30	—	—	10	1	8	—	—	—	40	1	8
2. Ellister (Wester) & Port Wemyss	310	—	20	150	1	—	296	—	—	756	1	20
3. Ellister (Easter)	117	—	—	149	—	—	430	1	—	696	1	—
4. Ballimony & Arrichalloch	163	—	—	460	—	—	210	—	—	833	—	—
5. Losset (Rhinns)	268	3	—	40	—	—	178	2	—	487	—	—
6. Kelsay	192	—	—	100	—	—	104	1	—	396	1	—
7. Tormistle	250	—	—	150	—	—	173	—	—	573	—	—
8. Coulstoon	100	—	—	250	—	—	62	2	—	412	2	—
9. Olistle	120	—	—	100	—	—	237	1	—	457	1	—
10. Grarach (sic)	200	—	—	136	1	21	100	—	—	436	1	21
11. Greamsay	100	1	—	211	—	—	549	3	—	861	—	—
12. Octofad	280	1	—	194	2	—	200	—	—	674	3	—
13. Nerabols	180	1	—	34	1	—	135	2	—	350	—	—
14. Craigfad	103	3	—	32	2	—	83	—	—	219	1	—
15. Torronich	68	3	—	21	—	—	134	—	—	223	3	—
16. Carn Pt. Charlotte	150	—	10	21	—	—	100	—	—	271	—	10
17. Glassins Lots	350	—	—	100	—	—	122	1	13	572	1	13
18. Kilchiaran	300	—	—	500	—	—	224	—	—	1024	—	—
19. Oct(o)more	506	3	—	55	—	—	479	3	—	1041	2	—
20. Cultorsa	81	—	—	53	—	—	34	1	—	168	1	—
21. Gartachara	108	3	—	51	3	—	132	3	—	293	1	—
22. Conisby	453	1	—	80	2	—	740	—	—	1273	3	—
23. Kilchoman	428	2	—	453	3	—	945	1	—	1827	2	—
24. Smaal	305	3	—	73	—	—	189	—	—	568	—	—
25. Sanaigbeg	49	3	—	100	—	—	124	—	—	273	3	—
26. Sanaigmore	318	3	—	178	2	—	872	—	—	1369	1	—
27. Kandrochid	154	—	—	130	—	—	315	—	—	599	—	—
28. Grulint (sic)	66	1	—	40	—	—	130	—	—	236	1	—
29. Carondonachy (sic)	125	1	—	52	1	—	279	2	—	457	—	—
30. Gruinart	753	1	16	150	—	—	250	—	—	1153	1	16
31. Leckgruinart	172	2	33	51	—	—	300	—	—	523	2	33
32. Kilnave	210	2	—	65	3	—	430	3	—	707	—	—
33. Ardnave & Breakachy	391	—	—	291	—	—	624	1	—	1306	1	—
34. Island Knave (sic)	—	—	—	69	—	—	—	—	—	69	—	—
35. Cor(s)apoll	343	3	36	73	—	—	966	—	—	1382	3	36
36. Coulabus	250	—	36	14	—	—	300	—	—	564	—	36
	8003	3	31	4641	2	29	10453	—	13	23098	2	33

Parish of Kildalton

	Arable			Green Pasture			Heathy Pasture			TOTAL		
	Acres	R.	P.	Acs.	R.	P.	Acs.	R.	P.	Acs.	R.	P.
1. Proaig	89	1	19	—	—	—	2739	—	—	2818	1	19
2. Ardtallay	233	—	—	264	—	—	1038	—	—	1535	—	—
3. Claigin	102	2	—	337	—	—	710	—	—	1149	2	—
4. Trudernish	105	2	36	67	2	12	676	—	—	849	1	8
5. Craigeen	116	—	—	223	—	—	886	—	—	1225	—	19
6. Kentoor	249	2	5	60	—	—	129	—	—	438	2	5
7. Stoain	74	2	16	66	—	—	100	—	—	240	2	16
8. Ardmanach	169	1	29	—	—	—	14	2	12	184	—	1
9. Ardmore & Islands	100	3	31	190	—	12	31	1	39	322	2	2
10. Kildalton	100	—	—	326	—	38	918	—	—	1344	—	38
11. Ard-Ellistry & Islands	104	—	10	388	1	38	599	—	—	1091	2	8
12. Knock	140	1	15	630	3	13	780	—	—	1551	—	28
13. Ardimarsay & Islands	114	2	27	201	3	39	194	—	28	510	3	14
14. Arinambiast	55	3	4	82	—	—	100	—	—	237	3	4
15. Ardbeg	108	—	—	122	—	—	—	—	—	230	—	—
16. Lagavullin	87	3	36	40	—	—	—	—	—	127	3	36
17. Collumkill	61	—	—	100	—	—	123	—	—	284	—	—
18. Solam	—	—	—	225	—	38	974	3	6	1200	—	4
19. Balinaughtonbeg	—	—	—	166	1	13	—	—	—	166	1	13
20. Balinaughtonmore	151	3	13	100	—	—	624	—	—	875	3	13
21. Kilbride	189	3	37	25	1	15	379	—	—	594	1	12
22. Surnaig	30	2	14	50	—	—	—	—	—	80	2	14
23. Ardinastle	70	3	38	126	—	—	—	—	—	196	3	38
24. Isle Texa	—	—	—	119	—	—	—	—	—	119	—	—
25. Torradale	197	1	29	37	—	37	133	—	—	367	2	26
26. Ballyneill	162	2	—	54	—	—	—	—	—	216	2	—
27. Tayndrome	136	—	—	22	1	10	284	—	—	442	1	10
28. Taycarmagan	160	—	—	120	—	—	169	—	—	449	—	—
29. Balivicar	163	—	18	245	—	30	351	—	—	759	1	8
30. Loairin (Lower)	94	2	6	100	—	—	281	1	36	476	—	22
31. Loairin (Upper)	172	3	37	56	2	36	525	2	29	755	1	22
32. Aryvoachallum	66	—	32	42	2	34	202	3	38	311	3	24
33. Machry	129	2	29	649	2	—	1395	1	2	2174	1	31
34. Glenegidale	386	—	—	398	1	—	1867	—	—	2651	1	—
35. Kintra	88	1	—	237	2	29	158	2	10	484	1	39
36. Kilnaughton & Cornabus	212	1	37	81	1	37	200	—	—	493	3	34
37. Lyrabus & Coslybus (sic)	366	1	34	100	—	—	351	—	—	817	1	34
38. Cragabus	200	1	24	67	—	—	298	3	8	566	—	32
39. Balichatrigan	332	—	—	31	—	—	200	—	—	563	—	—
40. Stremnishmore	173	2	2	100	2	14	131	—	—	405	—	16
41. Assabus	80	2	—	45	1	32	150	—	—	275	3	32
42. Stremnishbeg	131	—	—	152	—	—	354	—	—	637	—	—
43. Kinabus	122	1	38	155	1	13	69	1	—	347	—	11
44. Kileyan (Upper)	125	2	24	168	2	16	158	2	36	452	3	36
45. Kileyan (Lower)	174	2	24	129	—	—	100	—	—	403	2	24
46. Gioll	340	—	—	201	3	1	241	3	1	783	—	1
47. Glenastle (Upper)	164	1	30	70	1	24	162	1	18	397	—	32
48. Glenastle (Lower)	146	3	27	88	—	24	258	1	38	493	2	9
49. Tokamall	66	3	38	58	—	—	257	3	25	382	3	23
50. Grassdale	150	2	36	195	3	35	479	3	21	826	2	12
	67001	1	34	7519	1	30	19786	2	26	34307	2	10

Parish of Killarow or Bowmore

	Arable			Green Pasture			Heathy Pasture			TOTAL		
	Acres	R.	P.	Acs.	R.	P.	Acs.	R.	P.	Acs.	R.	P.
1. Loarabus & Blackrock	200	—	—	53	1	—	576	—	—	829	1	1
2. Bunanuilt												
3. Corghorton	377	3	6	355	—	—	3962	1	34	4695	1	—
4. Killanallan												
5. Scarrabus	205	—	—	61	—	—	500	—	—	766	—	—
6. Octavullin	175	1	8	80	—	—	300	—	—	555	1	8
7. Carrabus Knockdon & Blackrock	119	3	—	93	1	—	415	—	—	628	—	—
8. Kinabolls												
9. Lagbuy Islay												
10. Kilarow House	500	—	—	82	2	23	100	—	—	682	—	—
11. Glebe Farm												
12. Surn												
13. Ealabus	100	2	—	—	—	—	91	—	—	191	3	—
14. Skirrolls	193	3	8	28	—	—	—	—	—	221	3	8
15. Taynoknock	63	2	32	—	—	—	—	—	—	85	2	32
16. Eorabus	200	—	—	34	1	26	—	—	—	234	1	26
17. Daill	251	—	—	111	—	—	446	—	—	808	—	—
18. Kilbranan	92	3	17	100	—	—	245	—	—	437	3	17
19. Dluich	200	—	—	49	3	—	—	—	—	249	3	—
20. Balitarsin	216	2	28	59	1	—	—	—	—	275	3	28
21. Gartachosan	400	1	29	41	—	—	—	—	—	441	1	29
22. Gartloist & Gartmain	230	3	19	115	—	—	86	—	—	431	3	19
23. Grobolls	300	—	26	100	—	—	22	—	—	432	—	26
24. Ardlarrach	554	3	—	79	—	—	600	—	—	1233	3	—
25. Tallant	176	2	36	64	1	34	231	2	—	472	2	30
26. Curralach	90	—	—	—	—	—	482	—	—	572	—	—
27. Corrary	140	3	32	—	—	—	410	—	—	550	3	32
28. Laggan	282	1	39	100	—	—	500	—	—	882	1	39
29. Island	156	3	—	—	—	—	833	—	—	989	3	—
30. Duich	323	1	—	265	3	—	1627	—	—	2216	—	—
31. Torra	31	2	—	—	—	—	471	—	—	502	2	—
32. Avinvogie	23	3	28	—	—	—	427	—	—	450	3	28
33. Avinlussa	75	3	—	—	—	—	684	—	—	759	3	—
34. Killinan (Upr)	79	—	—	—	—	—	1399	—	—	1478	—	—
35. Killinan (Lwr)	90	—	—	—	—	—	1023	—	—	1113	—	—
36. Mulindry	263	2	35	102	3	—	313	—	—	679	1	35
37. Nosebridge	126	3	—	103	—	—	200	—	—	429	3	—
38. Nereby	137	3	—	100	—	—	33	—	—	270	3	—
39. Roskern	103	3	19	62	2	36	110	2	—	277	—	15
40. Barr	189	—	3	—	—	—	386	2	—	575	2	3
41. Cattadale	90	—	—	—	—	—	610	—	—	700	—	—
42. Kynagary	273	3	—	—	—	—	1509	—	—	1781	3	—
43. Allalay & Pendicle of Nosebridge	—	—	—	—	—	—	936	—	—	936	—	—
	7036	3	35	2263	1	39	19528	3	34	28829	1	28

Parish of Kilmeny

	Arable			Green Pasture			Heathy Pasture			TOTAL		
	Acres	R.	P.	Acs.	R.	P.	Acs.	R.	P.	Acs.	R.	P.
1. Balole	199	2	—	61	—	—	466	—	—	726	2	—
2. Leek	112	—	—	147	—	—	—	—	—	259	—	—
3. Duisker	126	1	—	33	1	—	504	—	—	663	2	—
4. Balimartin	118	—	—	38	2	—	49	3	—	206	1	—
5. Baliharvie	99	3	—	35	—	—	745	—	—	879	3	—
6. Balliclaven	144	2	14	131	—	14	1000	—	—	1275	2	28
7. Shangart (sic)	122	—	—	54	—	—	107	—	—	283	—	—
8. Portnellan	200	1	12	59	—	—	680	2	12	939	3	24
9. Stoainsha	157	1	34	115	1	1	1091	—	—	1363	2	35
10. Mergavale (sic)	25	1	22	—	—	—	569	—	—	594	1	22
11. Dudlemore	33	1	24	—	—	—	1411	—	—	1444	1	24
12. Dudlebeg	26	—	—	—	—	—	454	2	—	480	2	—
13. Gortantoaid	54	2	24	26	1	26	882	—	—	963	—	10
14. Bolsa	50	—	35	36	2	—	1214	—	—	1300	2	35
15. Cove	50	—	8	156	3	22	1095	—	—	1301	3	30
16. Ardnahoe	117	1	18	324	2	—	1627	—	—	2068	3	8
17. Balulve	159	2	28	100	2	—	451	—	—	711	—	28
18. Balighillin 19. Loagin	103	—	20	145	1	12	128	—	—	376	1	32
20. Torrabolls	50	—	—	165	—	—	100	—	—	315	—	—
21. Persabus	101	—	—	—	—	—	48	—	—	149	—	—
22. Mulreesh	65	2	16	61	1	—	—	—	—	126	3	16
23. Scanistle & Uchdruiclach (Auchnaclach)	252	2	—	300	—	—	—	—	—	552	2	—
24. Kiells	90	3	30	100	—	—	56	—	—	246	3	30
25. Portaskaig	38	1	12	—	—	—	88	2	—	126	3	12
26. Carnbeg	102	—	—	23	1	28	72	3	22	198	1	10
27. Kilslevan	154	3	—	100	—	—	124	—	—	378	3	—
28. Lossit	266	3	—	170	2	—	128	2	—	565	3	—
29. Baliochdrach	100	3	—	47	—	—	191	3	—	339	2	—
30. Baliclach	100	2	—	57	—	—	228	—	—	385	2	—
31. Eachvarnach	129	2	—	100	—	—	400	—	—	629	2	—
32. Knocklerock	134	—	—	84	—	—	162	—	—	380	—	—
33. Glasgowvey (sic)	16	2	16	—	—	—	11	—	16	27	2	32
34. Ardochy	121	—	—	83	1	—	162	1	—	366	2	—
35. Kilmenny	184	2	—	37	3	28	128	2	—	350	3	28
36. Baligrant	84	—	—	20	—	—	39	—	—	143	—	—
37. Robolls	172	2	38	121	—	—	100	—	—	393	2	38
38. Kepollsmore	240	2	—	38	—	—	62	—	—	340	2	—
39. Esknish	264	—	—	48	3	16	74	2	—	389	1	16
40. Tirvaigain	109	2	13	30	3	28	25	—	—	165	2	1
41. Arighuary	129	—	—	100	—	—	291	—	—	520	—	—
42. Storkaig	111	—	—	100	—	—	1412	—	—	1623	—	—
	4919	—	34	3252	1	15	16379	3	10	24551	1	19

ABSTRACT

	Arable			Green Pasture			Heathy Pasture			TOTAL		
	Acres	R.	P.	Acs.	R.	P.	Acs.	R.	P.	Acs.	R.	P.
Parish of Kilchoman	8003	3	31	4641	2	29	10453	—	13	23098	2	33
Parish of Killarow or Bowmore	7036	3	35	2263	1	39	19528	3	34	28829	1	28
Parish of Kilmeny	4919	—	34	3252	1	15	16279	3	10	24551	1	19
Parish of Kildalton	7001	1	34	7519	1	30	19786	2	26	34307	2	10
Scots Acres *TOTAL*	26961	2	14	17676	3	33	66148	2	3	110787	—	—
Imperial Acs.	34003	2	—	22293	3	20	83425	1	20	139721	—	—

This Survey is most likely to have been done by Stephen MacDougall in the period when he was making the Map of Islay. Only a nineteenth Century copy exists among the Islay Estate papers, which was produced at the time of the Sale of the Island to James Morrison of Basildon, 1853, when it is referred to as 'a very old survey'. It is several times quoted during the Eighteenth Century, *vide* the Surveys of Kintra, Grastill and Balenachtan More. No other Surveyor was employed by the Campbells until the early Nineteenth Century when William Gemmell was employed to make individual surveys of Farms and Distilleries and updated MacDougalls Total Scots Acres to give the equivalent Imperial Acres.

8 Map of Islay, 1749–51. The first modern map by Stephen MacDougall, Surveyor. He was the father-in-law of General Alexander MacDougall. Original in Islay Estate Papers.

Early Leases

The Lease granted to Archibald Campbell in Sannaig in 1752 is typical of the terms being offered as the various Wadsets were redeemed; it was for nineteen years at a rent of £38. Sterling money (gradually the Scots pound was being faded out). One condition was the growing of flax, and lint mills were erected at Skerroles and Lagavuline to process the crop, which was sold as yarn on the mainland.

Because the island had very little suitable timber for roofing purposes, except driftwood or timber from wrecks on the coast, it was customary for the Incoming Tenant to pay the value of the Roof Tree or the outgoing Tenant could take it with him. The local woods were mostly of scrub Birch, Willow, Alder and Rowan. Oak trees grew in the deep glens and in sheltered places but were so twisted that they were of little use except as knees for boats. Shawfield was therefore making walled enclosures in which to grow hardwood trees, but the heavy salt content of the air and the force of the gales made this a heart-breaking enterprise. The woods around Islay House were planted three times and were only successful when it was discovered that the sycamore tree, a completely alien tree to the country, would withstand these conditions and were planted as a windbreak.

Regt Tack betwixt
Campbell of Shawfield
&
Campbell — [Archibald]
M F   1752
Compd. C. M.
unpd

(The original is among the Kildalton Papers and is written on four pages of a double foolscap, signed at the foot of each page by Hu: Forbes.)

AT EDINBURGH the Nineteenth day of December one thousand Seven hundred and fifty two years In presence of the Lords of Councill & Session Advocates as pro'rs for Daniel Campbell and Archibald Campbell both after designed on the one and other parts and gave in the Tack underwritten desiring the same might be Registrate in the Lop books to the effect therein Specified which desire the said Lords found reasonable and ordained the same to be done accordingly whereof the Tenor follows at KILLAROW the . . . . . . day of August Imoyo and fourty years It is Contracted and Agreed betwixt Daniel Campbell of Shawfield heretable proprietar of ye Lands afterment On the one part and Archibald Campbell in Sannaigmore on the oyr part in manner following THAT IS TO SAY The said Daniel Campbell has set & hereby for the Maills & Dutys aftermentd Sets and in Tack and Assedation Lets to the said Archibald Campbell his heirs and Successors Excluding assigneys and subtennents except wt the sd Daniel Campbell's consent ALL and HAILL the three Quarter Lands of Sannaigmore Scarabolls & Upper Stainsha wt houses biggings yards pendicles & pertinints thereof whatsor Lying in the Parish of . . . . . . Isle of Islay and Sherriffdom of Argyle and that for the space of Nineteen full & Compleat years and Cropts next and Immediatly ffollowing his Entry thereto which is hereby Declared to be and begin to the houses grass & Pasturage at the term of Whitsunday next and to the Arable Land at the Saparation of the Cropt from the Ground the sd year. To be from thence furth peacably Laboured Enjoyed & possessed by him and forsds during the said Tack which the (said) Daniel Campbell obliges him To warrand at all hands & agt all deadly ffor the which Causes the said Archibald Campbell binds and obliges him his heirs Executors Successors & Intromiters wt his Goods and Gear whatsoever to Content and pay to the said Daniel Campbell his heirs & Assigneys or to his factors and Chamberlains in his name ALL and HAILL the sum of Thirty Eight pounds Sterling money In full of the Silver and Teind duties Dyr Multure Stot & oyr Casuallity formerly in use to be paid out of the said lands and that at the term of Martinmas yearly beginning the first years payment yrof at Martinmas Imoyc & fourty one years and so furth at each Martinmas yrafter during the Tack with Six pound money fooorsd of Liqt Expences for each year's faillie And to bring the Haill Grindable Corns of the sd Lands to the Miln of ------ and pay one peck of Schilline for each boll of Shilline thereof in law of Multures & Kneaveship Likeas he binds & obliges him to make payt of one Equall proportion wt ye rest of the tennents of Ilay of the Schoolmr & Surgeons fees & whole publick Dues Cesses taxations burdens and Impositions whatsoever Imposed or to be Imposed on the saids Lands with four days Service of Eight horses and four men a day for each Quarterland and so in proportion for a Greater or less Extent Land And for reparation of the Sucken Miln and Common Smiddy as use is And to Compear before Bailliy Court of Ilay when Called thereto & observe & obtemper the Acts yrof under the pains and fynes Imposed or to be imposed on the transgressors of the samen and to make payt to the Chamberlain yearly for the Behoof of the Bailly of Ilay of the Court Mail Duties being two pound Scots out of each Quarterland, And also to make payt to the saids Chamberlain yearly for the behooff of the Clarke of his proportion of the Compearance money of said Lands being fifteen Shillings Six pennies Scots out of each quarterland and to cut

& Cause cut their peats on the said Lands regularly as they shall be directed by the Bailly of Ilay and to pay ffive pounds Scots money for each Transgressions or Irregular Cutting toties quoties, and that they shall not have nor keep any Changehouse OR Maltkiln on the sd Lands wtout ye sd Daniel Campbell's Licence had and obtained yrto & in case they do in the Contrary they forfiet the benefit of this tack and Incur a fyne of Twenty pound Scot money to be levied by the Bailly of Ilay for the time being And in case one years rent run in the second unpaid then this present tack shall become void & null & it shall be lawfull to the sd Daniel Campbell to Sett use & Dispose of the sd Lands wtout Declarator of process of law as if these presents had never been Granted And it is hereby provided & declared that in case the forenamed persons or any of them shall set harbour of Encourage theive Vagabonds or other Vagreant persons of a bad character who are convicted as such or who shall Import reset buy keep or sell any Irish Cattle brandy or oyr foreign Spirits & shall be Convicted before the Bailly of Ilay of being guilty art or part of the offences afforsd or any of them that the person so convicted shall forfeit the benefit of this Tack and the same shall become void & null And it shall be Lawfull to the Sd Daniel Campbell Immediatly after the sd Conviction to sett use and Dispose of the said Lands as if this tack had never been granted and further he obliges him & forsds to uphold & maintain (sic) the haill houses & biggings of the sd Lands and leave the Samen in a Sufficient habitable Condition at the Expiration herof BUT prejudice to him to Claim payt from the Intrant tennent of the price of the Timber thereof according to the Antient practice of the Country And thay oblige them to allow the Inhabitants of Ilay to carry off Sand Limestone & Marle from the sd Lands they paying for the Damages the grass and Corn thereof sustained thereby at the Sight two Sworn Birlimen But Declaring that no marle is to be caryed off from the sd Lands wtout the sd Daniel Campbell's Licence had & obtained thereto in writing and likewise obliges him and forsds to sow Lintseed in the said Lands yearly at the rate of half a boll in the Quarter Land and to renew the said Seed once every two years During this tack, and to bring the Lint to be Dressed at the Lint Miln to be erected for that effect and to fflitt & remove from the sd Lands at the Expiration hereof wtout any proces of Law to be used for the Effect and both parties oblige them to perform the premisses hinc inde to oyrs under the penalty of ffourty pounds Scots money to be paid by the ffaillier to the observer or party willing to observe Attour performance Consenting to the Registration hereof in the books of Councill & Session or oyrs Competent That letters of horning on Six days and oyrs needfull may pass and be direct thereon as Effiers & Constitute Messrs. Robert Dundas & John Grant Advocates Their prors in witness whereof both partys have subscribed these presents written on this and the preceeding page Stampt paper by ffarqd Campbel writer in Ilay Place day month & year of God writen before these witnesses Mr. Alexr McMillan Writer to the Signet & Hector McLean his Servant ffiller up of the date Tack duty Tacksmen & witnesses names & Designations & Sundry oyr Blanks

(Signed) Daniel Campbell Arch: Campbell Al: Drummond witness Alexr McMillan witness Hector MacLean witness EXTRACTED upon this & the three preceeding pages By (signed) HU: FORBES

This Lease to George Campbell of Persibus is the first of the new type which would develop into the Standard Leases of 1777.

No. 7
Tack of Persabus
& Baloch Roy Changehouse
to
George Campbell
Son of Arch. Campbell of Losset.
20. 11. 1748
to start at Whit. 1760

(The original written on three pages of a double sheet of foolscap, is among the Islay Estate Papers Very torn and fragile.)

ATT WOODHALL the Twentieth day of November One Thousand Seven hundred and fourtie Eight years It is contacted and Agreed betwixt the parties following viz Daniell Campbell of Shawfield Esq. Heritable Proprietor of the Lands and Oyrs underwritten on the one part and George Campbell son of Archd Campbell in Losset one the Ane and other part in Manner following. That is to say the said Daniell Campbell has Sett and in Tack & Assedation lett and by these presents for the yearly Tack Duty and Other Destations aftermentioned SETTS AND LETTS to the said George Campbell his heirs and Successors (secluding Assignees and Subtenents except with the said Daniel Campbell's consent) All and Haill the three learhess of Persabus & Changehouse of Balachroy with the acre and pertinents yrto belonging as presently possessed by the Tenants of Kilcolumkill with the House biggings Yards parts pendicles and pertinents of the same as the said haill lands are presently possessed by any person whatsoever present possessor of the same all lying within the Parish of Kilmeny Island of Ilay and Sherriffdom of Argyle and that for all the days Space and Terms of Nineteen full and Compleat years and Cropts next and immediately following the said George Campbell of his foresds their Entry yrto which is hereby declared to be and begin to possess the houses grass and pasturage of the said lands ATT THE TERM OF WHITSUNDAY One thousand Seven hundred and Sixty years and to the arrable ground of the said Lands at the Separation of the Cropt from the ground the said year to be thencforth peacably laboured enjoyed and possessed by the said George Campbell or his foresaid during the currency of the Tack WHICH tack the said Daniell Campbell binds and obliges him his heirs and Successors qtsoever to warrant att all hands againt all Deadly, FOR THE WHICH CAUSES the said George Campbell Binds and Obliges him his heirs Exectrs Successors and Intromitters with his goods & gear qtsoever to content and pay to the sd Daniell Campbell his heirs or assignees of to his ffactors of Chamberlains in his NAME haill the sum Sixteen pound four shilling eightpence in full of silver rent teind duty dry Multure stot and oyr Casualitys formerly in use to be paid out of the said lands and that at the Term of Martinmas yearly beginning the first Terms payt of the said Tack duty at the Term of Martinmas One thousand Seven Hundred and Sixty years and so furth yearly yrafter during this Tack with Three pounds money foresd of Liquidate penalty for each Term's failzie and to bring the haill grindable corns of the said lands to the Milns as use and wont And to pay one peck Shilling for Each Boll Shilling in lew of Multure and Knaiveship LIKEAS the said George Campbell obliges & forsds to Make payment of an equal proportion with the rest of the tenants of Isla of the Schoolmaster and Surgeon fees and of the haill public burdens Cesses and Impositions qtsoever imposed or to be imposed on the said lands and of four days Service yearly of four Men and Eight Horses a Day Each Quarterland and so on in proportion for a larger of lesser extent and for reparartion of the Sucken [miln] and Common Smiddy as use and to compear before the Bailly Courts of Isla when Called thereto & to observe & obtemper the Haill Acts yrof under the pains and Fines imposed or to be imposed on the Transgressors of the same and to make payment to the Chamberlain's yearly for the behoof of the Clerk of Yr proportion of the Compearance Money being Fifteen Shillings & Six pennys Scots on Each Quarterland and to Cast and cause Cast yr peats regularly as they shall be directed by the Bailly of Islay & to pay five pounds Scots for Each irregular Cutting toties Quoties and that they shall not have nor keep a Changehouse or Malt Kiln on the said lands without the said Daniel Campbell's consent to set up and to dispose of the same and thay incurr of fine Fourtie pounds to be levied by the Bailly of Islay and if one years rent run into the second unpayd then and in that case this shall become void and Null LIKEWISE, And the said George Campbell obliges him & forsds to uphold and maintain the Haill houses and Biggings on the said lands during the Tack and to leave the same in a good sufficient and habitable condition at the Expiration hereof but prejudice to them to claim paymt from the Interant Tenants of the price of the timber of the said buildings according to the Ancient Custom of the Country and that they shall not Resett harbour or anywise countenance Theives Vagabonds or other Idle and vagrant persons under a bad character or buy keep or sell any Irish Cattle. Brandy or other foreign Spirits Under the Penalty of forfeiting this Tack and oblidges him and his forsds to sow Lint Seed on the said lands at the rate of half a Boll the Quarterland yearly & to renew the said Seed once in Two Years and to bring their lint to be dressed to the Lint Milns to be built in Ilay for that purpose and obliges him and foresds to allow any Inhabitant of Ilay to carry Sand limestone and Marle from the said lands they paying the damage the Corn and Grass sustain thereby at the sight of two Sworn Birlymen but declaring that no Marle is carried from the said sands without the said Daniel Campbell's consent and also that the said George Campbell obliges him & forsds to make payment of the Chamberlains yearly for the behoof of the third Erection for a Minister in Ilay being Two pound Scots out of each Quarterland & that at the Term of Martinmass after the said Third Erection take place and during this Tack and LASTLY obliges him & forsds to flitt and remove from the said lands at the Expiration hereoff without any Warning or process of Law to that Effect both partys oblige themselves to perform their respective parts of the Premises hinc inde to Each others under penalty of Fourtie pds Scots money to be paid by the party failzie to the party observer or willing to observe By and atouer Performance Consenting to the Registration hereof in the books of Council and Session or oyrs Competent that Letters of horning on six days and all Execution needfull may pass hereon in form as Effiers & Constitutes.

Their PRORS. In witness whereof Both parties have subscribed these presents (written on this and the two preceeding pages of Stampt paper by George Campbell son to [Archibald] Campbell Tacksman of Lossitt in Isla Place Day Moneth and year of God aforesd and before these Witnesses Duncan McIntyre Servr to Sir Duncan Campbell & Gilbert McCulloch Sert to Shawfield the Witnesses names and designations written and the blanks filled by Gilbert McCulloch witness hereto

(signed) DUNCAN McINTYRE witness   DANIEL CAMPBELL
        GILBT McCULLOCH witness   GEORGE CAMPBELL

Daniel the Second

Old Shawfield had also endeavoured to place the lead mines on a sounder basis, but his efforts were not very successful owing to the disturbance caused by the 1745 Rising [Book of Islay]. However, in spite of all the difficulties, Daniel had set the pattern for the future development of the Island. His son, John, predeceased him in 1746 and his heir was his teenage grandson and namesake who, at this moment – 1753 – was abroad rounding off his education with travel on the Continent, in the fashion of the age. Among the now missing papers are the accounts of his widowed Mother, Lady Henneret, for the education and clothing of her three sons.

There are two delightful portraits of this second Daniel and his immediate younger brother, John, as boys – handsome lads, the former in a long blue velvet coat, trimmed with gold braid, and the latter in one of hunting pink. Like all the Campbell men, Daniel was exceptionally tall and acquired the nickname of "the Long Love". He was described by his great-grand-nephew, John Francis Campbell, as a "great Dandy, who travelled, bought books and fiddles, possibly pictures, abroad and assisted Wodrow to publish his version of OSSIAN'S POEMS. He kept hounds, subscribed to rare publications and went the pace . . . . . His wardrobe of grand coats was in Islay and later sold as 'theatrical dresses'. " Much of this, and more, is borne out by the catalogue of his books. He was deeply involved in politics and as Member of Parliament for Lanarkshire, 1760/68, is recorded in history as one of the four Scots who, with a small minority of English Members, had the courage to divide the House when Bute presented his unpopular Preliminaries of Peace in 1762. His Constituents must have held him to account, as he was unseated in the Election of 1768.

Nevertheless, Daniel was not slow to implement his Grandfather's schemes in Islay. In 1762 the matter of the third erection was re-opened with the Synod and, in October 1763, we find him "perambulating" the parish bounds with the Presbytery of Kintyre, some of whose "valetudinarian" members were replaced by more active gentlemen from the Presbytery of Inveraray. The Glebes were, in due course, marked out next the Churches of Kildalton (on the lands of Surnaig) and Kilchoman and at

Bowmore. By 1767 the new Round Church, costing "above £700" was built at the head of the Main Street at Bowmore: the second entry in the Day Book, written in the hand of fferquhard Campbell, the Notary Public, is the stilted Latin inscription which appears on the tablet in the face of the Church tower.

Formation of Parishes

Originally there had been six Parishes in Islay – Kildalton, Kilnaughton [which covered the Oa], Kilarow, Kilmeny, Kilchoman and Kilchiaran. After the Reformation, the shortage of ministers was very badly felt in remote and Gaelic speaking areas. For the greater part of the 16th and 17th Centuries, there were never more than two in Islay and often one or none. By the end of the 17th Century the two ministers were given Glebes and manses at Kilarow. But as Daniel I had said, this was an inadequate arrangement and his offer, confirmed by his grandson, Daniel II, was to erect three parishes and supply the ministers with stipends, communion money, manses and glebes, agreed to unanimously by the Presbytery of Kintyre and Synod of Argyll. This meant, in fact, that there were three combined Parishes, Kildalton and Oa [the previous Kilnaughton], Kilarow and Kilmeny, and Kilchoman and Kilchiaran, which covered the Rhinns, with two churches in the most thickly populated area of Kilarow & Kilmeny, to be served by one Minister.

There were two Acts of the Synod of Argyle in August 1762 and August 1763, confirming the offer, and another of the Presbytery of Kintyre, meeting in Islay to mark out the sites of the Churches, Manses and Glebes for the three Parishes and to decide on the boundaries. In accordance with the agreement, the Synod duly applied to the King [George III] for the Valued Teinds of Islay to be given to Daniel Campbell of Shawfield and this application was duly granted by a Deed dated 29th November 1765.

These Acts are reproduced here in full, verbose and repetitive though they are, but of particular importance because they were resurrected a hundred years later in a Court of Session Case of the Ministers of Islay v. John Ramsay of Kildalton & the Heritors. One of the Ministers had discovered the figure of £600 Scots stipulated as the Stipend of each Minister in the Decreet of February 1769. No amount of explanation satisfied the Ministers that this sum was the equivalent of £50 Sterling (their actual Stipend) and not, as they claimed, £600 Sterling. Needless to say, the Ministers lost their case.

THREE EXTRACT ACTS
of the
PROVINCIAL SYNOD ARGYLE.
<u>dated</u>   *3rd August 1747*
5th August 1762
5th August 1763

and

ONE EXTRACT ACT
of the
PRESBYTERY OF KINTYRE
<u>DATED</u>   *18th October 1763*

An extract ACT of the provincial SYNOD OF ARGYLE At Inverary, Monday 3rd day of August 1747 years-Sederunt, the Provincial Synod of Argyle, session quinto ante meridiem. After prayer, roll called marked, Mr. John and Mr. Alexander Campbells being now called upon to exhibit the scheme concerning a new erection in Islay, they gave in a paper, which was read, ane whereof the tenor follows:– Proposals with regard to the erection of a new parish in Islay, humbly offered to the Very Reverend the Synod of Argyle, in name of Daniel Campbell of Shawfield, Esq., by Mr. John Campbell, minister of Killarow, and Mr. Alexander Campbell, one of the Ministers of Inverary, that three ministers be legally settled in Islay, with £600 Scots of yearly stipend each, £18000: that for furnishing communion elements yearly for the whole Island, there shall be allowed £60 money; that the three parishes shall be provided with Churches, manses, and glebes, according to law. Total sum, without taking in the expense of these last articles, which must be considerable £1860 Scots. To make up this sum, Shawfield undertakes, besides providing the parishes in the necessary accommodations of churches, manses and glebes, to give up all the value teinds of that island, which, including £73 Scots of tack duty payable yearly by him to the Synod, amount to £1333 : 6 : 8 Scots money, though he and the former heritors there have since the Reformation enjoyed about a third of said sum, and he in particular has been at no small expense to expede the grants and tacks usual in such cases, £1333 : 6 : 8 But then he expects that the Very Reverend Synod, shall first transfer to him all their right to the above tack-duty of £73 Scots, and to the feu-duty payable by him out of Islay to them, which is yearly £267 : 6 : 8 Scots and grant the needful recommendations to the proper Court or persons for ascertaining the said sums for the maintenance of the above three ministers, £267 : 6 : 8 Scots Money: Secundo, as there will by be still wanting of the above sum of £1860 Scots, £259 : 10 : 3 money forsaid, Shawfield, considering the burden he takes upon him in this affair, hopes the Synod will, in the most earnest manner, recommend the design in view to the royal bounty by representing to them the great necessity of it in the way they shall judge most proper and effectual, £259 : 6 : 8 total £1860 Scots; Tertio and lastly, to induce the Synod more readily to promote this scheme, Shawfield declares that he shall not claim the benefit of any grants that shall be now made him by the Synod in case it do not take place, and the above Mr. John Campbell hereby obliges himself to give up all the rights he has by acts of Synod or otherways to the augmentation of £266 : 13 : 4 Scots money, which he has now yearly from the Synod, so that the same shall return to them how soon the designed erection in Islay obtains. The above designed ministers think themselves sufficiently warranted from Shawfield by letters under his hand and otherwise, to make the above proposals in his name. In witness whereof they have subscribed these presents at Inveraray this 3rd day of August, 1747. Sic Subr J. Campbell, Alex. Campbell – Which scheme and proposals above engrossed having been maturely considered by the Synod, they heartily and unanimously approved thereof, and do hereby, towards executing their part of the said scheme, enact and appoint that the sum of £73 Scots money, being the feu-duty payable out of Islay, to both which the Synod have the right – Be (under the express provisions and conditions underwritten), allocated and appropriated towards carrying on the said new erection, hereby assigning, transferring, and disponing both the said sums to and in favours of Daniel Campbell of Shawfield, Esq., his heirs and successors, to be by them applied toward supporting three ministers in manner specified in and intended by the foregoing scheme, and the Synod do hereby, under the provisions and conditions underwritten, recommend it to the Lords of the Treasury or other competent Court, to grant their act of concurrence for securing and ascertaining the sums aforesaid for the purposes above mentioned; and further, the Synod do earnestly recommend it to the committee for managing the royal bounty, to grant the assistance expected from them for carrying on so desirable a work, provided always, as it is hereby provided and declared, that this present act and the recommendations above specified are made and granted on express condition that Daniel Campbell of Shawfield shall, in the first place, obtain from the said committee the assistance expected from them and shall in the next place, by a proper writing under his hand, oblige himself, his heirs and successors to allocate the whole valued teinds of the Island of Islay for supporting the three ministers of Islay, and also to accommodate them in churches, manses and glebes, conform to law, and provided likewise, that the said Mr. John Campbell shall overgive and discharge all right, title, or interest he has or can pretend, to the above 400 merks of augmentation formerly granted to him by act of Treasury or otherwise, under which provisions and declarations this act is agreed to and granted by the Synod, and not otherwise, so that is the foresaid sum expected from, the committee of the royal bounty shall not be obtained, or if Shawfield shall not become bound in manner foresaid, or if Mr. John Campbell shall not renounce the benefit of the acts of Synod and Treasury above mentioned – Then, and in any one of these cases, these presents shall be to all intents and purposes entirely null and void. Further, as the Synod consider this matter as of great importance to the interest of religion in these bounds, not only in the way of public instruction, but also as it may lay a foundation for executing a new Presbytery there (a thing extremely wanted for the safety of the ministers, and more regular and speedy dispatch of Church discipline) – they do therefore appoint the said Mr. John and Alexander

Campbell to wait upon Shawfield, if required, to give their assistance for bringing this whole affair to perfection, and if needful, to wait upon the said Committee, and in the Synod's name, to represent the usefulness and expediency of the foregoing scheme. Extracted furth of the minute of the said Synod, upon this and the preceding pages, by me, (Signed) JOHN CAMPBELL, Clk.

Item, Another extract of the said Provincial Synod of Argyle, whereof the tenor follows:– At Inveraray, the 5th day of August 1762 years – Sederunt, the Provincial Synod of Argyle, sessio tertia hora decima ante meridiem. After prayer, roll called and markt. At this sederunt the Synod resumed the consideration of the letter from Daniel Campbell of Shawfield, Esq., which, having been now again read and maturely considered by the Synod, together with the act therein referred to anno 1747, and the overture thereanent from the Committee of Overtures, and they finding that the difficulties which formerly stood in the way of obtaining a new erection in Islay are now happily removed by the expiry of their grant in favour of Mr. John Campbell late minister at Killarow, and by the engagements which Shawfield now voluntarily agrees to enter into, the Synod therefore did and hereby do, allocate and appropriate the sum of £73 Scots money, being the tack duty of the valued teinds of Islay, and the sum of £267 : 6 : 8 Scots Money, being the feu-duty payable to them out of Islay extending both to the sum of £340 : 6 : 8 Scots money, towards supporting a minister to be planted in the said new erection, hereby assigning and disposing the feu and teind tack duties above specified to an in favour of the said Daniel Campbell of Shawfield, and his heirs and successors, to be by them applied for the purpose aforesaid, and they do not only agree and consent, but earnestly recommend to the Right Honourable the Court of Exchequer and Lords for Plantation of Kirks and Valuation of Teinds, or any other person or court competent to interpose their sentence and authority for appropriating the foresaid sume in manner intended by this act, and they appoint their clerk to make out an obligation by which Shawfield shall be bound to pay £50 pounds sterling money of stipend with a fund for communion elements, and to build and provide a legal manse, glebe, and churches for the minister, to be settled in the said new erection: Moreover, to the end this affair may be brought to a conclusion with all convenient dispatch, the Synod appoint the Presbytery of Kintyre to repair to Islay, before the first day of September next, and while Shawfield is upon the spot, to mark out the limits of the several parishes, and the proper places for manses, churches and glebes, and Mr. Robert Thomson and Mr. John McAulay are appointed to bring a draft of a letter to Shawfield, signifying the Synod's entire satisfaction in this conduct concerning this matter, and the regard he thereby manifests for the interests of religion in that large and populous Island: Lastly, The Synod hereby declare, that nothing in this act shall be so constructed as to deprive them of the power of allocating and disposing of the sums now granted till the intended new erection shall actually take place. Whereupon, and upon the whole premises, Dugald McTavish of Dunardry, Procr. for Shawfield, asked and took instruments in the clerks hands and craved extract, which was allowed. Extracted, (Signed) Jo. Campbell, Clk. Item, Another act of the said Provincial Synod, the tenor whereof follows:– At Inveraray, the 5th day of August 1763 years – Sederunt the Provincial Synod of Argyle, sessio quarta hora decima ante meridiem. After prayer, roll called and markt. The Synod having read and maturely considered the following papers laid before them concerning the intended new erection in the large and populous Island of Islay, viz:– Two missive letters to the Synod from Daniel Campbell, Esq. of Shawfield, and a plan made out by him and the heritors of that Island for ascertaining the limits of the said erection, with the report of the Presbytery of Kintyre touching their proceedings on this matter, and the plan made out by them for the foregoing purpose, and having also read the acts of the last and former Synod thereanent, thay did, after mature deliberation thereupon, unanimously agree to the following scheme or plan for establishing the said erection, viz:– Primo, That the Parish of Killarow be disjoined from the Parish of Kilchoman, and the Parish of Kilmenzie disjoined from the Parish of Kildalton, and these two Parishes of Killarow and Kilmenzie be united and erected into a new Parish and separate charge, excepting the Lands of Culabolls and Crossabolls, which are to be annexed to the Parish of Kilchoman, and the Lands of Duich and Proaig, which are to be annexed to the Parish of Kildalton, so that the new erected Parish of Killarow and Kilmenzie shall be bound by the water or river of Ballivogie, and the Lands of Leribols on the west, the sea on the north, the Lands of Proaig on the east, and the waters or rivers of Duich and Laggan on the south, and that in this new erected parish there be two churches, the one at Kilmenzie and the other at Bowmore, and worship equally divided betwixt them, endowed with the stipend, partly payable by Shawfield and partly out of Synod's funds, as mentioned in thier act of last year, and which church, manse, and glebe, on the Lands of Bowmore, to be built and mortified by the said Daniel Campbell of Shawfield: Secundo, That there be but one place of worship in the Parish of Kilchoman, where the church, manse and glebe are to be built and mortified by the said Daniel Campbell: Tertio, That there be but one place of worship in the parish of Kildalton and that at Laggavulline, and the manse and glebe thereof on the lands of Surnaig, all to be in like manner built and mortified by him the said Daniel Campbell, and the Synod appoint the Presbytery of Kintyre to meet at Killarow, in Islay, upon the 10th day of October then next, in order to carry this plan or scheme in all its parts into proper execution, and according to the true intent and meaning thereof; and in regard several members of that Presbytery are valetudinary, and many of them at a great distance, the Synod do therefore appoint Messrs Archibald Lambie, Archibald and Hugh Campbells, from the Presbytery of Inveraray, to be conjoined with the members of the Presbytery of Kintyre, in order to bring the whole of this matter to a desirable issue; declaring, however, that these presents are granted and agreed to under the burden of the provision contained in the said act of last Synod, touching the Synod's right to dispose of those parts of their funds therein specified until the intended new erection shall take place, and under this further provision and declaration, that nothing contained herein, or in the said former acts shall be so construed or understood as to hurt or prejudice the interest of the two ministers now settled in Islay, or their successors in office, in any degree: Lastly, the Synod appoint Messrs. John McAulay and Robert Thomson to make out the draft of a letter to Shawfield signifying the Synod's resolution concerning this affair. Whereupon and all and sundry the premises Dugald McTavish of Dunardary, as procurator for, and having ample power for that purpose from the said Daniel Campbell, asked and took instruments in the clerks hands, and craved extract, which was allowed. Extracted from the minutes of the said Provincial Synod, & c. (signed) Jo. CAMPBELL, Clk.

Item, An extract Act of the Presbytery of Kintyre, whereof the tenor follows:– At Killarow, in Islay, the 12th day of October 1763 years – Sederunt, the Presbytery of Kintyre and Commissioners from the Synod of Argyle, After prayer roll called and marked, there was presented to the Presbytery, by Daniel Campbell, Esq., of Shawfield, a plan made out by him and the other heritors of the new parish to be erected in the large and populous Island of Islay, and an Act of the Synod of Argyle, dated at Inveraray the 12th day of August last, approving thereof, of which plan the tenor follows:– Primo, That the parish of Killarow be disjoined from the parish of Kildalton, and these two parishes of Killarow an Kilmenzie united and erected into a new parish and separate charge, excepting the lands of Cuilabolls and Crossabolls, which are to be annexed to the parish of Kilchoman, and the Lands of Duich and Proaig, which are to be annexed to the PARISH of Kildalton, for that the new erected parish of Killarow and Kilmenzie shall be bounded by the water or river of Ballivogie, and the lands of Leribolls on the west, the sea on the north, the lands of Proaig on the east, and the waters of Duich and Laggan on the south, and that in this new parish there be two churches, one at Kilmenzie and the other at Bowmore, and worship equally divided betwixt them, endowed with the stipend, partly payable by Shawfield, and partly by the Synod of Argyle, out of their lands, as particularly specified in their Act, dated at Inveraray the day of August 1762 years, amounting in all to the sum of £50 pounds sterling of stipend, and £5 sterling as the allowance for communion elements, with a church, manse, and glebe, on the lands of Bowmore, to be built and mortified by the said Daniel Campbell of Shawfield: Secundo, That there be but one place of worship in the parish of Kilchoman, and that at Kilchoman, where the church, manse and glebe are to be built and mortified by the said Daniel Campbell: Tertio, Therebe but one place of worship in the parish of Kildalton, and that at Lagavulline, and the manse and glebe thereof on the lands of Surnaig, all to be in like manner built and mortified by him, the said Daniel Campbell. The Presbytery having perambulated the several parishes above designed, and having read and maturely considered the scheme or plan of new erection above mentioned, sis and hereby do, unanimously approve thereof, upon the condition and provision that the ministers of the old parishes of Kilchoman and Kildalton shall be continued in possession of the stipend they at present enjoy, an a proper allowance for communion elements. Thereafter, the Presbytery did, with the advice and consent of Daniel Campbell of Shawfield, proceed to design a glebe out of the lands of Bowmore, for the minister of the then parish of Killarow and Kilmenzie – Compeared, Alexr. Campbell land measurer, Hugh McKay at Bowmore, and James McDonald at Bunanuisq, honest men in the parish, and the said Alexander Campbell did, in presence of the Presbytery, measure out 41/2 acres of arable ground out of the lands of Bowmore, for a glebe and stance for the minister's manse, garden, and office-houses, and the presbytery did, with the advice and assistance of the said honest men, design and mark out as much ground contiguous thereto as would be sufficient

D

for four soums grass, bounded in manner following, viz.– the water of Bunanuisq on the north, Lochindaul on the west, a line drawn from a rock on the side of Lochindaul to Gordonmore on the south, and a line as now marked and meithed from the angle on Gortanmore to the water of Bunanuisq on the east, which glebe and grass the Presbytery did, and hereby do, design as glebe and grass for the minister of the new parish of Killarow and Kilmenzie in all time coming, the Presbytery finding that, by the scheme of erection agreed to betwixt Daniel Campbell of Shawfield and the Synod of Argyle, the glebe for the parish of Kilchoman is to be designed out of the lands of Kilchoman, and the glebe for the parish of Kildalton out of the lands of Surnaig, and finding that the two old glebes belonging to the ministers of Islay ly contiguous to the old kirk of Killarow in the new parish, did, with the advice and consent of Daniel Campbell of Shawfield, and Mr. John Woodrow, and Mr. John McLea, minister of Islay, agree to make choice of James Campbell of Ballinaby, and William Campbell of Ormsary, as proper persons for estimating the present glebes of Islay, and also for estimating the grounds on the respective parishes of Kilchoman and Kildalton to be given as an equivalent for said glebes, and they agreed that the said James and William Campbells should proceed to estimate the old glebes, and condescend upon so much of the lands of Kilchoman and Surnaig as thay shall judge a full and adequate equivalent for the said old glebes at Killarow, and report to Shawfield and the Presbytery of Kintyre.

(signed) ROBERT THOMSON,
Pres. Clk., as the said writs bear.

VIII. – Gift of the Valued Teinds of the Island of Islay in favour of Daniel Campbell of Shawfield, Esq. Dated 29th November, Registered 19th December 1765.

George, by the grace of God, King of Great Britain, France and Ireland, Defender of the Faith, to all and sundry whom these presents do or may concern – Whereas we, considering that her late Majesty, Queen Anne, by letters under the Privy Seal of Scotland, bearing date the 14th day of July 1705 years, did grant to the Synod of Argyle All and Haill the rents, revenues, casualties, and emoluments of the Bishopricks of Argyle and the Isles during Her Majesty's pleasure, and until the said grant should be recalled by Her Majesty or her Royal Successors, to be applied in settling schools, repairing churches, educating ministers, and supplying such of them as had small stipends, and for other pious uses, in the Highlands of Scotland; and we being informed that the valued teinds of the Island of Islay, amounting to £111 : 2 : 2 2/3 sterling, and an a rent feu duty of £22 : 5 : 6 2/3 sterling, payable from Daniel Campbell of Shawfield's estate, in the said island, to us, as coming in the place of the Bishops of Argyle and the Isles, have been since leveyed by the said Synod as part of the revenues of Islay is of great extent, containing about 4000 inhabitants, and that there are only two ministers therein;

and that the said Synod of Argyle, and the said Daniel Campbell of Shawfield, apprehending a third minister to be necessary there, had agreed to allow the said Daniel Campbell to levy the valued teinds of the said island, and to retain the feu-duty paid to them out of his estate, and that he had engaged to pay annually to each of the said three ministers £51 : 13 : 4 sterling, and to procure them manses and glebes according to law, upon our ratifying and confirming the said agreement: and we being desirous to promote religion and morality in that part of the kingdom Therefore wit ye, as with the advice and consent of Robert Ord. Esq., Lord Chief Baron of our Court of Exchequer in that part of Great Britain called Scotland, John Maule, John Grant, William Mure, and George Winn, Esquires, Barons of the said Exchequer, – to have given, granted, and disponed, like as we, by these presents, with advice and consent foresaid, give, grant, and dispone, to our lovelite, Daniel Campbell of Shawfield, Esq., his heirs and assignees whatsoever, during our pleasure, and until the foresaid grant from Her Majesty Queen Anne shall be recalled, All and Whole the valued teinds due and payable out of the lands and Island of Islay, and the yearly feu-duty payable from his land and estate in the said Island, to us and our royal predecessors, as come in place of the Bishops of Argyle, and the Isles, and which have been in use to be uplifted by the Synod of Argyle and their factors, he paying yearly to each of the three ministers of the said island the sum of £51 : 13 : 4, and procuring them manses and glebes according to law. And we, for us and our royal successors, during the space aforesaid, ratify, approve and confirm all agreements entered into between the Synod of Argyle and the said Daniel Campbell of Shawfield, and his predecessors, for the purpose aforesaid, and ordain the same to be carried into execution. – Given at our Court at St James', and under our Privy Seal of Scotland at Edinburgh, the 29th day of November 1765 years, in the sixth year of our reign.

Written to the Privy Seal, and registered the 19th, and sealed at Edinburgh the 21st days of December 1765.

DEECREET

OF

DISJUNCTION and NEW ERECTION

against

The Synod of Argyle.

22nd February 1769

and

PETITION

OF

The Synod of Argyle

28th June 1769

VI. – Decreet of Disjunction and New Erection, No 34 of process, Daniel Campbell of Shawfield, Esq., against The Synod of Argyle, – 22nd February, 1769.

At Edinburgh the 22nd day of February 1769, anent the summons and action of disjunction and new erection, raised and pursued before the Lords of Council and Session, Commissioners appointed from Plantation of Kirks and Valuation of Teinds, at the instance of Daniel Campbell of Shawfield, Esq., against Mr. Archibald Campbell, Minister of the Gospel at South Knapsdale, and present Moderator of the Synod of Argyle: Mr. George McClish, Minister of the Gospel of the United Parishes of Skipness and Carradale, and Moderator of the Presbytery of Kintyre: Mr. John Woodrow, Minister of the Gospel at Kildalton, in Islay: Mr. John McMillan, Minister of the Gospel of Kilchoman, in Islay: James Riddell, Esq., proprietor of the lands of Torrobols, in the island of Islay; Robert Campbell of Senerland, and Donald Campbell of Ballinabie. The which summons maketh mention, That whereas the Provincial Synod of Argyle, by their Act, dated at Inverary the 5th day of August 1747 years, after maturely considering a scheme and proposal made by Shawfield, the pursuers grandfather, at length mentioned in the above Act concerning a new erection in Islay, whereby it is agreed, primo, That three ministers be legally settled in Islay, with £600 Scots of yearly stipend each; Secundo, That for furnishing communion elements yearly for the whole island ther shall be allowed £60 Scots; Tertio. That the three parishes shall be provided with churches, manses, and glebes according to the law. To make up this sum, Shawfield undertakes, besides providing the parishes in the necessary accommodation of churches, manses and glebes, to give up all the valued teinds of the island, which, including £73 Scots of tack duty, payable yearly by him to the Synod, amounts to £1333 : 6 : 8 Scots Money, though he and the former heritors there have, since the Reformation, enjoyed about a third of said sum, and he, in particular, has been at no small expense to expede the grants and tacks usual in such cases. But then he expected that the very reverend

Synod should first transfer to him all their right to the above tack duty of £73 Scots, and the feu-duty payable by him out of Islay to them, which is yearly £267 : 6 : 8 Scots, and grant the needful recommendations to the proper courts or persons for ascertaining the said sums for the maintainance of the above three ministers: Secundo, As there will be still wanting of the above sum of £1860 Scots, £259 : 6 : 8 money foresaid, Shawfield considering the burden he took upon him in this affair, hoped the Synod would in the most earnest manner recommend the design in view to the countenance, and assistance of the Committee for managing the Royal Bounty, by representing to them the great necessity of it in the way they should judge most proper and effectual, did unanimously approve thereof, and thereby enacted and appointed that the sum of £73 Scots money being the tack-duty payable for the teinds of Islay, and the sum of £267 : 6 : 8 Scots money, being the feu-duty payable out of Islay to both which the Synod have right – Be (under the express provisions and conditions under-written), allocated and appointed towards carrying on the said new erection, thereby assigning, transferring, and disponing both the said sums to and in favours of the said Daniel Campbell of Shawfield, Esq., the pursuers grandfather, his heirs and successors, to be by them applied towards supporting three ministers in manner specified in, and intended by the foregoing scheme, and the Synod did thereby recommend it to the Lords of the Treasury, or other competent Court, to grant their act or concurrence for securing and ascertaining the sums aforesaid for the purposes above mentioned, and the said Reverend Synod by their other act, dated at Inveraray the 5th day of August 1762 years, after maturely considering their act above narrated, and finding the difficulties which formerly stood in the way of obtaining a new erection in Islay, are now happily removed by the expiry of the grant in favours of Mr. John Campbell late minister at Killarow, and by the engagements which the pursuer had voluntarily agreed to, did therefore by their said act allocate and appropriate the sum of £73 Scots money, being the tack-duty of the valued teinds of Islay, and the sum of £267 : 6 : 8 Scots money, being the feu-duty payable to them out of Islay, extending both to the sum of £340 : 6 : 8 Scots money towards supporting a minister to be planted in the said new erection, thereby assigning and disposing the feu and teind tack dutied above specified to and in favours of the pursuer and his heirs and successors to be by them applied for the purposes aforesaid, and they did not only agree and consent, but earnestly recommended to the Right Honourable the Court of Exchequer and Lords for Plantation of Kirks and Valuation of Teinds, or any other person or court competent to interpone their sentence and authority for appropriating the foresaid sums in manner intended by this Act, and they appointed their clerk to make out an obligation by which the pursuer shall be bound to pay £50 sterling money of stipend, with a fund for communion elements, and to build and provide a legal manse, glebe and churches for the minister, to be settled in said new erection: Moreover, to the end this affair may be brought to a conclusion with all convenient despatch, the Synod appoint the Presbytery of Kintyre to repair to Islay before the 1st day of September then next, and while the pursuer was on the spot, to mark out the limits of the several parishes, and the proper places for manses, churches and glebes: and the said reverend Synod, met at Inveraray the 5th day of August 1763, after maturely considering the above Acts, and the obligations given in by Shawfield, in consequence of the same, and the report of the Presbytery thereanent, and the plan made out and laid before them for carrying the above new erection into execution, did unanimously agree to the following scheme or plan for establishing the said erection, viz. – Primo, That the parish of Kilarow be disjoined from the parish of Kilchoman, and the parish of Kilmenzie be disjoined from the the parish of Kildalton, and these two parishes of Kilarow and Kilmenzie be united and erected into a new parish and separate charge, excepting the lands of Culabolls and Crossabolls, which are to be annexed to the parish of Kilchoman, and the lands of Duich and Proaig which are to be annexed to the parish of Kildalton, so that the new erected parish of Kilarow ad Kilmenzie shall be bounded by the water or river of Ballivogie, and the lands of Leribolls on the west, the sea on the north, the lands of Proaig on the east, and the waters of Duich and Laggan on the south, and that in this new parish there be two churches, one at Kilmenzie and the other at Bowmore, and worship equally divided betwixt them, endowed with the stipend, partly payable by the pursuer, and partly out of the Synod's funds, as mentioned in their Act of last year, and with a church, manse and glebe on the lands of Bowmore, to be built and mortified by the pursuer: Secundo, That there be but one place of worship in the parish of Kilchoman, and that at Kilchoman, where the church, manse and glebe are to be built and mortified by the pursuer: Tertio, Therebe but one place of worship in the parish of Kildalton, and that at Lagavulline, and the manse and glebe thereof on the lands of Surnaig, all to be in like manner built and moritified by the said pursuer, and the Synod appoint the said Presbytery of Kintyre to meet at Killarow in Islay, upon the 10th day of October then next; and in order to carry this plan or scheme in all its parts into proper execution, and according to the true intent and meaning thereof and the Presbytery of Kintyre, as Commissioners from the Synod, in virtue of the above Acts, having met at Killarow on the 12th day of October 1763, when the pursuer laid before them the above plan and Acts of Synod anant the above questions, did, after perambulating the several parishes, as in the said Acts, unanimously approve of the same, on the condition therein mentioned, and thereafter, by the pursuer's consent, proceeded and designed a glebe out of the new parish of Killarow and Kilmenzie, conform to a plan and measurement of a land measurer and honest men of the parish, in terms of the statutes thereanent, made and in manner particularly inset in the said Act of Presbytery, as in the said Acts of Synod and Presbytery at more length is contained; and whereas the pursuer having, in consequence of the said agreement with the Synod of Argyle, for carrying the same into execution having applied to the Lords of the Treasury for a confirmation of the above Acts, and for a gift of the vaued Teinds of Islay agreeable thereto, and for the purpose therein and above mentioned, did accordingly obtain the same, conform to the Royal grant, dated at the Court of St. James, and under the Privy Seal of Scotland at Edinburgh the 29th day of November 1765 years: And true it is, that the pursuer has implemented his part of the above agreements with the said Synod of Argyle, and built at a great expense a church at Bowmore, with manses, glebes, & c., as by the said agreement stipulate: Therefore, in terms of the same, and the royal grant above mentioned, the Lords of Council and Session, Commissioners, appointed for Plantation of Kirks and Valuation of Teinds, in virtue of the several powers lodged in them by the several statutes made thereanent, for dividing large parishes, erecting new kirks or dividing and uniting kirks, changing kirks incommodiously situate, and to place them more centrically, with consent therein mentioned, obtained against the pursuer, who is possessed of the whole island, except for a few small farms, ought and should by their decreet, disjoin the said parish of Killarow from the said parish of Kilchoman, and these two parishes of Killarow and Kilmenzie should be united and erected into a new parish and separate charge, excepting as mentioned in said Acts, and bounded as therein particularly described, and the places of worship in the parishes of Kilchoman and Kildalton ought to be fixed and stipulate and agree to by the pursuer and the said Synod, and the said Acts of Synod and Presbytery ought and should be ratified and confirmed by our said Lords Commissioners in the whole heads and articles thereof, under the conditions therein and above mentioned, and the stipend payable to the ministers of the above three parishes ought and should be declared to be now and in all time coming, agreeable to and in terms of, the above agreement, and the kirks planted accordingly after the form and tenor of the said Acts of Synod and Presbytery, and the royal grant confirming the same in all points: And anent the charge given to the said defenders to having compeared before the said Lords at a certain day bygone, to have heard and seen the premises sufficiently verified and proven, and decreet and sentence of disjunction and new erection given forth and pronounced by the said Lords, conform to the above libel in all points, or else to have alleged a reasonable cause in the contrary why the same should not have been sone with certification, as the said principal summons and execution thereof at more length is contained, the which being called, and the said pursuer compearing by Mr. Walter Campbell, advocate, his procurator, who for verifying the points and articles of the libels, produced viz. – Imprimus, February instant, and both parties compearing by their procurators foresaid, their Lordships continued the said cause till that day eight days, and ordained parties' procurators to be ready to debate against that day, and also ordained parties to put into the Lords' boxes a note of the particulars on which they were to plead: Thereafter, upon the day and date of these presents, the said action and cause being called in presents, the said action and cause being called in presence of the said Lords, and both parties compearing by their procurators foresaid, the said pursuer's procurator repeated his libel, and represented that in August 1747 a scheme was laid before the Synod of Argyle in name of the deceased Daniel Campbell of Shawfield, the pursuer's grandfather, by Mr. John Campbell, minister of Killarow, and Mr. Alexander Campbell, one of the ministers of Inveraray, with regard to the erection of a new parish, and a third minister in Islay, whereby it was proposed – Primo, That there should be three ministers settled in Islay, with £600 Scots of stipend each, is £1800 Scots: Secundo, For furnishing communion elements for the whole Island there be allowed yearly £60 money – in all is £1860 Scots. That to make up this sum Shawfield should undertake, besides providing the parishes with the necessary accommodations of churches, manses, and glebes, to give up all the valued teinds in the Island, which, conform to the decreet of valuation anno 1636, amounted to 200 merks; and it was proposed that the Synod, on their part should transfer to him, towards making up the above stipends, the rents and emoluments which belonged to the Bishop of Islay, to which the Synod had right by a gift from Queen Anne during pleasure, being a teind duty of £73 Scots, and a feu-duty of £267 : 6 : 8 and as there would be still wanting of the above sum of £1860 Scots, £259 : 6 : 8 Scots, Shawfield proposed the Synod should recommend the scheme in view to the countenance and assistance of the committee for managing the Royal Bounty for what aid could ber obtained from them; that the scheme being maturely considered by the Synod, they unanimously approved thereof, and appropriated the above feu and teind duty towards carrying on the said new erection, and for that end assign and dispone to them the said feu and teind duty, and recommended to their Lordships as Commissioners for Plantation of Kirks and Valuation of Teinds, to interpone their authority for carrying the above proposal into execution. That this proposal, so unanimously agreed to by Shawfield and the Synod, was prevented from being carried into execution by the late Shawfield's death, and the present Shawfield being a minor, and abroad, but soon after his return home, and the proposal being laid before him by the Synod, he heartily approved of the same, and the Synod, by their Act dated 5th August 1762, after having maturely considered the above Act 1742, with a letter from the pursuer thereanent, they finding the difficulties which formerly stood in the way of the new erection, were removed by Mr. John Campbell's death, and the voluntary concessions made by the pursuer did again renew their right and appropriation in the pursuer's favours of the above feu and teind duties, to be applied as aforesaid, with the usual recommendations and appointed the Presbytery of Kintyre to repair to Islay and mark out the limits of the three parishes, with the proper places for manses, churches, and glebes; and the said Reverend Synod met at Inveraray 5th August 1763, after maturely considering the above Acts and obligations givewnin by Shawfield, and reproet of the Presbytery thereanent, and the plan made out and laid before them for carrying the erection into execution, and unanimously agreee to the said plan for carrying on the new erection, therein particularly mentioned and here referred to; and in order to carry the plan in all its parts into proper execution, they appoint the Presbytery of Kintyre to meet at Killarow in Islay on the 10th October then next; and the Presbytery having accordingly met, they unanimously approved of the plan laid before them by the pursuer, and at the same time designed a glebe for the third minister; and matters being thus settled betwixt the Synod and the pursuer, he applied to the Lords of the Treasury, and obtained a gift, whereby His Majesty, on a narrative of the above Acts of Synod, gives, grants, and dispones to the pursuer, his heirs and assignees. All and Whole the valued teinds of 2000 merks, payable out of the Island of Islay and the above feu and teind duties, the pursuer paying yearly to each of the ministers of the said three parishes £51 : 13 : 4 sterling, and procuring them manses, glebes according to law, and His Majesty, by the said gift, ratifies and approves the whole agreements betwixt the pursuer and his predecessors, and the Synod of Argyle, in relation to the premises and this gift, is expede under the Privy Seal December 1765; and the pursuer, in consequence thereof, has built a church in the new parish, which has cost him above £700, and the present process now before the Court is a process of disjunction and new erection, in which it is hoped their Lordships will have no difficulty, after the solemn agreements cofirmed by so many Acts of Synod, and the gift from the Crown, and therefore craved that their Lordships, as Commissioners foresaid, would by their decreet disjoin, and of new erect, the said third parish into a new parish and separate charge, confirm to the plan approven by the Synod and Presbytery by the Act 1763, as repeated in the pursuer's libel, and to find that the whole valued teinds of the Island are exhausted, and belong to the pursuer, for payment of the three ministers stipends therein mentioned. Solicitor Dundas, for the Synod of Argyll, answered that he could by no means agree to the facts as stated on the part of Mr. Campbell of Shawfield, the pursuer, for that the question turns upon the following short state of the case:— The late Shawfield being desirous to have a new erection in the Island of Islay, applied to the Synod of Argyle, as having right to the bishop rents of Argyle and the Isles by grant form the Crown, in order to obtain the Synod's consent to the proposed erection of a new parish, and procure from them such of the Bishop's rents as were payable by them out of Islay to the Synod, in order to assist him in making up a stipend for the minister serving the Cure at this intended parish, and it appears that the Synod, at the request of the two ministers of the old parishes in Islay, were willing to comply with Shawfield's demand; however, as the Synod had made a grant of part of these funds previously to the now deceased Mr. John Campbell. Minister of Killarow, the affair was dropt, but in the year 1762, Mr. Campbell, now of Shawfield, made application to the Synod by letter proposing to have the new erection carried on, and it was then expressly covenanted betwixt the Synod and Shawfield that the new erection formerly proposed should be carried into execution. The Synod by their Act in process, assigned and disponed the feu and teind tack duties payable to them, in virtue of the grant from the Crown out of the Island of Islay, being £340:6:8 Scots, to and in favours of Shawfield and his heirs and successors, to be applied by them for the purpose of making up a stipend for the use of the ministers of the said new erected parish, in manner intended by that Act, – 'And they appointed their clerk to make out an obligation by which Shawfield shall be bound to pay £50 sterling money of stipend with a fund for communion elements and to build and provide a legal manse, glebe, and churches for the minister to be settled in the said new erection and by this Act of Synod, the Presbytery of Kintyre were appointed to mark out the boundaries and limits of the new parish, as well as of the two old parishes from which it came to be disjoined, reserving power to the Synod to dispose of the sums thereby assigned to Shawfield, until the new erection should actually take place, and upon these particulars, Dugald McTavish of Dunardary, as procurator for Shawfield, who had conducted the treaty with the Synod, took instruments in the clerk's hands. By a subsequent Act of Synod, stated in the year 1763, upon considering two missive letters from Shawfield, with a plan made out by him for ascertaining the limits of the said new erection, with the report of the Presbytery of Kintyre, the manner in which the said erection was to take place as particularly mentioned, and according to it the Interlocutor to be pronounced by the Lords in this cause, fall to be regulated as to the limits and boundaries, places of worship, manses, and glebes, but this Act of Synod has the following express condition and provision that the Synod should not only have the right to dispose of the teinds assigned by them until the new erection should actually take place, but also, 'that nothing contained herein or in the said former Act shall be so constructed or understood as to hurt or prejudice the interest of the two ministers now settled in Islay, or their successors in office, in any degree'. This being the true state of the case as concerted between the Synod and Mr. McTavish, who attended all the meetings of the Synod, it is contended that no mention whatever is to be made in the Interlocutor ascertaining the stipend of the two ministers already established in Islay, who are not to be hurt in the temporal concerns by this new erection for that the judgement of the Court ought to go out for erecting a new parish according to the bounds and limits specified in the Act of Synod 1763, and finding that the minister of the said new erected parish is to be provided in a stipend of £50 sterling per annum by Shawfield and his heirs and successors, with a suitable provision for communion elements, as the Synod have already assigned in Shawfield's favour the feu and teind-duties payable to them out of the whole Island of Islay, to enable him to endow the said parish with the said stipend, and it is by no means proper in the present question to give any sanction to what is represented to Shawfield of the whole teinds of the parish being valued at £1333 : 3 : 8 for there appears no evidence in this process of the fact further than bare allegations, nor is it hujus loci, and therefore it is humbly hoped the Court will not extend their Interlocutor in this case, beyond the point relative to the new erection, which was the only thing that appears to have been under the consideration of the Synod, while treating of with Shawfield and Mr. McTavish, his factor, as appears by a letter from the Moderator of the Synod and Mr. McTavish to the agent for the Synod, produced in process – Whereunto the procurator for the pursuer replied that he thought it quite unnecessary to make any particular answer to the long state of the facts in the answer for the Synod. The Act 1747, with other Acts of Synod relative thereto, and the grant from the Crown and decreet of valuation were all laid before the Court when the cause was pled, and if the Lords think proper to cast their eyes over them, they will see the fact to be as pled by the pursuer. In the Act 1747, the provisions to the old as well as the minister in the new erected parish, are as plainly settled as figures can make them, and by the subsequent Acts, all relative thereto and ratified by the Crown, the places of worship of the three parishes and boundaries &c. are all settled betwixt the Synod and the pursuer, and can never have the effect to destroy the plain words of these Acts all ratified by the Crown, and by this the interest of the two old ministers cannot be hurt as the teinds are exhausted, and therefore craved a decreet in terms of the libel. Which debate above written, with the libel being upon the day and date of these presents, heard, read, seen, and considered by the said Lords, they separated and disjoined the Parish of Killarow from the Parish of Kilchoman, as also separated and disjoined the Parish of Kilmenzie from the Parish of Kildalton, excepting, as was hereby excepted, and united and erected the said Parishes of Kilchoman, as also separated and disjoined the Parish of Killarow and Kilmenzie, excepted as said is into a new, separate, and distinct parish to be called in all time coming up the United Parishes of Killarow and Kilmenzie; excepting from the said disjunction, union, and erection, the Lands of Cuilabolls and Crossabolls, Duich, and Proaig, and annex the said lands of Cuilabolls and Crossabolls to the Parish of Kilchoman, and annex the said Lands of Duich and Proaig to the Parish of Kildalton, and found that the new erected Parish of Killarow and Kilmenzie is bounded by the water or river of

Ballivogie, and the Lands of Skribolls upon the west, the sea on the north, the Lands of Proaig upon the east, and the waters of Duich and Laggan on the south, and ordained the two churches mentioned in the Act of Presbytery libelled on, dated the 12th day of October 1763, the one at Kilmenzie and the other at Bowmore, to be the churches of the said new erected Parish of Killarow and Kilmenzie and worship to be equally divided betwixt these two churches, and ordained the church of Kilchoman, mentioned in the said Act of Presbytery, to be the Parish Church of the Parish of Kilchoman, and ordained the church at Laggavulline, likewise mentioned in the said Act of Presbytery to be the Parish Church of Kildalton, and decerned and ordained the whole inhabitants within the bounds of the said parishes to repair to the respective kirks above mentioned, for hearing the Word, receiving the sacraments, and all other acts of public worhsip, and to subject themselves to the ministers of the said respective parishes, as their own proper pastors, in time coming and modified, decerned, and ordained the constant stipend and provision of the minister who shall serve the Cure of the said new erected Parish of Killarow and Kilmenzie, to be yearly, in all time coming, £600 Scots money for stipend, and £20 money foresaid for communion elements, and decerned and ordained the said stipend and communion elements money to be paid yearly to the minister to be settled in the said new erected parish, and his successors in office, at the terms of Whitsunday and Martinmas yearly, by equal portions, and that by the pursuer and his successors in the manner specified in the Act of the Provincial Synod of Argyle, dated the 3d day of August 1747, likewise libelled on. That is the sum of £93 : 6 : 8 Scots, being the superplus Teind, conform to Decreet of Valuation of the Island of Islay (including therein the teind tack-duty of £73 Scots, formerly payable to the Synod of Argyle), after payment of the stipends and communion element money of the Parishes of Kilchoman and Kildalton: Reserving, nevertheless, to all parties concerned to challenge the said Decreet of Valuation as accords of law. Item, the sum of £267, and £67 : 6 : 8, being the feu-duty payable by the pursuer to the Crown, as come in place of the Bishop of the Isles, and of the lands and Island of Islay, to which teind and feu-duty the Synod of Argyle had right by a grant from Queen Anne, and to which the pursuer has now right by a gift from his present Majesty, in consequence of the Acts of Synod libelled on, and of consent of the pursuer, the remainder being £259 : 6 : 8, by the said Daniel Campbell of Shawfield, Esq., pursuer himself, and his successors, extending in whole to the sum of £620 Scots money, and decerned accordingly. Thereafter there was a petition given in and presented to the said Lords by the Very Reverend the Synod of Argyle, shewing that in the process of disjunction and new erection at the instance of Daniel Campbell, Esq., against the petitioners, their Lordships, of this date, 22d February 1769, signed the 8th March, thereafter pronounced and Interlocutor which, inter alia, bears, modify, decern, and ordain the constant stipend and provision of the minister who shall serve the Cure of the said new erected parish of Killarow and Kilmenzie to be yearly in all time coming, £600 Scots money, for stipend and £20 money foresaid for communion elements, and decern and ordain the said stipend and communion element money to be paid yearly to the minister to be settled in the said new erected parish, and his successors in office, at the terms of Whitsunday and Martinmas yearly, by equal portions, and that by the pursuer

and his successors, in the manner specified in the Act of the Provincial Synod of
Argyle, dated the 3d day of August 1747, likewise libelled on, – That is the sum of
£93 : 6 : 8 Scots, being superplus teind, conform to decreet of valuation of the
Island of Islay (including therein the teind tack-duty of £73 Scots, formerly
payable to the Synod of Argyle) after payment of the stipends and communion
element money of the Parishes of Kilchoman and Kildalton, reserving, nevertheless, to all parties concerned, to challenge the said decreet of valuation, as accords
of law. Item, The sum of £267 : 6 : 8, being the feu-duty payable by the pursuer
to the Crown, as comes in place of the Bishop of the Isles, out of the lands and
Islands of Islay, to which teind and feu-duty the Synod of Argyle had right by
a grant from Queen Anne, and to which the pursuer has now right by a gift from
his present Majesty, in consequence of the Acts of Synod libelled on, and of the
consent of the pursuer, the remainder being £259 : 6 : 8, by the said Daniel
Campbell of Shawfield, Esq., pursuer himself, and his successors, extending in
whole to the sum of £620 Scots money, and decern accordingly. Of that part of
the interlocutor which modifies only £20 Scots for communion elements, the
Synod hunbly intreats a review. Their Lordships have never, it was believed, in
any case given so small an allowance for communion elements, and in the
circumstances of this parish now erected by their Lordships, the sum is altogether
inadequate, although, perhaps, in no greater bounds than any of the other parishes
in Islay it contains an equal number of people to both of them put together, and
the numbers are daily increasing by reason of the new discovered mines, and very
extensive operations consequential thereof within said parish. The only port or
harbour in the island to which there is any resort of shipping is also within it. In
short the sum specified in the Interlocutor bears so small a proportion to the
expense which must be incurred in dispensing the sacraments in that parish, that
the petitioners are much afraid the dispensation will not be frequent unless some
addition is given. It will perhaps be said that the circumstances of this case are
particular, that in order to make up the fund for the minister of this new parish,
Mr. Campbell of Shawfield has been obliged to contribute a yearly sum out of his
own pocket, and that by the transaction between him and the Synod, it was to be
understood that no more was to be allowed either for stipend or communion
elements that the sum specified in the interlocutor. Upon this idea their Lordships
probably went in modifying so low a sum. But with submission, when the Acts
of Synod agreements with Shawfield are examined, the fact with regard to the
matter of communion elements casts up a different light. It is true that when the
first proposal of a new erection was made in 1747, by the present Shawfield's
grandfather, it appeared from the Act of Synod in August said year, that the two
ministers who reported Shawfield's proposal to the Synod, mentioned £60 Scots
as the allowance to be given for communion elements to the ministers of the
whole three parishes – But the scheme then proposed never was carried into
execution – it was only approved of under certain conditions by the Synod,
failing which conditions, they declared that their consent should be to all intents
and purposes void and null. Sundry obstacles came in the way, and nothing was
done in consequence of that proposal. In 1762 a similar scheme was set on foot,
but with some variations, and the whole Acts of Synod, and other evidence this
new scheme shows, that the members of the Synod ere careful of two things – in

the first place, not to affect in any shape the interests of the ministers of the two old parishes; and secondly, to have £50 sterling settled as a stipend to the minister of the third parish, besides a reasonable sum for communion elements, which reasonable sum is specified in one of their Acts to be £5 sterling, of £60 Scots, for the use alone of the said new parish. It was under these conditions that they agreed that Shawfield desire to give up the rights which they had from the Crown to the teind and feu-duties payable to them out of the Island of Islay, amounting to £340 : 6 : 8 Scots, and that they allowed Shawfield to obtain a grant for them from the Treasury to serve as a fund in part of the new minister, he contributing the rest as best he could out of the teinds in his hand, or out of his pocket, so far as these are deficient. The Act of Synod 5th August 1762, after agreeing to make over their right to the forsaid £340 : 6 : 8 of teind and feu-duty for the purpose aforesaid, proceeds in these words: – 'And they appointed their clerk to make out an obligation by which Shawfield shall be bound to pay £50 sterling money of stipend, with a fund for communion elements'. The Act of Synod 5th August 1763, after specifying the boundaries of the new erected parish, which parish is 'to be endowed with the stipend partly payable by Shawfield and partly out of the Synods funds, as mentioned in the Act of last year, declares that nothing contained herein, or in the said former Act, shall be so construed or understood as to hurt or prejudice the interest of the two ministers now settled in Islay, or their successors in office, in any degree. Both these Acts of Synod bear that upon all and sundry the premises Dugald McTavish of Dunardry, as procurator for, and having ample power for purpose from the said Daniel Campbell, asked and took instruments. The Presbytery of Kintyre, and Commissioners from the Synod of Argyle, have met at Killarow, in Islay, upon the 12th October 1763, the Act drawn up by them on that occasion, after settling the boundaries, & c., bears that said new erected parish is to be endowed 'with the stipend, partly payable by Shawfield, and partly by the Synod of Argyle, out of their funds, as particularly specified in their Act, dated at Inveraray the day of August 1762, amounting in all to the sum of £50 sterling of stipend and £5 sterling as the allowance for communion elements'. The Act farther says that the Presbytery, having peram- bulated the several parishes above designed, and having read and maturely considered the scheme of plan of new erection above mentioned, did, and hereby do, unanimously approve thereof, upon this provision and condition, that the ministers of the old parishes, Kilchoman and Kildalton, shall be continued in possession of the stipend they at present enjoy, and a proper allowance for communion elements. That all parties did then understand £5 sterling to be the sum fixed and agreed upon for communion elements of these new erected parishes most certain. A letter is produced in process from the Reverend Mr. Paul Fraser, Moderator of the Synod, dated 3d November 1768, setting forth the meaning of the Synod all along to have been that they gave their £340 : 6 : 8 of teind duty and feu-duty to Shawfield, upon condition of his 'erecting a new parish in that Island, the emoluments whereof to be £50 sterling, and £5 sterling for communion elements, with a manse and glebe, according to law, which glebe was already designed by the Presbytery of Kintyre, and that a decreet of disjunction and erection should pass accordingly,' – To which letter is subjoined an attestation under the hand or Mr. McTavish of Dunardry, who appeared through the whole transaction as Shawfield's procurator, and as having full powers from him, in these words, – 'Having this day had the honour to converse with the Committee of the Very Reverend the Synod of Argyle relating to the new erection, Islay, and after perusing the above letter, am fully satisfied the same contains the true and honest meaning of the parties, and am humbly of opinion Shawfield shall desire the decreet to pass agreeable to within the letter.' Their Lordships, in place of giving what was thus understood by all parties to be fixed as the sum for communion elements, have allowed only the third part of it, being no more than the trifling sum of £1 : 13 : 4 sterling, and you seem thereby to have had in view a tripartite division of the 5 among the three parishes. But with a submission, this has proceeded from a misunderstanding of the agreement, and it is the only part of the Interlocutor in which the interest of the other two parishes is in any way touched. The petitioners have all along understood that the other two parishes were to be left on their present footing, without being affected more or less by this transaction. They have hitherto been provided in communion elements out of their funds, and there is no reason why any part of the small sums which have been appropriated to the new erected parish should be taken away in order to be applied to them. What would render the case of this new parish the harder if so trifling a sum were to be allowed for communion elements, as there is no fund out of which the stipend of £50 can ever be augmented, at least if the allegation made on Shawfield's part be ture, that the teinds of the Island are already more than exhausted, and craved that it might therefore please their Lordships to alter their Interlocutor, so far as regards the sum modified for communion elements, and to modify such larger sum as shall appear adequate, as the said petition bears. Which petition being, upon the 28th day of June 1769, advised by the said Lords, they refused the desire thereof, and adhered to the former Interlocutor. And so the Lords gave and pronounced their decreet and sentence in the said matter, in disjoining and erecting, modifying, decerning and ordaining, in manner at length above mentioned.

9 Mr Freebairn's House and Smelter Building at Freeport on Sound of Islay. Original in British Library. *Photograph courtesy of Royal Commission.*

Improvements

In 1762, Daniel II succeeded in leasing the lead mines to Charles Freebairn for thirty-one years at a payment of 1/8th share, or "dish", of all ore raised during the first fifteen years and 1/7th share, or "dish" of that raised during the remainder of the Lease. Freebairn had no better luck than his predecessors and died a Bankrupt. The mines employed several hundred men.

The possibilities of a fishing industry were also considered and William Moffet produced a report on the matter for Daniel in 1776 [Book of Islay]. The Salmon fishings were leased out and the salmon fisher was accommodated with a cottage on Laggan river.

Daniel I was well aware that the 'rentier' system of the Tacksmen was not conducive to good husbandry nor to the best welfare of the lesser people and he was determined to put an end to sub-setting. There is an interesting document in the Appendix to the Book of Islay, setting out his views. It points out that there are

> two class of tenants, viz. the great, or gentlemen tenants, and the small tenants, the gentlemen possessing several quarterlands extending to three and four thousand acres and upwards. They mind husbandry very little, only the yearly sett of these large farms to a sett of poor people they call their farmers. The small tenants, four, five, six, or eight of them, enjoy a quarterland promiscuously among them. The manner of both classes are destructive to husbandrie – the great only minding their yearly sett: their farmers what soil and climate gives in their year; and the small farmers being unequally yoked, live in indolence and debate. These manner of holdings the proprietor is determined to alter. And, in regard to the first class [of] tenants, that each is only to enjoy such an extent of lands as may rationally fall under the cognizance and management of a good improver. And as to the second class of small tenants, that their farms be new modeled, each to have an establishment for himself, and to occupy individually.

Proceeding on these lines, Daniel II gave interim leases to some tenants in 1769 for nine years. The form and terms of these leases were finalized and over ninety (to come into force at Whitsun 1779) were written out in duplicate during 1777. Besides their Money Rents, the Tenants were bound to pay the Public Burdens attached to each quarterland. All Leases had Clauses whereby the tenants must help erect March Dykes between their farms: reclaim heath and moss land: follow certain rules of husbandry: cut their peats regularly; allow other tenants to have access to sand, limestone and marle (they paying for any damage incurred in the removal of same).

All flax was to be taken to the Lint Mills of Skerrols or Lagavuline for processing: woollen cloth to the wauk mill and all iron work to the local smiddy. In accordance with the Disarming Act, they were forbidden to carry or use firearms, nor were they to keep greyhounds, setting dogs or others harmful to game: nor to kill Black Fish (presumably late Salmon) with nets, rods or spears, nor to use "bleezes" on any of the rivers or burns. Neither might they keep Change Houses (or Tippling Houses) without special Licence. All woodlands were protected and mineral rights reserved to the proprietor, he making reparation for any damage caused by his activities in this direction.

The improvements on his estates, the redemption of the Wadsets, his political interests (an expensive ploy in the Eighteenth century) and his personal extravagancies (typical also of the young men of his period) made it necessary for him to find more capital. Thus, in 1767, with the consent of his younger brother and heir, John, he granted Bonds over the Estate of Islay to William Stewart, the King's Remembrancer, and to Lord George Germain (notorious as having been courtmartialled for cowardice at the Battle of Minden: he later succeeded as Viscount Sackville) for £6000 and £20,000 respectively.

Daniel II, in 1768, projected the village of Bowmore, as his grandfather had planned, though as all heritable jurisdictions were abolished after the Rebellion of 1745, it could not claim to be a Burgh of Barony. It was built on the quarterland of Ardlaroch of which the Tacksman was a representative of the MacKays of the Rhinns, a family which had held office under the Lords of the Isles. After the fall of the Lordship and the later flight of the MacKay Chief to Ireland, the remaining members of the Clan had remained low and, on the incoming of the Campbells of Cawdor, had signed, in 1618, a Bond of Obedience to them. Little is heard of them until John MacKay emerges as Tacksman of Bowmore and members of his family became the earliest feuars there. They also acquired, by lease, some of the lands granted to Brian Vicar MacKay by Donald of Harlaw, Lord of the Isles, under the Gaelic Charter of 1408 (now one of the most treasured possessions of the Edinburgh Register House). It had been dramatically found and rescued from a tin box buried in the garden of two elderly ladies, of MacKay descent, in Northern Ireland, who believed that some day they might be able to lay claim to the lands therein mentioned.

10 View of the Town of Bowmore, 1771, by John Clevely, Junior. Original in British Library. Photograph courtesy of Royal Commission.

Building Leases and feus, together with small crofts on the outskirts of the village, were available, one of the conditions being that the houses should be built of stone and lime, with built-in chimneys in the gables, and slated. The height and measurements are given for single and two-storeyed houses in the Day Book. Such houses had already been built in Kilarrow and the Tacksmen had also built their own houses in this fashion, though it was a long time before even they were slated.

The people's cottages were built of double dry stone walls stuffed with peat for insulation, having a central fire on the floor with a hole in the roof above for the egress of smoke: specimens of these were to linger on for another century. The original cottages were illustrated by the artists who accompanied Thomas Pennant during his Tour of the Highlands and Islands in 1772.

Daniel had only been 16 when his Grandfather died and he was sent abroad to complete his education and make Le Grand Tour. On his return to take up his responsibilities he was in close contact with John, Lord Lorne, who, with his wife Elizabeth Gunning, widow of the 6th Duke of Hamilton, had been on the Continent themselves at the same time as Young Daniel of Shawfield and Islay was on his Grand Tour. Very little was done to complete the new village of Inveraray during the period of the 4th Duke of Argyll (1761–1770), though John managed to do some work, before he succeeded his father, as 5th Duke, when the plans really went ahead. But quite obviously there had been conversations with young Daniel in regard to the creation of Planned Villages. The enthusiastic young man, having been much impressed by the hilltop villages of Italy, crowned by their churches, quickly adapted John Adam's 1758 discarded plan of a round church for Inveraray as ideal for the focal point of the projected village of Bowmore, with which his Grandfather, for a variety of reasons had been unable to proceed.

The requirements of Inveraray had been a division of the church, so that in one half an English service could be held and in the other half a Gaelic service. This was unnecessary in Islay, so the dividing wall was disposed of and the building much simplified, having a single Square Tower, which forms a porch and holds a staircase leading to the gallery.

Confirmation of this came from Duke Niall (10th Duke, 1872–1949) who was steeped in the muniments of Argyll and the traditions of the family, as perhaps no-one else has ever been. It was he who told Captain Iain Ramsay of Kildalton, a friend of many years, of this matter. Certainly, from the time of John's accession to the Dukedom in 1770, there was close contact between the family at Inveraray and that of Islay and later there were intermarriages.

During his travels on the Continent, Daniel had met and formed a friendship with the Princess Daschkaw, Lady of Honour to Catherine II,

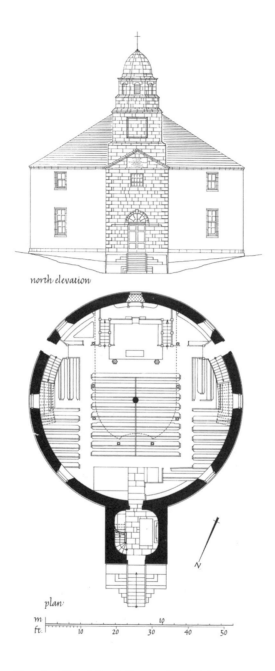

north elevation

plan

11 North elevation and floor plan of Round Church, Bowmore 1769, built by Daniel Campbell, Yr., 2nd Laird of Shawfield and Islay. *Photograph courtesy of Royal Commission.*

Empress of Russia. Owing to the intrigues of that Court, this fascinating lady, now widowed, fell from favour and, leaving Russia, brought her son to be educated at the University of Edinburgh. Family tradition asserted that she visited Daniel at Woodhall and that he gave her the Shawfield pearls. Though her portrait certainly hung there, there is no proof either of this visit nor, indeed, of the existence of the pearls, but the strong family belief in the legend led to a strange sequel about sixty years later. It is best told in the words of the youngest witness, John Francis Campbell. He found the following entry in his Mother, Lady Eleanor's Diary:–

"Tuesday January 25th 1830 Mr. Robinson of Lochopp called we broke upon the curious old strong box found it contained only papers – dinner 5. We visited all the poor people and the beasts about." I perfectly remember this event thus recorded after my lessons in the Library of Woodhall. I was allowed to join the party. I scrambled up a flight of wooden steps behind the window in the passage, where the machine contrived by my Father to produce perpetual motion and which never went at all used to stand. Scrambling through the low open door at the top I found my Mother seated in state on an arm chair amidst a lot of dusty lumber. "Before me was an old iron bound brown box which had been a plate chest . . . . on his heels beside the box was John Campbell the piper in his Kilt, his good natured pock marked face lighted up with curiosity and eagerness, my decorous nervous little tutor, Mr. Loudon, stood near, Guyot, the butler, my Father's travelling servant when abroad a very handsome dark Swiss with glossy curly hair like the hair of the late Duke of Hamilton was chattering broken English, and a carpenter with some tools in a basket was standing ready for action. The box had been found in the lumber room, no one knew anything about it, no key in the House would fit it: It might contain the long lost Shawfield Pearls which the Princess Dashchoff was supposed to have carried away: so the box was to be broken open –".

At it they went with a will I well remember the nervous anxiety of watching wondering what would appear when the lid was opened. Some one had suggested a Skeleton.

At last with a wrench and cheer the lid rose and there were only layers of yellow papers. Still hoping for the pearls or for a snuff box at least, layer after layer was unpacked and tossed on the floor. No one heeded the dusty old papers. At last his voice cracked with keeness the piper shouted and a rough tin with a parchment dangling to it was handed to the light of day. I see that group now as in a picture though I saw it only once thirty five years ago. The light came down from a garret window in the roof. The piper with the parchment in his hand stood before my Mother, the handsome head of the Swiss butler bent over his brown nervous hands, which were struggling with the rust on the tin box, my Tutor with keen eyes & eager face watched them & an urchin in a kilt stretched his neck to see what marvellous thing would come out of the tin box. It might be a pearl necklace worth thousands of pounds. "Huch" said the Piper "its only a seal. But its a very queer one" The box contained nothing but papers and we were all grievously disappointed. We ate our luncheon & went a round of the Farm Labourers Cattlesheds and pigsties with the gentlemen who came from Lauhcop. On the 27th Feb my Father & Col. John Wildman [brother-in-law of Lady Eleanor] started for London and on March 7 my Mother & I went to Gosford [the home of Lady Eleanor's father, the Earl of Wemyss] returning through E'burgh on the 15th we started for London where we staid till July 7th. On the 17th of July Mr. McInnes the Edinburgh Doer went away from Woodhall having transacted a deal of business. In April MacInnes returned a verification of the Infeftment of Ilay in the Parliament holden in ANNO 1617 to Sir John Campbell of Calder marked (No. 4). This was one of the papers found in the old chest and it was supposed to make Bowmore in Islay a "Burgh". [The right to erect a "Burgh of Barony" was invalidated by the abolition of Heritable Jurisdiction]. The chest contained the title deeds of the estates which Daniel Campbell purchased, and a great mass of accounts, letters bonds and securities, all carefully arranged numbered and packed. I have no doubt these papers were so packed by the Curators of Daniel Campbell on the death of Daniel Campbell 1st Shawfield in 1753. They may have been so packed on the Death of Daniel in 1777, when Walter his brother succeeded to the estates. Anyhow none of the generation who found them knew anything about them. I well remember the joking that passed over the bills of Lady Heneret Cunningham for the clothing and Education of her sons the last of whom was my Father's Grandfather "old Shawfield". The papers were taken out of their box & the box was mended & made to look venerable & taken to Islay. Some of the parchments were sent to the Edinburgh Doer some were stowed away in drawers, and carried about in desks. The bundles of letters, etc., were opened & some at least were sent to Charles Sharpe & returned by him. One bundle is marked in his hand "Letters from Woodhall". In another hand, I think my Mother's or my Aunt Julia's, it is directed to Charles Kirkpatrick Sharpe, Esqr, Princes Street. This particular bundle contained a lot of family Autographs some apparently selected for something quaint in the letter. The conclusion to which I have now arrived is that Charles Sharpe got the pick of the letters and sent a few to my Mother in 1830. Many are missing about 1715–1745 the most interesting periods historically.

Since J. F. Campbell wrote even more of these papers are missing. Those of Daniel's Trading activities from 1695–1714, the personal letters and Estate papers were again rescued, this time by John Ramsay of Kildalton (who, together with J. F. Campbell, acted as Trustee for Walter Frederick Campbell at the time of the Sequestration). The removal men had packed the books in the Woodhall Library for sale in Edinburgh in 1862, strewing the papers, which they found in the drawers, on the floor as worthless. Ramsay collected them and sent all the Factory and personal papers to

Campbell, keeping those affecting Islay: a few days later Woodhall was destroyed by fire.

The Factory papers, edited in Ms by J. F. Campbell, appeared on the London market in 1959, from an anonymous source, and were purchased by the Mitchell Library, Glasgow. The fate of the personal letters of the Eighteenth Century is unknown beyond the fact that in 1866, John Francis did not wish them to be published [The Campbells of Shawfield, by J. F. Campbell].

All the Islay papers up to the beginning of the Eighteenth Century formed the nucleus of the BOOK OF ISLAY, which was completed by Gregory Smith after John Ramsay's death in 1892, on the instructions of his widow. Lucy Martin of Auchendennan [entry in the Sederunt Book of Kildalton]. More than half of the edition of the Book of Islay was destroyed in an air-raid fire, Glasgow, Easter 1915. The original Mss. of the Stent Book and the Road Book of Kildalton were deposited in the Register House by Captain Iain Ramsay of Kildalton in 1955. [Part of the residue of the Eighteenth Century Estate papers are transcribed in this volume]

The Wadset of Killinallen and other lands, listed in the Rent Roll of 1686 to the "Wnquile" Alexander Campbell, is probably the earliest of the Wadsets. By 1733 it included Ardnahow and Ardnave, and by 1741, Alexander Campbell II of Killinallen seems to have handed over Ardnahow and Cove to his grandson Colin: Ardnave and Breachachie to John Campbell, who married the widow of Colin Campbell, Alexander's son: and Killinallen to his widow and her son Angus. At his death it appears that the Wadset was disponed to his grandson, Colin Campbell of Ardnahow. When the Wadset had been finally redeemed, Colin "left this Kingdom" [Stent Book p. 91, 95] in 1778. The Lease of Ardnahow was then given to Archibald Campbell of Kintour.

Copy Stated Accot betwixt Daniel Campbell of Shawfield Esq. & Colin Campbell, Wadsetter of Ardnohow Copied 8th day of September 1773

Dr				Cr	
To Ardnahow's acceptance to Shawfield	£75. 14. 10⅓		By Wadsett money of Killinallan £211. 2. 2⅓		
payable at Whits 1760 for £126 whereoff					
paid £50 [5] − [1]⅔ inde a Balance			Disponed to Ardnahow & payable		
of ——[5] − [1]⅔			by Shawfield		
To Interest on Do. Balance from Whits. 1760	12. 19. 8		By Int. Do. Sum from Whits.	36. 19. —	
to Marts. 1763——3½ years ——			1760 to Marts 1763——3½ years		
To Sixpence of Diligence incurred on Do.					
Bill . . .	1. 6. 9				
To a Balance due by Shawfield to Ardnahow	159. 19. 11.				
	£248. 1. 2⅓			£248. 1. 2⅓	

At Killarow the Eighteenth day of October, One Thousand Seven Hundred & Sixty three years The above Accompt of Debt and Credit betwixt Daniel Campbell of Shawfield, Esq., and Colin Campbell, Wadsetter of Ardnahow are by them instantly examined and finds the same justly stated & bearing a Balance of One Hundred & fifty nine pounds Nineteen Shillings and Eleven Pence Str due by Shawfield to the said Colin Campbell and of which said Balance above stated the said Colin Campbell hereby acknowledges to have instantly received Shawfield's order on the Bailie of Isla for the sum of Fifty nine pounds Nineteen Shillings & Eleven pence money foresaid which reduces the foresaid Balance to the sum of One Hundred Pounds and this last Balance is all that remains unpaid of the Wadset money of Kilinallen & bearing interest from Marts next in regard the above Calculations are carried down to that date In Witness whereof these presents (written by Gilbert McCulloch servt to the said Daniel Campbell) are subscribed by both parties Place day month and year above written And before these Witnesses Duncan Campbell Bailie of Isla and the said Gilbert McCulloch writer hereoff as also Witness to the Delivery of the acceptance entered on the Debtor side hereof and of the Diligence that followed thereon.

(signed) Dan: Campbell Witness   (signed) D Campbell
(signed) Gilbt McCulloch Witness   (signed) Colin Campbell
Balance BALANCE £100. Str

Improvements in Agriculture

In 1764 the Island was visited by "The Mad Minister" of Moffat, the Reverend John Walker. His epithet had been acquired because of his obsession with the wild plants of Scotland ('weeds' according to his Parishioners). He was, in fact, a very fine naturalist and was given Commissions by the Board of the Annexed Estates to make a Report on the conditions and resources of the West Highlands and Islands with a view to their improvement; the S.P.C.K. and the General Assembly were glad to have him complete the work of two ministers who had set out a few years previously to ascertain the size and problems of the Parishes and to survey the state of Education. Thomas Pennant, the English Zoologist, also seized the opportunity to ask him to observe the wild life and note any "rare Marine substances, insects and small fishes". He was given the use of the Custom House Wherry from Greenock and funds were made available; the Assembly arranged pulpit supply for the duration of his trip. He made many interesting observations but was at times inaccurate in his estimation of size of population. Daniel

II had just taken over and many of the improvements suggested by Walker were already in hand. Walker was a friend of Lord Kames and the Campbell family had benefited from the great agricultural Improver's advice on the occasions of his visits with John Ramsay of Auchtertyre, to Inveraray Castle.

Interestingly, Walker mentions the steady flow of Emigrants to the New World and reports that on the 1st August, 1764, about 80 young men and women embarked for Ireland to join the Emigrant ships which sailed from Loch Foyle to America. He also reported that innoculation had not yet reached the Island and that there was a heavy toll, particularly among the adults, every year from Smallpox. Children, he said were carried off annually by measles. Unfortunately, there are very few reliable shipping lists and it is often very difficult to pick up the families on the other side of the Atlantic. In some cases the descendants do have some information as to their origins, but mostly it is very vague.

Potatoes had been introduced about 1750 and were used to break in new ground; the people were already relying on them heavily as a staple and some doubts were expressed as to the wisdom of this – alas, the doubts were to be fully justified in the Nineteenth Century with the arrival of the Potato Blight and the disaster of the great famine in the 1840's.

The experiments of the Campbells in growing a variety of sown grasses, clover etc., were already making improvements in animal feed and wheat and improved grains showed a good return in favourable summers. But the great disadvantage to good crops was the lack of fences and, as Pennant was to observe in 1772, the cattle roamed freely over the fields destroying the crops. Hence the insistence on the building of stone dykes around the cultivated fields. At first these took the form of turf and stone walls 2 or 3 feet high, which were not at all satisfactory, but in the next century drystane dykers were brought in from Durham, Northumberland and Galloway to teach their craft and many of these wonderful walls have survived intact for well over a hundred years.

Rules with Regard to the Cutting of
Moss
8th Sept., 1767

(This foolscap sheet of paper is very fragile, and quite gone in the ninth line, where one of the folds comes. The original is among the Kildalton papers.)

That such as will be indwellers at Bowmore & Ardlarach (except fewers,) after the Term of Whitsunday 1768, must cutt their Turf in a regular Beng as will be shown them:– Those residing at Bowmore are to begin cutting at the beginning of the moss betwixt Knocknafirah and the Church Those in Ardlaroch to begin beg[i]ning of the moss nearest their Houses and corn.

That the Moss must be Cutt regular to the Bottom, and the parings laid regular after them.

That if any person or persons DO cutt Terf contrary to the Intention of the above Rules such person or persons SHALL be liable to the sum of Ten Shillings Stirling for the first offence twenty for the second and his, hers or theirs Turf thrown into the Holes in which they were cutt.

It is strictly ordered that all conserned will comply with the above RULES as Timeous nottice will be given them.

I Daniel Campbell of Shawfield do hereby order that the above three Rules be strictly observed and that under the Penalties above expressed:– FOR WITNESS whereof I have subscribed these presents at Isla-House the eight day of September Seventeen Hundred and Sixty seven years Before these Witnesses fferqd Campbell of Lagganlochan and Angus Taylor in Daill.

(signed) D. CAMPBELL

COPY
INVENTARY
of
TACKS and CONTRACTS
Granted by late
SHAWFIELD got of
W McK by N McGibbon
to
SUNDRIES in ISLAY
1775

Woodhall
10th January 1776
The tacks & Contracts mentioned in this Inventary delivered up to Gilbt
McCulloch at Woodhall by N MG

(The original is among the Kildalton Papers.)

Inventory of Tacks and Contracts Granted by the deceased Daniel
Campbell of Shawfield Esqr. to Sundries in Islay Got up from
W. MKay by N MG

1. Tack to James Campbell of Balinaby of the Miln of Breckacy
2. Tack to Idem of the Lands of Tormistle and Leckgrunart & c
3. Tack to Colin Campbell of Ardnahow of the Lands of Kilenailen & Balsa
4. Tack to Idem of the Lands of Gortantoid
5. Contract and prorogation of Wadsett betwixt the said D. Campbell of Shawfield and James Campbell of Ballinaby
6. Contract and prorogation Bewixt Idem and John Campbell of Sultown [Cultoon]
7. Tack to George Campbell son of Archd Campbell in Lossitt of the Lands of Persabolls & c
8. Tack to Angus Campbell Smith in Killarow of a House and Kiln & c
9. Tack to Allan McLean of the lands of Gortan nantra
10. Tack to Donald Campbell Officer of a House
11. Tack to Archibald MacLachlan Mercht in Killarow of a house there
12. Tack to Patrick Colquhoun of a House
13. Contract Betwixt the Deceast Shawfield and Colin Campbell late of Ardnahow
14. Tack to Mathew Hunter of the lands of Taynacnock
15. Tack to John McEachern Smith in Killarow

Rentall of Ilay
To Commence at Marts 1779

(The original is among the Kildalton Papers and is written on three pages of double foolscap.)

Rentroll of those parts of the Estate of Islay sett in Tack from and after Whitsunday 1779 exhibiting the present Rent and the New Rent payle at the aforesaid period of 1779

Names of Lands	Tenants' Names	Present Rent Crop 1774			New Rent payle at Marts 1779		
Aryhalloch	Archd Carmichael	£17	—	—	£35	—	—
Avenlussa & c	Gilbert McArthur	8	10	—	28	6	—
Easter Ellister	Dond McDermitt	14	—	—	50	—	—
Grulent	Dugal McDuffie	5	—	—	15	10	—
Persabolls	Charles Freebairn	16	4	6	32	9	4
Bolsa	Duncan Brown	6	—	—	20	—	—
Upper Learin	John Campbell	10	—	—	15	—	—
Duisker	Archd Campbell	20	4	—	30	6	—
Buninuilt	Archd McEacheran	8	—	—	25	—	—
Balligally	Archd Carmichael	12	12	3	70	—	—
Ardmore & c	Baillie Dun: Campbell	80	16	11½	93	8	1½
Clagingarroch	John Carmichael	11	11	—	30	—	—
Balligillen	John Campbell	14	6	—	42	18	—
Millrish	John & Archd Campbells	6	10	6	19	11	6
Gruinard	Dond McGillespy	14	—	—	40	—	—
Tirevagan	Finlay McDermid	8	5	—	22	—	—
Trudernish	John Campbell	9	9	3	28	7	9
Corsplan	Alexd McNivan & c	14	—	—	40	—	—
½ Grobolls	Duncan Brown	5	13	9	15	—	—
Talent	John Brown & Co	12	15	—	31	17	6
Cattadill	Malcolm Mcffadzen	7	10	—	18	—	—
Mulindra	Archd Campbell	17	9	—	43	12	6
Gortantyde	John Bell	3	—	—	25	—	—
½ Nosebridge	Nicol Keith	8	12	6	35	—	—
Balulve	Dun: Carmichael	15	—	—	45	—	—
Roskeran	Dond McNivan	6	15	—	16	17	6
Torronich	Neil McCore	8	10	—	25	10	—
Balliclach	Dond McVurrish	7	5	—	14	10	—
Echvernach	Patrick Currie	13	17	6	38	—	—
Smail & c	Alexr McEcheran & c	26	15	—	60	—	—
Kinindrochid	Dond McMillan & c	14	16	2	36	—	—
Connisbay	Archd Bell & c	22	10	—	54	—	—
Leck Gruindard	Duncan Currie	13	12	6	36	—	—
Gartacher	Dond McCallman	7	—	—	20	—	—
Shingart	Duncan McCallum	13	3	8	30	—	—
Skerrols & Waulk Miln	John Taylor	15	19	8	39	—	—
Balligrade & Meal Miln yrof }	Angus Taylor & c	20	7	⅓	50	—	—

Names of Lands		Tenants' Names	Present Rent Crop 1774			New Rent payle at Marts 1779		
Kellsay		John Ross	17	—	—	34	—	—
Ballivicar & c		Willm Grahame	26	19	3	64	19	9
Ballimertin & c		Alexd McLauchane	23	6	2	50	—	—
Lossit in Harries		McVurrichs & c	30	15	—	62	—	—
Lossit in Rines		Duncan McAula & c	19	1	—	60	—	—
Balliclavan		Mr. Campbell of Sunderland	8	12	2	45	—	—
½ Correry & c		Rond Johnston	6	11	11	15	—	—
½ Island		John McVorren	4	19	6	10	—	—
Gortanilivory		Alexd McEwen	5	11		14	—	—
Gartloisk		John Stewart & c	12	12	6	27	—	—
Portenolen		Alexr McEcharan & c	18	17	—	53	—	—
Esknish		John Campbell & c	19	—	—	40	—	—
Ballitarsen		Alexr McCowaig & c	12	—	—	30	—	—
Kilinave		Martin McAlpin & c	15	10	—	36	—	—
Tormistill		John McArthur	17	10	—	38	—	—
Killmeny		Dond McMillan	19	—	—	40	—	—
Killbranan		Dond McNab	12	—	—	18	—	—
Nerabols		Peter McDonald	18	—	—	40	—	—
Kepilsmore		John McKay & c	22	—	—	50	—	—
The two Kilhomans	X	Mr. Campbell Knockomily	49	—	—	120	—	—
Upper Gremsa	X	Do	10	—	—	35	—	—
Ardnahow & Cove	X	Archd Campbell	5	3	1½	40	—	—
Miln of Oa	X	Do	6	4	6	20	—	—
			£901	13	8½	£2198	15	5
		Present Rent Deducted				901	13	8½
		Balance of Increase on the Rental at Martin-Mas 1779				£1297	1	9

The Farms of Kintraw
Grastill
Ballinachtan More

(The original is among the Kildalton Papers and is written on two sides of foolscap paper.)

The only lands that are open or out of Tack at present in Isla are the two ffarms of Grastill and Ballinachtanmore.

The History of each is thus – The lands of Grastill were part of a larger ffarm and then called the ffarm of Kintraw and Grastill and Kintra according to the denomination of extent of that Country was what is called 2 Leohrass or 16 Shilling Land---- Grastil is a 3 Leohrass or 24 Shilling LAND AND THESE FIVE Leohrass or 40 Shilling Lands were set by the late Shawfield to his Brother in law Mr. McNiel of Knocknaw for a 19 year Tack from Whits. 1760 to Whits. 1779 for a Grassum of and a yearly rent of £19. 5. 4. The present Mr. McNiel suspecting the Lands would not again be given in Tack without a far more considerable increased Rent of Grassum than formerly and as he had a liberty to subset he therefore in January 1770 proposed to sell the benefitt of the Tack for the 9 years then to run and the lands were carried by Shawfield at £300 Str. and since has sett that part of them called Kintraw for a 19 year Tack at £31. Str. yearly

Kintraw 2 Leorhess or a 16 Shilling Land	£31.
In proportion Grastill falls as 3 Leorhess or 24 Shilling to give	£46. 10.
	£77. 10.

This will be found to be about 4 times the former Rent of £19. 5. yearly and Shawfield could not have much less for the 9 years to recover this £300 he paid and the current Rent of £19. 5. 4.

There is a Survey of Grastill and contains of acres as per the other side [of the paper].

GRASTILL

110 arrable acres rated at 5/ each	£27 – 10
169 of Green Pasture at 2/6 each	21 – 22 – 6
300 of Level Moss @ 6d each	7 – 10
347 of Mountains @ 6d each	8 – 13 – 6
962 acres at the yearly Rent of	£64 – 16 –

If set in proportion to Kintraw which contains

88 arrable acres at 5/	£28.
66 Green Pasture at 2/6	8. 5.
330 Level Moss at 6d	8. 5.
484 Acres	£38. 10.

So Kintraw is set within £7 of the Acre Rate (i.e.) for £31———————So if Grastill Setts for £46. 10. it will be £18. 6. below the acre rate and fully cheaper than Kintraw which formerly was one and the same ffarm with Grastill. BAL- LINACHTAN MORE was formerly [was] part of the farm lately possessed by one of the ffactors at °116 Rent and 11 years of the Tack purchased by Shawfield at °1210 Str. but not sure at present what the extent of it is whether a 16 a 24 or a 32 Shilling Land But it was sett for 19 years to a young man at °60 yearly and who died soon after and the widow not thinking herself equal to such a charge beged of Shawfield to take up the Tack which he did and thereby the lands of Ballinachtanmore are open and the survey is as follows

151 Arrable Acres at 5/.	£37. 15.
110 Green Pasture at 2/6.	12. 10.
624 Mountain at 6d.	15. 12.
	£65. 17.
The former Rent.	£60.
Short of the Acre Rate	£5. 17.

Catalogue
of Books belonging to
Shawfield left in Isla
House Nov. 1776—
Excepting those within
marked which are to be
brot to Woodhall

(The original is among the Kildalton papers and is written on a foolscap sheet.)

Catalogue of Books belonging to Daniel Campbell of Shawfield, Esqr left at Islay House November 1776.

Vollums		
	3	Haughton's Husbandry
	1	ffarmer Letters
	1	Practical Husbandman
	1	Dickson's Agriculture 2d vol. only
	2	Mill's Husbandry 2d & 3d do. do.
	2	Ellis's Husbandry
	2	Siecle de Louis 14th
	1	Juvenalli Delphinii
	1	Stirling's Virgil

		2	Mistakes of the Heart 1st & 3d vol. only
		4	Retz's Memoirs
		1	Virgilli Opera
Returned	X	1	A view of the Internal Evidence of the Christian Religion
		3	Origin of Laws
		1	Buchanan's History – ffolio
		2	Sketches of the History of Man – do.
		1	Boutcher on fforst Trees
		1	Valuable old Manuscripts
		2	An inquiry into the nature and Causes of the wealth of nations
		3	Bryant's Mythology
		3	Dr. Henry Exposition of the Book of Job – ffolio
Returned	X	1	another copy of Boutcher on fforest Trees
,,	X	1	Dr. Beattie's Essays
		1	Essays on Agriculture
		1	Guthrie's Geographical Gramer
		1	Buchanan's Salms
Returned	X	6	Langhorn's Plutarch
do.	X	1	Horatii Opera
		1	Penal Statutes
		2	ffowls Tasso
		1	Description of the Western Isles
		1	Milton's Paradise Lost
		1	Large Map Book
		1	The Map Book of Islay
		1	Taylor & Skinners map of the Roads in Scotland
Returned	X	1	Mason's Poems
do.	X	1	C Offices (the first word is blotted)
do.	X	5	Histoire des Indes – the 2d vol: missing
		1	Speech of Edmond Bourk
		1	The Edinbr Mag: & Review
		1	L'Evangile Du Jour

Walter: New Industries and Development

Daniel II died in 1777, leaving personal debts to the amount of £22,275:4:8, and heritable debts amounting to £61,000. His brother John (who had been given Skipness in 1756 on the failure of the senior line of the family) had died in the previous year, so that all the Estates and Debts were inherited, rather unexpectedly, by Walter the youngest of the brothers.

Walter was an advocate in Edinburgh and a close friend of Henry and Robert Dundas, Ilay Campbell and other notables of the legal world. It was on their advice that he very soon applied for and obtained a Disentailment Act to enable him to sell certain lands, retaining Woodhall, Skipness and Islay. The Memorial drawn up for Walter's benefit in 1780 and the State of Process of Declarator and Sale, 1781, give a very clear account of Islay at this period. Though by this means many of the debts were cleared, the heritable debts remained, and, alas, were to grow and prove the millstone around the neck of his grandson, Walter Frederick, the last of the family to hold the remnant of old Daniel's acquisitions.

Walter had married, in 1768, Eleanor, daughter of Robert Kerr of Newfield, by whom he had eleven children. She died in 1785 and shortly afterwards he married Mary, daughter of Nisbet of Dirleton and widow of Major Hay. This marriage brought about a closer relationship with the Dundas family as Mary's brother, Hamilton of Pencaitland, was married to Henry Dundas's niece.

The bulk of the entries in the Day Book are by Walter and show that he spent most of his time between Woodhall and Islay, using Skipness as a half-way house. The new schemes now began to show some results: by Whitsunday, 1779, almost all the farms were held under Leases (which show Daniel's name erased and Walter's substituted). The building of farm steadings and cottages was slowly progressing, enclosures prevented the spoilation of crops and woodlands by grazing stock, burns were bridged and canalized to help drainage. The newly introduced potatoes and later, turnips, together with better types of grain and sown grasses provided more food for men and beasts. A cattle fair had been instituted at Bowmore, to which Dealers came from all over the country, and it was estimated that an average of 3,000 black cattle were exported annually.

One factor, however had not been foreseen and that was the enormous rise in population figures: in 1742 it has been estimated at 4,000, in 1771 at 7,500, and in 1791 it had risen to 9,500. It was to reach its height of nearly 15,000 in the next forty years and provide great problems. Walter, as his entries show, was anxious to promote local industries, other than farming, such as tiles and glass, to employ this surplus population. The latter manufacture did not materialize, though suitable sand was exported to the mainland for this purpose for many years. Bricks and tiles were baked in the kiln at Foreland during the next eighty years and Walter's grandson was to be described as a "brick and tile Manufacturer". The former were rather porous and are still to be found in the construction of some of the older chimneys: samples of the somewhat heavy pantiles may still be seen on the Boathouse of Kildalton. Linen yarn was next in importance to cattle raising and Pennant stated that in 1772, about £2000 worth was sold to the mainland. Fishing, kelp-making, weaving and legal Distilling were growing industries towards the end of the Century. Tradesmen were also increasing – masons, joiners, saddlers, and smiths were all required to serve the increased farm and traffic demands.

With the outbreak of the Napoleonic Wars, a Militia Company was raised in 1798 and commanded by Walter's eldest son "Long John" (who had been in the Guards). Four battery towers were erected, of which two remain – one on the ridge above Carnaan and the other on the old Gallow's Hill at the entrance to Islay House: those at Bowmore and Portaskaig were demolished and the cannon of the latter formed the bollards on that pier. There was also a gun chained to the naked rock, below a signal staff, on the summit of Knock in Kildalton; while the chains which held it in position and the stump of the staff may still be seen on the hill top, the gun is now in the Museum of Islay life.

Walter purchased the Estate of Sunderland in 1786 from the heirs of Robert Campbell, who had been Pennant's host in 1772. The Sunderland Campbells had been the first members of the Calder family to take up their residence in Islay and it was from them that most of the Tacksmen were descended. They had held a feu of Sunderland, Foreland, Coul, and Cladville. Walter conveyed this Estate to his third son, Walter (a Captain in the Hon. East India Company's Shipping Service), in 1814. His second son, Robert, an Advocate, was to have Skipness but died in 1814: However, it was left to Robert's son, another Walter, who succeeded on his Grandfather's death in 1816. Walter's fourth son, Colin, became an Admiral and inherited Ardpatrick, on West Loch Tarbert. The estates of Woodhall and Islay were inherited by John's son Walter Frederick.

The amusing list of the weights of the family and guests in the Day Book was probably the result of the acquisition of a new weighing machine: it was at this time that Walter and the Stent Committee were endeavouring to enforce a standard of weights and measures in the island.

Day Book
of
Daniel Campbell
of
Shawfield
1767

1

[a] 36 yards make a Tale.
40 Tales make a Rood.
4 Rood make an Acre.
A Square of 76 yards nearly encloses an acre as 5760 square.
Ells is the contents of a Scotch Acre
[b] In pietatus studium veri, honestique sultum
Hoc templum deo optimo maximo sacrum
Daniel Campbellus hujus Insuly Dominus
Anno Millesimo septingentisimo sexagesimo septimo propriis suis sumptibus posuit

These notes are written by Gilbert MacCulloch, clerk to Shawfield.

(a) An Ell = 45″. There was also an Ila Ell, used by the Weavers, of which no exact measurement is given but that it was over a yard is stated in the Stent book, pp. 133/34, when the Stent Committee condemned the Weavers of Kilchoman Parish for reducing their measure to an English yard, 36″, but charging at the higher rate for an Ila Ell.

1 yard = .99 Scottish Ells, i.e. Ell = approx. 1 metre (1 yard 3 inches)

(b) Inscribed on a tablet on the face of the tower of the Round Church in Bowmore, built by Daniel II in 1767 at "the cost of more than £700". Daniel Campbell, Laird of this Island/Devoutly in search of truth and honesty/At his own expense built this holy Church/In seventeen hundred and sixty seven/To the greatest glory of God.

This note is written in the hand of fferquhard Campbell, (a member of the family Lagganlochan) Notary Public, whose artistic signature is usually accompanied by a Latin tag.

2

[a] Estimate of different prices of Building Stone
& Lime Work either Houses of Dykes The Materials
being laid down viz.
Parks of Garden walls not exceeding
Six feet high 20/– per rood
Do. Nine or Ten feet high 25/– per rood
Office houses or other houses Nine or ten feet high side walls 30/–
Houses two story high eighteen or twenty feet in the side wall 35/–
[b] Estimates of building dry stone dykes six yards to the pole
Two feet high 8d. Three feet 1/– four feet 1/4d
five feet 3 1/8d.
Dry stone sunk fences to be built four feet
and a half high at 1/– pr pole the Earthern
fence being cleared by the Employer.

(a) A great deal of building was being done at this time, particularly in the new village of Bowmore, where Feus and Building Leases, with crofts and grazing in the vicinity were being granted: one of the conditions was that the houses must be constructed of stone and lime with built-in chimneys.

(b) The new Tacks to start at Whitsunday 1779 contained the following Clause:–
"It is highly material for the improvement and good order of the Country that the marches be streighted and proper March Dykes built betwixt the different farms" and tenants were required to join with their neighbours in building dry stone dykes where required.

3

Given to Archibald Hill in payment of the
[a] Wheels formerly and to be just now delivered

Given him	£3...3
Do	5...5
Do	5...5
Do	4...15
[b] July Do. for tyle	1...18
20	1
Now 23 paid John Tenant for his order	3
	£24...6

[c] Mr Grahames 12 stots to be delivered
to Robert MacKenzie writer Dumbarton

(a) For the past thirty years the Stent Committee had annually supervised the construction of roads and bridges. Vehicular traffic was now possible, at least in the Middle Ward, and this is the first mention of wheels in the Islay papers. Ten years later, in 1788, Mr. MacNeil Ardelistry, and Captain Godfrey MacNeil were able to report to the Meeting "that the Bridge over the water of Duich has been clayed and gravelled ----- and that it is in their opinion perfectly sufficient, not only for foot passengers but also for Horses and Carriages". (Stent Book)

(b) This is the first mention of Tyles, but whether for drainage or for the carrying of water to Islay House (p. 31) it is impossible to say.

(c) Archibald Graham, Baillie of Islay from 1764. He farmed Dail, Lower Grimsa, Doudle and one half each of Allaly and Nosebridge.

4

Memorandum. . . . .
The new Tacks of Persibus[a], Kilcolmkill[b] & all
in the neighbourhood of the Port[c]
to be burdened with the Servitude of
allowing the cattle of the Island to be
shown on their Grounds[d] . . . .
The Farm of Cruach will sow 18 Bolls
Corn and keep 20 milk cows[e] . . . .
The Farm of Sanig Begg will winter
120 Stots and Summer the same number
for six weeks[f] . . . .
A Rent to be put upon the Seats[g]
in Bowmore Church and arrears paid
up . . . .
Sunderland[h] and Knockhamily[i] to be
settled with for the possession of the Glebe[j]
at Kilchoman since the commencement of the
present lease . . . .
Enquire whether Sunderland is liable
for his proportion of Church repairs &
whether he paid his part when Kilcho
man was last repaired. . . . .

(a) Over ninety new Tacks were granted as from Whitsunday 1779, most of them to endure for nineteen years, but a few for 20, 23, or 25 years, one or two for 14 and 16 years, and one for thirty years. They had a common form, to which special clauses were added where applicable.

(b) Persibus, the Change House of Ballochroy and Glasgow Beg were leased to Charles Freebairn, who was also the Lessee of the Lead Mines at this period. Ballochroy, at the head of the narrow glen leading down to Portaskaig Ferry, stood at the point where the island drove roads converged: it was really on the lands of Kilcolumkill but, for some time, had gone with the Persibus Tack. Glasgow Beg lay on the Southern part of Ardochy, where the richest lead vein had been found. Many of the miners were housed here and the Furnace and Tool shed were situated close by.

Columkill in Harries [Kilcolumkill: Kiels] Harries was the name often applied to the Middle Ward of Islay, comprising the two Parishes of Kilarrow and Kilmeny had been tenanted by Duncan McLachlan, the Ferryman of Portaskaig. He seems to have died at the end of 1777 or beginning of 1778 after the new Tack (to begin in 1779) had been agreed upon. Notes on the following pages show that Walter was anxious to provide for his widow and family, but to relieve them of the too great responsibility of the Ferry. The matter was finally settled in 1780, when the Tack of the Ferry and half of the farm of Kiels was taken over by John Hill and his father-in-law, Neil Brown (from Kiels in Knapdale – the mainland end of the Lagg Ferry). This new agreement also provided for an excambion with the possessor of Persibus whereby another part of the farm of Kiels might be exchanged for the Changehouse of Ballochroy. See Appendix p 242.

(c) Portaskaig

(d) A Clause in the Tacks of these two farms in the neighbourhood of Portaskaig provided that they should allow grazing for the island cattle gathering to cross the Sound of Islay on their long trek to the mainland Trysts. Their route lay via the Ferries of Portaskaig – Feolin and Lagg – Kiels (on Loch Sween) to the local Tryst of Kilmichael-Glassary and thence to Dunbarton or Creiff and, later, Falkirk. The improvement in Agriculture showed in the increasing numbers and better quality of the beasts exported from now on. It was estimated that between two and three thousand black cattle were sent out from the Island annually: English graziers were said to prefer the beasts from Argyll and Islay to those from any other part of the Highlands, as they fattened more readily and better on the rich lowland pastures.

(e) Daniel wished to promote dairying as well as cattle-raising.

(f) Until now very few cattle had been wintered owing to the lack of fodder, but the growing of green crops and improved hay was being encouraged for this purpose.

(g) The seats in the Round Church of Bowmore were, at this period, benches of wood supported by pillars of stone at either end: the floor was composed of flagstones. These were replaced by the present wooden pews and floor in 1878.

(h) Robert Campbell of Sunderland, descendant of Colin, the first of the Calder family to take up residence in the island. He was granted a Feu Charter by Sir John Campbell of Calder, of Sunderland, Foreland, Coul and Cladville. Robert was host to Pennant during the latter's visit to Islay in 1772.

(i) Henry Campbell of Knockhamily, Tacksman of Kilchoman. He was descended from Margaret, daughter of George Campbell of Airds, Tutor to the Fiar of Calder, and Archibald Campbell of Knockhamily (a cadet of the Auchinbreck family).

(j) The Glebe had been taken out of the lands of Kilchoman in accordance with the Act of Presbytery, dated 12th October, 1763. See pp 76, 77.

5

look through Gilbert MacCulloch's[a] papers
at Woodhall in order to find out the
terms upon which Dr. Robertson[b] got
possession of the Mill and House of Alibus[c]
it was in the year 1747 and the Mill was
then Sclated . . . . . . greatest part of which
was done by my Grandfather[d] after
Baillie Coll's[e] death . . . . look for the Doctors
lease at Woodhall (*this sentence has been inserted by Walter*)
A good tenant from Sunderland
wants Gartachare[f]
(*From this point the entries are in Walter's writing*) Two
MacIvers from Balligrant want
part of Portinellon[g] alongst with the present
Tenants who are but weak . . . . this may be
granted provided they get their Tacks from me[h]
The inhabitants of Bowmore to be compelled to
cut their peats regularly[i], and bridges to be
made between their breast and the Great Road . . . those that
have cut this season upon the upper side of the
Rode (sic) to be fined for making irregular
holes . . . . . . Duncan MacKenzie in Kelsa and
Charles MacArthur have offer £26 for that

(a) Gilbert was described as "Servant to Shawfield (i.e. Daniel II)". He seems to have been a confidential servant, who acted as this Clerk; his signature appears, as Witness, on many of the documents and some of the papers are written in his hand, as also some of the notes regarding measurements in the Day Book, (p. 1, Note (a)). It is possible that the papers referred to were those finally found in the Plate Chest, as described by J. F. Campbell (see Introduction).

(b) Lease was lost.

(c) Dr. John Robertson was the Physician in Islay for many years and held a Tack of Ealabus and its Miln. In the 1741 Rental (Book of Islay), the house is shown to be in the hands of Baillie Coll "during pleasure". Dr. Robertson was granted a Tack of the lands of Robolls and Keppelslachlan to commence at Whitsunday 1779 (Tack 25) and was succeeded in Ealabus by the new Surgeon, Dr. Samuel Crawford, who, in later years, was to become Factor of Islay. During the period 1755/85, Dr. Robertson was a very active member of the Stent Committee. In the Process of Declarator and Sale 1781 he is listed as a Creditor of Daniel I and II.

(d) Daniel I of Shawfield and Islay.

(e) Coll MacAlister was Baily of Islay to Daniel I from 1724 (when Daniel became Wadsetter of Islay) until his death in 1747.

(f) A farm in the Rhinns of Islay. The Tenant in 1774 was Donald MacCallman, paying £7 Rent. In 1779, it was let to Donald McDonald, Samuel and Angus Johnstons, paying a total of £25. See p 197.

(g) The Present Finlaggan Farm.

(h) Walter, pursuing the family policy, frowned on subsetting by the Tacksmen, and, where holdings were divided between several Tenants, each one received a direct Tack from him for the portion of land he farmed.

(i) The necessity of cutting peats in regular banks proved difficult to get across to the inhabitants.

6

half of Colton that is not presently possesed
by Balinaby[a] He has also offerd for Oshnish
£12 and £20 in part of the value of the moor
Neil Curry[b] in Sunderland Dougal & Archibald
MacLean's[c] in Foreland & Finlay Ferguson
Conisby, £40. For Leck Oshnish
or £48 for Coltoon . . . . . . & Donald & John
Leitch[d] present tenants in Leck and Malcolm
Curry[e] there, join in their offer for that
place . . . . . . .The Green Meadow below Skerrolls
most shamefully cutt, this is to be stoped in the future
and those who did it this year fined . . . . . . the
Road below that meadow would require a
drain to let off the water . . . .
Donald MacEachern Malcolm and Neil Mac
Duffies[f] in Leck and Angus MacIntaire offer
£45 for Leck . . . . . .[g]
Duncan and Hugh MacDougal and those
in Kilsleven offer £45 for Robus[h] with
the burden of one fourth of it to Mrs. Campbell
during life . . . .
William Curry Schoolmaster at Kilmeny[i]
wants a grot land[j] of Portaneillan. . . . .

(a) The Beatons, or MacBeths, Surgeons of the Isles, had held the lands of Ballinaby "beyond the memory of man" and were confirmed in them by a Charter from James VI, dated 10th July, 1609 (Book of Islay). These lands, however, were purchased from John Beaton by Archibald, Lord Lorne, in 1629 and thereafter they were held on a feu charter direct from the House of Argyll by the Campbells of Ballinaby until the end of the Nineteenth Century. Ballinaby was Wadsetter of a number of lands in Islay belonging to the Calders: these were redeemed by Shawfield and a Tack given for some of them (including Coltoun) instead.

(b) The 1779 Rental shows Neil Curry as a Tenant in Leck Gruniart.

(c) The names of the Feuar's subtenants do not figure in the Rental.

(d) See (e).

(e) Dougal and Archibald MacLeans, with Malcolm Curry, were granted that part of Leck Oshinish lying in the Grulin (or Eastern) side of the Burn of Leog (which runs from Loch Corr to Loch Gorm) at a rent of £25 and (d) twenty-four dozen eggs and twenty-four hens. Mrs. Betty Campbell of Ballinaby and Donald and John Leitch were to have the Western part of this land, paying £15 rent, four dozen eggs and four hens from the Leitches. See p 218.

(f) Malcolm and Neil MacDuffies appear as Tenants of Dluich in the 1779 Roll and a Rent of £17.

(g) Leck Oshnish: through Clerical errors, this has now become known as "Leek" and is so written in MacDougall's Map of 1750. "Leac = a flagstone".

(h) A Clause in the Tack of Robolls granted to Dr. Robertson, reserves a quarter for the previous Tacksman. Ronald Campbell, for his life. The Mrs. Campbell here referred to is presumably his widow.

(i) William Curry was still a Schoolmaster at Kilmeny on the 8th of August, 1780, with a yearly salary of £5. 11. 1 4/12.

(j) a groatland = 4/- (Scots) = 4d. Sterling.

7

Offered for Coltoon by John Beaton
at Kilchoman, Hugh Lesly at Coltoon
Donald MacLellan at Ballinaby
Archibald and Neil Smiths at Gruinart
and Angus MacIntagert at Sunderland
£50 . . . . The Marches between Barr
and Storgaig to be settled . . . . . . Enquire of
Mr. MacGibbon[a] if the old man Campbell
at Kinesby[b] had any promise from my Brother[c]
of a House or Farm. . . . . . . the marches betwixt
Cornabus and Frachkell[d] to be settled . . . . also
those of Knochleroch (sic) . . . . . . is any part of
Ballahatrigin not let; Donald McGowan
present possessor wants a two pence land
of ot . . . . Janet Campbell widow of Alex
Currie in Ballichrach wants a farm
The tennants in the whole estate to be time
ously and duely warned, those in Kilarrow
to be warned directly . . . . . . Neil Anderson
and three others in Tormastle[e] want an
eighteen part[f] of land in Lease. . . . . . .

1) Daniel Campbell, Yr., 2nd Laird of Shawfield and Islay: born c. 1732, died 1777; unmarried. Eldest grandson of Daniel Campbell, 1st Laird. Writer of The Day Book, 1767-77. Succeeded to Shawfield and Islay, 1753. Succeeded to his cousin in Skipness, 1756. Member of Parliament. *Photograph by Allan Wright.*

2) John Campbell, second grandson of Daniel Campbell, 1st Laird of Shawfield and Islay. **1776:** predeceased his elder brother, Daniel Campbell, 2nd Laird. *Photograph by Allan Wright.*

3) Shooting party at Woodhall, Lanarkshire, the mainland residence of the Campbells of Shawfield, c. 1780. Artist unknown. Original Watercolour in Kelvingrove Art Gallery.

(a) Neil MacGibbon, Writer in Inveraray, Shawfield's Factor for Islay and Jura.
(b) No Campbell appears among the tenants of Kinesby (Conisby) in 1778 unless he is one of the Bell's, a contraction of Campbell. See p 219, in which Donald Bell declares he cannot write and instructs the Notaries Public to subscribe for him. The Lease is signed by Archibald Bell, presumably a younger man.
(c) Daniel II.
(d) Frachkell – Fracadale in the Oa. All Marches between the farms were being defined and a clause in the Tacks provided for the building of March Dykes to prevent the straying of one tenant's cattle on to the lands of his neighbours.
(e) Tormastle: Tormastill: Tormisdale: a farm in the Rhinns.
(f) This is an error very common in the Eighteenth Century. It should read "an Auchtenpart", or 16/8d. land: it was the half of a quarter, or 33/4d, land. (See Lamont: Old and New Extent in Islay).

F

8

Alex MacAlman offers for Gartchar[a]
                  (this is the son of the man who
twenty one Pound yearly (hás a missive of it, it may do
                  (for both
I am informed that Ronald Johnstone[b]
took a lease of the one half of Corrary, that
after dividing the Farm he got by far
the best half, and thereafter claimed and
carried two other fields that were possessed
by as belonging to Corrary and now
possesses both of theas (sic) fields one of which
certainly belongs to the other half of Corrary
                  (& John Johnstone to be settled
this is to be enquired into   (along with Ronald who has
                  (lost two sons. . . .
am Informed that Mrs. Cas Kilinalen[c]
has claimed by the assistance of Carnbeg[d]
a pendicle of Land as belonging to her
farm of Killinalen, of which another
small Tennant had got a Missive
                  (settled £20 given down of gressum[e])
from my Brother[f]
In the Infeftment Granted by Ballinaby
to Gartmar and Ardnave mention(ed) is made
and Infeftment given upon the lands of Garta
hold situate in the middle of Leck Oshnish[g]
and the whole of Ballinabys lands are said to amount
to a five merk land. . . . .

(a) MacAlman does not appear among the tenants of Gartachara in 1779.

(b) According to a Missive signed at Islay House on the 3rd September, 1773, Daniel agreed to grant a Tack for nineteen from 1779 of the half of the Lands of Corrary and Couralach, at that time sett to Ronald Johnstone, in the names of him and his two sons, Alexander and Archibald, on payment of a Grassum of £25 Sterling. The Tack was duly granted, but when it came to be signed on the 5th October, 1778, Alexander and Archibald are recorded as having died and it is only signed by Ronald. See p 223. The other half of Corrary was Sett to the Misses Simson. See p 142.

(c) Mrs Campbell of Kilinalen and her son, Angus, held Kilinalen, Rim, Ballinish, Sornusary, Croishvoir and one half of Eoribus for a Rent of £80.

(d) Colin Campbell, Tacksman of Carnbeg: he was at this time, the Contractor for the Pacquet, which made a weekly sailing between West Loch Tarbert and Portaskaig. See p 240.

(e) Gressum = Grassum = payment on the granting of renewal of a Lease.

(f) Daniel II.

(g) By a Missive, dated 1st November 1776, Donald Campbell of Ballinaby was to be given a Tack of Leck Oshnish, Cultoon, Sannaig beg and the Miln of Breackachy, with its Changehouse, for nineteen years from Whitsunday 1779. However, Donald "left this kingdom" (Stent Book) in 1778 and the two copies of the Tack among the papers of Islay House remain unsigned by either party. See p 240. These documents are of particular interest in that they list the Lands which were thirled to the Miln of Breackachy. Mrs. Campbell retained part of the lands of Leck Oshnish and the rest were disposed to other tenants.

9

Duncan MacAlman who took
Gartaharr[a] alongst with Archibald
McLugash must be sent for, in order
either to give up or abide by his lease. . . . . .
Donald MacNiven who took half of Rosquern
was bound to pay odds of £17[b] unable to pay
either this or his rent, must be sent for
and settled with . . . . So soon as Mr. MacGibbon comes
Duisker[c] to be sent for settled with and made to
give up his tack, with which or with Ballimartin[d]
Mrs. MacLachlan her children[e] and Mrs. Shaw
may be accommodated they having previously
given up the possession of Keils and the Port. . . . .
Some of the farms fittest for grain to be
made pay part of their Rent in Meal & Barley. . . . . .
the Meal to be estimated at fourteen Schillings the
ten stone weight. . . . .
One Donald Brown formerly a Merchant[f]
now at Grunart wants a Leorhess[g] of land
Has a letter of security for his rent from Mitford

(a) Both these tenants seem to have relinquished their Lease.

(b) The 1779 Rent Roll shows the farm of Rosquern to be held by Donald MacNiven and Duncan MacAlman at £16. 17. 6. of yearly rent.

(c) Archibald Campbell, Tacksman of Duisker in 1779 at a rent of £30. 6. 0.

(d) The 1779 Rent Roll shows Ballimartin and Stoinsha to be tenanted by Alexander and Archibald MacLaughlan at £50 rent.

(e) The whole matter of Mrs. MacLachlan's accommodation was settled by the Agreement, dated 8th February 1780, with John Hill and his Father-in-law, Neil Brown, to take over the Ferry, the Changehouse of Portaskaig and half for Mrs. MacLauchlan and her family. There are many references to John Hill and to the improvements made to, and at, the Ferry, during the years that followed, in the Stent Book.

(f) Donald Brown was given part of Carabus. Rent Roll 1779.

(g) Leorhese (lewirheis) = 8 Horsegang or 10/- land.

10

Archibald MacColman who took a Learhase
of Eachvernock[a], wants a March land in
Scaribus as it is nearer to Cospellan his
present possession . . . . Alexr Johnstone
in Kilnave wants a Groat land for himself
or son in law Alexr MacKay. . . . . .
Alexr MacDiarmid in Knock[b] Duncan
Carmichael and Hugh his Brother in
Knock and McQuilkan have this year carried a cargo
of Bark for sale to Kintyre; from the woods in
their Neighbourhood, after having
been warned by Archibald Kinture[c]
against this practise of which they have been
long in use . . . . Mr. MacGibbon when
on that side of the country to call them before
him and if the fact is proved they to be fined
part of the wood on that side of the country
to be preserved . . . . . a House and Croft for
the Salmon Fisher at Lagan to be marked out
in terms of the Missive to Hugh MacKay[d]. . . . . . .
Alexander Johnstone in Ballinachtan More
wants a Leahese or thereby. . . . .

(a) Eachvernock, at the head of the Big Glen, was a hill farm which the Laird now kept in his own hands for cattle grazing.

(b) The MacDiarmids and the Carmichaels are included among the tenents of Knock (Knockroanistle) in 1779.

(c) This bark was probably shipped to the Fisherman of Tarbert Loch Fyne who, by a special dispensation, were allowed to use the bark of oak and birch for tanning their nets (Teignmouth: vol. II p. 319).

(d) Archibald Campbell, Tacksman of Kinture, was, in 1779, to take over the Tack of Ardnahow, Colin of Ardnahow having "left this Kingdom" (Stent Book). Archibald was to be succeeded in Kenture by Colin Campbell, Tacksman of Eoribolls and his son John. See p 196.

(e) With the coming of the Shawfields, the representatives of the family of MacKay of the Rhinns come back into prominence. John of Ardlarach becomes the Tacksman of the new town of Bowmore and Hugh became Tacksman of Laggan, until finally they hold much of the land granted to Brian Vicar MacKay by the Lord of the Isles in 1408. This Gaelic Charter is now one of the most prized exhibits in the Register House, Edinburgh.

11

Peter MacCuag and two Maclennans
in Gortenillwory want part of Surn[a] or
any other lands. . . . .
Memorandums taken at Skipness
after the 20th October 1778. . . . .
The half of the Farm of Keils that Mrs.
MacLachlan gets ought to be £15.10/ rent[b]
the other half, Publick House croft and Fery
of Portaskaig ought to be £24. . . . . . .
To be sent to Skipness four May Duke
Cherries for a wall and four apple trees
for Do[c]. . . . . .

(a) 1779 Rental does not show these tenants in Gortenillivray.
(b) The suggested division of the lands held by the late Duncan MacLachlan, which was carried out by the agreement made with John Hill and Neil Brown in 1780. See p 241.
(c) Much attention was being given to the gardens of the Mansion Houses, especially with regard to the planting of fruit trees.

12

Memorandums taken at Woodhall after
1st December 1778 . . . . .
Robert MacKendrick Plasterer in Millers
Street Glasgow wants to feu six acres of the
lands of Shawfield lying next Polmadie Bridge
to pay ten shillings per acre of
Feu duty the remainder to be paid in Cash
as purchase Money. . . . .
13th February 1779 agreed with James Morrison
to grubb out and make fit for sowing
three acres of Natural woods and to level
the ground the Rocks to be carried off by
me where he has not an opportunity of
Burying them, the work to be finished
before the 1st May under penalty of
5 sh per day for each day he is longer
in finishing his work, He to be paid
Nineteen Pounds Sterling for the stone work
the money to be advanced as the work
goes on, a few mattocks to be furnished by
me, the expence of laying them to be paid
by the undertaker.

12 Cottage in Islay, 1772, by John Frederick Miller, who accompanied Sir Joseph Banks on his expedition to Iceland, and Pennant on his visit to Islay.

13 Cottage in Islay. Artist unknown. Original in British Library. *Photograph courtesy of Royal Commission.*

13

Send Mr. A. Douglas twelve stots
4 years olds if they can be got, of a midling
size. . . . .
Came to Islay 10th July 1779. . . . . .
The people of Kilmeny have again Cutt
their peats in the Green Meadow below the
Road – they must certainly be fined[a] . . . .
The People of Bowmore have also Cutt vile
Holes and taken out Peats above the Road
this must be stopt . . . . Stewart who was dis
possessed of his seat in the Church has as yet
got no other seat, that and the alteration of Mr.
Murdoch's seat must be done before Mr.
MacGibbon leaves the country. . . . . . .
two Barrells Clay for Brick and two Barrels
Sand for Glass[b] to be sent to Glasgow by
the Nancy . . . . The New line of Road
thro Tighcarmagn being altered it is
requisite that the Tennants who have now the
Burden of the Road should receive[c]

(a) The habit of cutting peats in irregular holes seemed strangely difficult to break. Dr. Smith of Campbelltown, writing twenty years later, deplored it and pointed out how dangerous to cattle the quagmires so formed could be and, also, how fatal to the reclamation of the land. Daniel II laid down definite rules for peat cutting in 1767 (See pp 105, 106 "Rules for Cutting Moss") and each lease contained a clause to the effect that a fine of £5, later raised to £6, would be exacted from offenders.

(b) These samples of Clay and Sand were sent to Glasgow in the hope that they might prove suitable for the making of Bricks and Tiles and Glass and thus provide another local industry. The two former were made locally and Walter's Grandson, Walter Frederick, was described as "a Brick and Tile Manufacturer" in 1848. Islay-Made tiles are still to be seen on some old roofs in Bowmore and on the Kildalton boat house. They were rather heavily made and required a very strong timber roof to support them. The bricks were very porous and often to be found in the older chimneys. Glass was not manufactured locally, but suitable sand was exported to the mainland for this purpose until the middle of the Nineteenth Century.

(c) The new road through Tighcarmagan was led down from the higher ground behind what is now the village of Port Ellen. It reached the shore near the corner of the bay, continued by the present Port Ellen Distillery, on behind where Cairnmore House now stands and on to the Big Strand at Kintra: here it was joined by a track from the Oa and at Knockangle, half way along the Strand another one came in from Lagavuline, Kilbride and Leoran. At the end of the Strand it ran up through the sandhills, by Island Farm and the hump-backed bridge to Bowmore. This was to be the main road between the East and West of the Island for the next eighty years. There were nine tenants on the Quarterland of Tighcarmagan at this time. See p 141.

14

Indemnification from the Tenants
on the other half of the farm, who formerly
received indemnification from the latter. . . . . . .
The Tennants of Small[a] either to build the
difficult piece of March Dike betwixt (Small) & Sanaig
Beg and to keep it up, Coll[b] being at half the
expense, or else the tennants of Small to
allow Coll to keep that part of Small to Mr.
MacGibbon to determine what recompense
Coll is to pay them . . . . Take some Rope
Fence to Skipness. . . . .
John Johnstone in Upper Corary complains
that the Miss. Simpsons[c] have not farmed
their half of Upper Corary but have subset it
to a very bad neighbour who has oversoumed
MacFarlane Fidler near Ardnahow
and young Campbell the Eagle Killer's son[d]
must be strictly reprimanded for shooting
and if a gun found in their hand to be sent to
the Army . . . . The Marches between Leck and Ballinaby[e]
and the affair as to the Glebe of Kilchoman[f] to be
settled by Archibald Graham[g] while Mr.
MacGibbon is in the Island . . . . the
submission in my hands.

(a) Tack No. 17, granted one third of the lands of Smaill and Migram to Neil McEachern and two thirds to Archibald McEachern, Alexander McNeill, Angus MacIlvoile and Ronald McVurrich from Whitsunday 1779. The missive, dated 9th February, 1773, states that the MacCheckerans, McIlvoile and McVurrich were then all in Grunart and Alexr. McNeil in Corrary. Their combined rent under the new Tack was £60. Sterling.

(b) Coll Campbell, Tacksman of Sannaig.

(c) The Misses Simson were the Proprietrices of the Ship Tavern in Bowmore, where the Stent Committee met annually from 1779 to 1798. In 1806 the Committee allowed Miss. Lily Simson the sum of £5. "for renting a house to render her situation more comfortable" and the amount was continued in 1807 (Stent Book).

(d) After the Jacobite Rising of 1745, when a new Disarming Act was rigorously imposed, official Eagle and Fox (there were and are no foxes in Islay) Killers were among the few people permitted to carry firearms in the Highlands. A Clause of the Act imposed a fine of £15, or enforced enlistment in the Regular Army, on anyone found carrying or hiding arms. The Highland Regiments raised during the mid-Eighteenth Century gave legitimate scope for the restless young men, with their warlike background. In the previous year, 1778, the Argyle Highlanders (the 74th Regiment) had been raised by John Campbell of Barbreck and was now, in 1779, seeing service in America against the rebellious Colonies. Barbreck had found it difficult to raise recruits in Argyll as most of the young men went to sea rather than into the Army. (S. H. S. Forfeited Estates – Rannoch and Brown's History of the Highlands).

(e) These were settled.

(f) The redemption of the Wadset on these lands entailed a definition of their Marches, as also in connection with the newly-made Glebe of Kilchoman.

(g) Archibald Graham, Bailie of Islay.

15

The Mill of Alibus to be comprised and an
estimate made what it will require to put
the house and mill in a Habitable condition with
a Sclate Rooff (sic)[a] . . . . If the wheels not
all disposed of two or three to be
given to Miss Murdoch[b] . . . . . The Tacksman
of the Miln of Alibus to be called out after Harvest
to finish the Mill Road all my workmen to
assist[c]. . . . . . .
Note of Fruit trees to be sent to Skipness[d]
winter 1779 – 3 Green Gages and Jargonal
Pears 2 Morrella Cherries 6 May Duke
11 Riders . . . . wood wanted for the
Castle 30 sparrs 19 1/2 long 3 1/2 inches
thick 7 1/2 inches deep – 30 Baulks 14 1/2 feet
long 15 joists 21 feet long 3 1/2 inches
thick 7 1/2 deep.

(a) The Mill was taken into the Laird's own hands but the charming house, which was now to be put into good condition, was leased to the new Surgeon, Samuel Crawford, "as a convenience to him while he continues to practice as a Surgeon in Islay". His Missive, dated 9th October 1778, offers a rent of £11, for the "Slated mansion house – kitchen – barn stable and bire. . . ." (Tack and Missives for Ealabus). Samuel continued to live there until his death in 1835. He married Margaret, daughter of James Campbell of Balinaby: his daughter, Eleanor, married Alexander Graham, Distiller at Lagavulin, who for many years managed the Islay Distillery Cellar at 5 Dixon Street, Glasgow. One son, John, was in the East India Coy's Medical Service and became well-known as an Orientalist, and another, James, was a Writer to the Signet in Edinburgh: on Walter's suggestion (letter to Dr. Crawford, dated 15th January 1813) he was appointed sub-Collector of Taxes in Islay. After the Doctor's death, Ealabus seems to have been used as a residence for some of the Laird's family, as the furnishings of the house were listed among the possessions of Walter Frederick at the Sale of the Estate. Later, under the new proprietor, it again became the House of the Factor having the Estate office built on to it. Since the sale of Islay House it has become the home of Lord Margadale.

(b) Miss. Murdoch was probably the sister of the Reverend John Murdoch, Minister of Bowmore and Kilmeny.

(c) Dr. John Robertson, Physician.

(d) The Estate of Skipness had been inherited by Walter's brother, Daniel II, on the death (26th April, 1756) of Colin, Captain of Skipness. (Colin was a nephew of Daniel I and husband of his daughter, Anna.) Daniel II died in 1777 and Skipness passed to Walter. He intended it for his second son, Robert, an Advocate in Edinburgh, but he predeceased his father by two years and, on the latter's death in 1816, Robert's son, another Walter, inherited this Estate.

16

Skipness June 1781
Whin seed to be sent from Woodhall
for the purpose of sowing upon the tops
of the ditches round the Laggan &
little parks[a] . . . . some plants of pale
Roses to be sent to Skipness.

(a) Whin still grows on the top of the ditches around Laggan and on the turf Dykes which
     separate the Bowmore Crofts.

17

June 1781 Memorandum of this date. . . . .
Look Dr. Robertson's security as in
state 1757 with my Grandfather[a] the
interest is stated at only 4 1/2 per Cent
at the same time let Dr. Robertson
be settled with for the repairs of the Mill
of Allibus[b] . . . . Neil MacArthur
in Ardlestir[c] wants an immediate
division of his farm by Mr. MacGibbon
referred to Malcolm MacNeil[d]. . . . .
The Tenants of Knock agree with the
people of Gigha & sell them liberty to
Cut their woods,[e] this is to be strictly
looked after and process to be brought. . . . .
Mem: taken at Skipss 3 Novr – 82
for the quarter five score apple
& one score pear trees – for the wall
in the garden twenty apple and four
pear trees – for the Castle four Duke
& one Morello cherry & three rider
Dukes – for Islay one Jargonel
Pear & two rider Dukes[f] . . . .

(a) Dr. Robertson was listed as a Creditor of Daniel I, Walter's Grandfather, in the State of Process.
(b) Presumably the repairs done in 1747.
(c) Duncan MacIntyre and Neil McArthur are shown as tenants in Ardlestir (Ardelestry) in 1779.
(d) Malcolm MacNeil, Tacksman of Ardtalla.
(e) Having been prevented from trading bark to Tarbert, the tenants were now trying to sell via the people of Gigha, with whom they had a long historical connection, the lands of Knockroanistle having been in the hands of the MacNeils of Gigha, as part of the Barony of Bar which Neil MacNeil had resigned into the hands of Mary, Queen of Scots. The MacNeils, however, continued to hold lands in the neighbourhood as Tacksman until the middle of the nineteenth Century.
(f) Islay House still has a productive orchard, though it is improbable that any of these pears and cherries are still extant.

18

The Lanark Boll of Oats exceeds
the exact Linlithgow standard in
4 per Cent of in half a peck & about
three fourths of a fourth part – but
the common country firlots exceed
the Linlithgow standard a trifle[a] . . . .

(a) In England the standard of Weights and Measures set in 1588 held good all over the country until 1824, when the Imperial Standard was adopted for the United Kingdom. In Scotland, however, they differed from district to district, which led to constant abuse. As a result of complaints, the Stent Committee, in 1788, recommended "to the Gentlemen in the different Divisions of the Country to be at pains by Proclamations at the Churches and otherwise, to establish the Barril Measure over the whole Island of Islay, and this meeting now fix and ascertain the Boll of Putatoes to be four Harring Barrils filled to the Brim. It being represented to the meeting that light or improper Weights are used in the Town of Bowmore, as well as in other parts of the Country, and in order, as far as possible, to rectify abuses of that kind, the meeting now appoint Lieut. Malcolm Campbell, Mr. David Simson, Mr. Archd. Adair, all in Bowmore, as a Committee who or anyone of them are hereby impoured to try and examine the difft Weights used in Bowmore of its neighbourhood. . . . . ." and offenders were "to be Fined or otherwise punished as the Law directs." In 1826 the Stent Committee recommend the purchase of a set of Imperial Measures and appointed Samuel Lamont to superintend the whole matter. (Stent Book of Islay).

19

Oats consumed at Woodhall betwixt the 15th May 1779 & do 1780
In the principal Stable 113. 2. 2
In the work Stable 53. 3. 2
In the Byre and Pig Stye . . . . 16.
By the Poultry 22. 2. 1
By the Pigeons[a] . . . .   3.
By the Hounds and Pointers[b] . . . . 50.

                                                                      258. 3. 5

Oats consumed at Woodhall betwixt the 15th May 1780 & do. 1781 –
In the principal Stable . . . . 112.
In the work Stable . . . . 64.
In the Byre & Pig Stye . . . . 18.
By the Poultry . . . . 20.
By the Pigeons . . . .   3.
By the Hounds and Pointers . . . . 40.

                                                                      254. 3. 0

return of the   + Oats sewn this Spring 43 Bolls. . . .
43 Bolls oats   Meal consumed this year
was 230   by Family & outservants . . . 54 Bolls. . .

(a) A dovecote still provided a considerable contribution to the Laird's table.

(b) Writing in 1872, Walter's great-grandson, John Francis, mentions that his great-great-Uncle Daniel II "kept hounds". There is no record that either Daniel II or Walter kept a kennel of sporting dogs in Islay, though it is more than probable that these pointers accompanied them to Islay.

In the New Tacks there is a Clause forbidding the tenants "to carry or use firearms [the Disarming Act of 1746 was not yet repealed] or kill game of any kind and that he shall not with Nets Rods or Spears slay or kill black fish or use bleezes on any of the waters or burns within the Island of Islay and that he shall not keep setting dogs Greyhounds or others dogs that may be destructive to game. . . . ."

In the old Kildalton Church there is a very interesting gravestone of "Charles McArthur who lived in Proaik [Proaig] and departed life the fiften day of Fevary 1696 yeares" on which is incised the outline of a typical Highland Flintlock, muzzle-loading gun, with its curiously curved butt, a powder horn and the head and shoulders for pointer-like dog: it is now so worn that the dog is almost indiscernible.

20

Oats, Beans & Barley consumed at
Woodhall betwixt 15th May 1781 & 1 June 1782.

In the principal Stable	96.	1.
In the work Stable	54.	3.
In the Byre & Pig Stye	12.	
By the Poultry	20.	2.
By the Pigeons	3.	
By the Hounds & Pointers	37.	
	213.	2.

Meal consumed this year by Family
and outservants 50 Bolls and 5 Bolls
& one half of wheat made into Flower
Oats sown this Spring 26 Bolls and 7 Bolls Beans.

Oats Beans & Barley consumed at Woodhall
betwixt the 1st June 1782 & the 23 June 1783

In the principal Stable	96.
In the work Stable	53.
In the Byre & Pig Stye	10.
By the Poultry	21.
By the Hounds & Pointers	34.
	214.

Oats sown this Spring 32 Bolls & 7 Bolls Beans & Peas & of Wheat 5 1/2 bolls
Meal consumed during the above period by
Family and outservants 61 Bolols one firlot

21

Oats Beans & Barley consumed at Woodhall
betwixt 23rd June 1783 & 12 June 1784

	B.	F.	p.
By the Groom in the principal Stables	48.	2.	—.
By the Postillions in ditto	51.	—.	—.
In the work Stables	60.	—.	—.
By the Poultry	19.	—.	—.
By the Byre & Pig Stye	10.	2.	—.
By the Pidgeons	3.	2.	—.
By the Hounds & Pointers	42.	2.	—.
	235.	—.	—.
Oats sown this season	43.	2.	2.

Wheat sown this season

22

Expences of the Family and Farm exclusive
of Public Works and law expences for the twelve
months preceeding April 1780   £3376
Expences preceeding April 1781

For the Family	£2171	
For the different Farms	761	
For the Public Works	379	
For Law Accts	514	£3825

As the above comprehends some articles that ought
to have been stated to the former years as also some
principal sums paid to old servants, the following
is the mode I intend in future to make out my
annuel account . . . .

Expended as per my Book	1755
[a] By John Aiton for Family, Farm etc	446
By Neil MacGibbon Do. & Publick works in Islay exclusive of Ministers Stipends	534
By Do. on Acct of Law but part whereof will be paid by the defaulters	42
[b] By Mr. Grant on Acct of Law	358
By Do. on Acct of Family, etc	197
[c] By Kintarbert on Acct of Family & Publik works at Skipness . .	82

Total expenditure of the year preceeding 10 April 1781 . . . . £3414

(a) John Aiton of Burnbank had been at this date (1781) Factor for Shawfield on the Estate of Kilsyth for eleven years.
(b) Mr. Isaac Grant, one of the foremost Writers to the Signet, was an old friend of Walter's and also his "Doer".
(c) Factor on the estate of Skipness.

14 Kilarow Town. Artist unknown. Original in British Library. *Photograph courtesy of Royal Commission.*

15 Kilarow ruined church and tolbooth, 1772, by John Cleveley, Junior, an artist who accompanied Sir Joseph Banks on his expedition to the Hebrides and later to Spitzbergen. The figure examining a gravestone is said to be that of Cleveley's patron, Sir Joseph Banks. Original in British Library. *Photograph courtesy of Royal Commission.*

23

6 June 1789

	St.	Lb.
[a] Mrs. Campbell	8.	$4\frac{1}{2}$
Miss. Sempill	10.	6
Miss. Ritchie	8.	2
[b] Miss. Campbell	10.	5
[c] Miss. H. Campbell	9.	4
[d] Miss. G. Campbell	9.	4
[e] Miss. M. Campbell	7.	4
Miss. Macdowall	8.	10
[f] Mr. Campbell	16.	2
[g] Mr. John Campbell	10.	9
Mr. D. MacDougall	12.	$9\frac{1}{2}$
Mr. Maitland	10.	1
[h] Mr. Gordon	10.	11
[i] Mr. Colin Campbell	2.	$5\frac{1}{2}$
[j] Miss. C. Campbell	4.	11
[k] Miss. Elizabeth Campbell	3.	2
Miss. Forbes	8.	2
Mrs. Dundas	7.	6
[l] Mr. Sol Dundas	10.	—
Charles Fox	1.	—
Virgin	1.	7

4) The Family of Walter Campbell, 3rd Laird of Shawfield and Islay.

5) Colonel John Campbell, eldest son of Walter Campbell, 3rd Laird. **1796:** married Lady Charlotte Campbell, 2nd daughter of John, 5th Duke of Argyll. Died 1809. *Photograph by Allan Wright.*

6) Lady Charlotte Campbell, wife of Colonel John Campbell; second daughter of John, 5th Duke of Argyll and Elizabeth Gunning, Duchess of Hamilton. 1796: married (1) Colonel John Campbell (d. 1809);

The next four pages (recorded in various hands) are in tune with the Stent Committee's pre-occupation with standardized weights and no doubt Islay House was furnished with the newest of weighing machines.

(a) Walter's second wife, Mary, daughter of Nisbet of Dirleton and widow of Major Hay. She was the Mother of his seventh and eighth daughters, Mary and Hamilton, and his sixth son, William, who died young. Her brother, Hamilton of Pencaitland, was married to a niece of Henry Dundas, at this time Treasurer of the Navy later to be Viscount Melville. Her daughters finally inherited the estates of Dirleton and Pencaitland.

(b) Eleanora, Walter's eldest daughter by his first wife, Eleanor, daughter of Robert Kerr of Newfield (who died in 1785). Born 5. 3. 1769, died unmarried at Woodhall and was buried in Bothwell Church.

(c) Harriet, Walter's second daughter, b. 10. 2. 1770, married Hamilton of Gilchristcleugh (Gilkerscleugh) and Finnart.

(d) Glencairn, Walter's third daughter, b. 27. 4. 1771, married T. Carter of Edgecott, Northamptonshire, and died without issue.

(e) Margaret, Walter's fourth daughter, b. 7. 2. 1774, married 31. 4. 1794 Francis Charteris, later 7th Earl of Wemyss. Her daughter, Lady Eleanor Charteris, who married Walter Frederick (Walter's grandson and heir), the last Shawfield Laird of Islay. Their son was John Francis, notable for his Collection of the Popular Tales of the West Highlands.

(f) Walter Campbell 3rd of Shawfield and Islay, 3rd son of John and Lady Henneret Cunninghame and grandson of Daniel I. m. (1) 1768 Eleanor Kerr, 5 sons, 6 dtrs; m. (2) Mary, dtr Nisbet of Dirleton, 1 son, 2 dtrs. He succeeded his brother, Daniel II, in 1777.

(g) John, eldest son of Walter, b. 3. 12. 1772, married in 1789 Lady Charlotte Marie, younger daughter of John, 5th Duke of Argyll and Elizabeth Gunning (widow of the Duke of Hamilton). He predeceased his father. He held a Commission in the 3rd Regiment of Guards and was appointed Colonel of the Argyll Militia in 1798. He was also M. P. for the Argyll and Ayr.

(h) John Gordon, Jr. of Earlston, W. S. TUTOR AD LITEM for Walter's seven elder children, born before the Act of Disentailment was introduced. He was a kinsman, descended from Catherine, youngest daughter of Daniel I.

(i) Colin, 5th son of Walter, born 4. 7. 1785, died 1859. He became an Admiral and married Harriet Royde. His father left him Ardpatrick, at the mouth of West Loch Tarbert, which had been part of the Skipness Estate.

(j) Catherine, 5th daughter of Walter, was born 24. 11. 1779, and married Charles (later Sir Charles) Jenkinson in 1803. She died in 1855.

(k) Elizabeth, Walter's 6th daughter, was born 28. 6. 1783 and died 1865. She married Stewart Moncrieff Threipland.

(l) Mr. "Soleecitor" Dundas was the Solicitor General, Robert of Arniston, a nephew of Walter's old friend, Henry Dundas (later Lord Melville), whose daughter Elizabeth he had married in 1787.

24

Mr. D. MacQueen	14.	9
[a] Mr. Isaac Grant	18.	—
Mrs. McDouall	16.	—
[b] Mr. Archibald Campbell	11.	2

20th August 1789

[c] Mr. Robert Campbell	8.	11
[d] Mr. Walter Campbell	6.	9
Mr. Johnston	12.	10

28th August

[e] Mr. Hamilton	14.	5

29th August

Mr. Stirling	12.	4
[f] Mr. Aitton	14.	6
Colonel Possoy	14.	
Miss. Margaret Campbell	9.	5
Mrs. Stirling	9.	5

(a) Isaac Grant W. S., one of the foremost Lawyers of his day and "doer" in Edinburgh for Daniell II and Walter. He was also a close friend of the Dundases.

(b) Archibald Campbell, the Tacksman of Kinture who gave evidence in the Disentailment Action. Tacksman of Ardnahow since 1779.

(c) Robert (Robin) Campbell, 2nd son of Walter, born 21. 2. 1775. He became an Advocate and married Eugenia, daughter of Richard Wynne of Folkinham, in 1805. His father had intended to leave him Skipness, but he died two years before his father, in 1814, and the estate was inherited by his eldest son, another Walter.

(d) Walter Campbell, 3rd son of Walter, born 5. 4. 1778. He entered the Shipping Service of the H. E. I. Company and, in 1814, bought the estate of Sunderland and Foreland from his father for the sum of £14,800. There is a persistent story in Islay that he was deprived of his East Indian riches on the Pacquet between Tarbert and Islay by John Paul Jones: but it is a fact that the latter was operating around the Western shores of Scotland during the month of this Walter's birth: his father at that date was an Advocate in Edinburgh and had not yet purchased the feu of the Sunderland Estate. He married Maryanne King and built the main portion of the charming Foreland House.

(e) Probably Alexander Hamilton of Gilkerscleugh and Finnart, who gave evidence regarding the value of the woods and plantations on the Woodhall Estate at the hearing for the Disentailment Act, and was to marry Walter's second daughter Harriet. OR possibly John Hamilton of Pencaitland, Walter's brother-in-law by his second wife, who was married to a niece of Henry Dundas.

(f) John Aitton, Factor on the Estate of Woodhall.

25

Captain Martin	12.	3
Mr. Royal African	8.	8
Mr. Boyer	8.	2

January 1793

Mrs. John Dunlop	9.	5
Mr. John Dunlop	11.	6
Captain Cragie	11.	3
Mrs. Campbell	8.	1
Miss. Harriet Campbell	9.	12

6 January 1794

[a] Lord Lorn	13.	$1\frac{1}{2}$
[b] Mr. Macneil	14.	$2\frac{1}{2}$
Miss. Margaret Campbell	9.	9
Mrs. Hamilton	9.	13
Mr. Hamilton	11.	4
Mr. McDowall Grant	14.	6

13 April 1794

[c] Mr. F. Charteris	11.	8
Ca: Gask	8.	12

(a) George, Lord Lorn, the future 6th Duke of Argyll, whose sister, Lady Charlotte, was to marry John, Walter's eldest son, in 1796.

(b) Probably Malcolm, the Tacksman of Ardtalla.

(c) Francis Charteris, the future 7th Earl of Weymss, was to marry Walter's daughter Margaret at the end of the following month.

26

13 April 1794

Mr. John Campbell	13.	2

June 29th

Mr. John Campbell	12.	4
[a] Mr. Kerr	12.	4

May 24, 1795

[b] Mr. Threipland	10.	3
Mr. Dalrymple	9.	8
Mr. R. Campbell****	14.	2!!
Mr. Traff. Campbell	12.	7
Mr. John Campbell	12.	$2\frac{1}{2}$

December 13th, 1795

John Campbell after dinner	13.	10

(a) Probably Walter's brother-in-law, his first wife having been a Kerr of Newfield.
(b) Stewart Moncreiff Threipland married Elizabeth, sixth daughter of Walter.

27

Woodhall 26 Jany 1784
Rough Bear of Woodhall weighed
42½lib per Bushell which is 16st. 3lb. the
Linlithgow Boll . . . .
Irish Oats weighted 34lib. per Bushell
which is 12st. 12lb. the L: B: . . . .
Woodhall Oats about 1½lb. heavier . . . .
Dantszac Beans weighed 55 pr bul.
which is 13st. 12lb. − L: B:
Woodhall Wheat weighed 54½
per bushell which is 13st. 10lb. − L: B:

Woodhall Beans weighed 57 per Bul.
which is 14st. 4lb. − L: B:
Jany 28th Burnbank White Wheat after
fallow weighed 54 per bushell . . . .

Woodhall Polish Oats weighed 37st. per
1Bl which is 13st. 14lb. − L: B:

Wheat from Islay House Farm
after clover lea in the month of August
weighed 56lib. per Bushel . . . .

Walter was trying various grains on his various estates and comparing the results.

28

Islay House farm 4th August 1784
Beans weighed 60lib pr Bushel
Common Oats weighed 35 p.b.
Tennants rough Bear weighed
$44\frac{1}{2}$ pr Bushel . . . .

Islay House 29 Sept 1784 – Oats
of the Farm cut green for seed
weighed 35lib pr Bushel – Do Oats
better ripened weighed 36lib pr B.
Do. Rough Bear weighed 46lib pr B.
[a] Do. two rowed Barley weighed $45\frac{1}{2}$ p. B.
[b] Do. Wheat all lodged weighed 51 pr Bus
N.B. All these weighed as put into Barn Yard
27 April 1786 Woodhall
Wheat after fallow weighed 56 pr B.
the grain not very good hurt with
the Bugg . . . .

(a) 2 rowed Barley is now obsolete, but was considered to be the best for Whisky distillation.
(b) Pennant, in the account of his visit to Islay in 1772, mentions that wheat had been successfully grown in enclosed ground by the Laird, but that otherwise it was not possible owing to the cattle grazing over the open fields.

29

List of Stock upon Islay Farm November 1781

Three year olds	13
Two year olds	53
Stirks bought	51
Wintering cows	5
Milk Cows	3
Two year old Scots of Farm rearing	22
Stirks of Do	5
Calf of Do	7
Bull	1
	140

Work Horses	4
Out laying Do	8
	12

English Sheep	24
Jura Wedders	19
Highland Ews	11
	54

Stock upon Skipness Farms November 1781

Four year olds Three Stots one Quaye	4
Three year olds Two Stots one Quaye	3
Two year olds Two Quay One Stot	3
One Bull one Stot	2
Year olds four Quays two Stotts	6
Calf four Quays Two Stots	6
Wintering cows	8
Milk cows	8
Heffer bought	1
	39

Horses

Work Horses	4
Outlaying Do	4
	8

Sheep

English Sheep in whole	35
Highland Wedders	7
Highland Ews	3
	45

30

Whole Stock of Black Cattle upon the
Farms of Islay House and Echvernoch[a]
Winter 1782–
        exclusive of Horses & Sheep 203
Do. Winter 1783
        exclusive of Horses & Sheep 228
Viz.
    24 Cows for wintering
    11 Heiffers summered in Echvernoch
     5 Ardnave Cows in Calf
    77 Stots two year old bought
     6 Do. farm rearing
    78 Stot Stirks – bought
     1 Do. farm rearing
    11 Calfs farm rearing
    10 Milk Cows farm rearing
     4 Bulls
     1 Heiffer from Hamilton
    ———
228

NOTE

(a) Eachvernoch, a hill farm at the head of the Big Glen in Islay, which the Laird retained
in his own hands for cattle grazing.

31

Jany 1784 – wanted for Islay
five Bolls of Rey[a] grass 60 red clover
35 white 20 Ribbed grass 16 turnip[b]
seed one half red the other white . . . .
Islay House 6th October 1784
in order to bring water into the
Skullery there will be wanted of
Clay pipes 252 yards and of lead
pipes 40 yards[c]
wanted for the Garden Islay House
36 Espallier Apple trees, and some
Gooseberries good kinds . . . .
Jacob Robinson Bank Head
North Shields . . . .

(a) Rye Grass.
(b) The first mention of turnips grown in Islay.
(c) The first piped domestic supply of water in Islay. It is probable that the clay pipes were manufactured in the Island, but there is no means of knowing whether the lead pipes were made of local lead.

32

To find out the contents of a
Hay Stack by measure –
Supposing the Stack to be 15 yards
Long, 5 yards wide, 3 yards
high from the ground to
the Easing, & from the
Easing to the Top 2 yds of
perpendicular hight, of which
take the half, which is one
yard & add to the hight
from the ground, to the Easing
making the whole hight
4 yards – the length is multiplied by the width
& that product by the hight, which gives the
Square Yards.

33

Mr. MacGibbon has given Duncan
Taylor[a] in cash prior to the 14th June
1782 . . . . £56. 10
Square Yards, & for each yard
Square, after the Stack has
Stood for 5 or six months and
duly subsided, allow Ten Stones
but if soon after it is only
been put up, allow only 8 stone
to the square yard.

Length	15 yards
Width	5 yds
	75
Hight	4
	300 total square Yards
at 8 stone	8
	2,400 Stones & if at ten
stone would be	3,000 stone.

NOTE

(a) Duncan Taylor was Clerk of Works at Islay House and particularly figures in the Stent Book of Islay in connection with the repairs to the Duich Bridge from 1785 onwards.

34

Mountain Yellow & White Carver Black
& White   Major Brown
[a]Post arrival at Tarbert from Inveraray
upon Tuesday, Thursday and Saturday
about six o'clock evening – Departure
for Inveraray on Monday, Thursday
and Saturday at one o'clock P.M.

(a) At this period Islay was served by a Sailing Pacquet which was contracted to make
     a return journey to West Loch Tarbert each week, "wind and Weather permitting". If
     the Pacquet master could not fulfill this he undertook to send the mail by runner over
     the ferries of Lag and Feorrlin. (Stent Book of Islay)
         Carnbeg's contract for the running of the Pacquet expired in October 1783 and as
     he did not wish to continue it, the service was undertaken by John Hill, the Ferryman
     of Portaskaig. The Pacquet remained in his hands until his death, when his son,
     Robert, the principal Postmaster of the Island, became responsible for it until the
     sailing Pacquet was superceded by a Steam Boat in 1824.

Memorial
ffor
Shawfield, regarding the
Island of Islay
1780

(The original is among the Kildalton Papers. It is written on 12 foolscap sheets, sewn together.)

Memorial Regarding the Island of Islay.

ISLAY is the Southernmost of all the western Isles, lies in view of Ireland and about four leagues from the continent of Argyle, its extent is about twenty six computed miles by eighteen, is served by three ministers but is divided into four parishes Vizt. Kildalton, Kilmeny, Killarow now called Bowmore & Kilchoman and contains about 9000 Inhabitants.

The whole of this Island excepting about £400 Str. p. annum which holds of Shawfield, is his own property and held by him of the Crown, the valued rent is £8878. 18 Scots, and the contents of this property as appears from a general survey which also specifies the paticular measurements of each farm is about 114,000 Acres

	acres
whereof in tillage	27720
Grass or Green pasture	8507
	36227

The mountainous part is upon the East towards Argyle, but of its extent it is in general and uncommon flat Country, its soil remarkable good, fine Kelp shores and plenty of sea ware along all Coasts and Rock marle, shell marle and Limestone in great abundance over the whole Island.

The above Survey affords evidence that the Island is but in its infancy of improvement, is naturally fertile and on account of its variety of manure is particularly adapted for grain of all sorts, of which indeed it already produces in general sufficient to serve itself, tho' hitherto its chief commodity has been black cattle, of these alone at an average it sends annually to market about 3000, the kind and size superior to any other from the higlands as is well known to all dealers, and that no drove from this country can be completely saleable without a mixture of them.

The lead mines of the Island are a great object tho' they have always misfortunately fallen into the hands of Adventurers unequal to the undertaking, but from the trials made their quality and appearances are admitted not to be inferior to any in Scotland or England, and to have superior advantage in point of situation as they cannot require three miles of land carriage and are within one days run of the Clyde and two of the British market. The late Shawfield obtained an irrideemable gift to these mines and a three nineteen years Tack of the King's tenth from Whitsunday 1769 at 20 merks yearly – In the 1762 he gave a lease thereof to the late Charles Freebairn for a 7th dish of the free produce, which notwithstanding his inability at any period to work them properly has at an average brought to the proprietor about £100 Str. p. annum.

The next chief export to that of Cattle, is yarn, the manufacture of which is carried on to a pretty considerable extent from Lint of the growths of the Island, but there are various other commodities which also bring money to the Country, in particular Kelp begins to be an article that will soon be manufactured to a very great extent.

Fishing is likeways an article thitherto entirely overlooked, tho' from the faint trials made, there are the greatest appearances, but the present proprietor's late accession has not allowed him time to be sufficiently acquainted with all the possible improvements of the Island, and the pen of a man of business, less acquainted with it, must be still more deficient, only it is abundantly obvious what a country upon which nature has bestowed so much and is so richly peopled, may and indeed must not long hence produce.

The Island forms several grand Bays and has two Harbours for Shipping Vizt. Lochindale on the South and Portaskaig on the North, and in each of these, Piers have been lately built at very considerable expence, some part of it advanced by Government.

Lochindale is about the middle of the Island, forms a Bason similar to that of Inverkeithing, but is sufficient for its extent and depth to accommodate ships of any number of burden, and it is of such easy access in all weathers that it is the resort of all shipping to or from the west, driven from their course by contrary winds or Storm, in so much that it is seldom without a dozen or twenty riding at anchor.

Islay House is situated upon the north end of this Bay, in the full view of it & of the Country round it which is the most improved and fertile part of the Island, Bowmore the post Town of the island and a thriving village lately laid down upon the side of that Bay, is also in the full view of Islay house from the windows of which Ireland is likeways discernable.

Upon account of the favourable situation of Lochindale, its easy ingress & egress and the great saving and conveniency it would afford the foreign merchant who deals in such American or western commodities as require to suffer British import before they can go to any other market, as well as for the particular conveniency of the export and import of the island itself, it has been in contemplation to apply for getting a Custom House established at Bowmore there being already two Customhouse Officers there, the one of them lately

16 Islay House, Steading and Bowmore in distance. Original watercolour in private collection by W. Heath. *Photograph courtesy of Royal Commission.*

vested with powers to give Clearances, which will be attended with most salutory advantages, as it will save the run to Campbeltown where vessells are often for weeks landlocked whereby the Cargoes not only suffer, but frequently lose market.

The present communication betwixt the Island and Continent is by a Pacquet that runs weekly from thence to Tarbet in Kintyre, the expence of which and of Runners to the different Districts is defrayed by the Tenantry who are bound by their Tacks to assess themselves with this and all the other Contigencies and public or private burdens of the Island, the feu duty and Ministers' Stipends only excepted.

There is no Court of law in the island, which has occasioned great inconveniency to the Inhabitants, but that is about to be remedied by the Sherriff's appointing a Substitute and constituting a Court there.

As already observed Shawfield is Superior and proprietor of the whole island excepting Sunderland of rent about £300 Str which holds of him for payment of a feu and teind duty of £15: 3: 4d Str, Torobols belonging to Mr. Riddle of rent £35 Str for which also holds of him for payment of £3. 5. 2⅓ of feu duty and Balinaby of Rent about £100 like money which alone holds of the Duke of Argyle, a circumstance omitted to be mentioned in the preceding part of the memorial.

The progress of writes are clear and from the Chartularly this Estate with the superiority and right of Forrestry of the island of Jura appears to have been the property of the Calder family from the 1614 will they sold the same to the Memorialist's Grandfather in 1722.

The ffeu duty payable out of Islay to the Crown is for the Crown lands 9000 merks whereof Lord Frederick Campbell has a gift during pleasure from the Crown. And for the Tenantry of Lossit formerly holding of the Bishop 40 merks of which last the late Shawfield obtained a Gift along with the valued Teinds of Islay as shall be afterwards noticed.

In 1636 Neil Bishop of the Isles, obtained Decree of the Commissioners of Teinds, valuing the teinds of the whole Island those of the above Fewars included at 2000 merks, which Decree is recorded as a probative writ in the Books of Council and Session 27 May 1737 and in the new Record of the Commissioners for teinds 19 January 1743.

The Synod of Argyle appear to have obtained a Grant from Queen Anne to the above Teinds and to the foresaid ffeu duty of Lossit, but they having agreed to allow the late Shawfield to procure the Grant in his name on his giving competent Stipends & c. to the ministers of the island, he accordingly applied for & obtained a Gift dated 21" Decr 1765 whereby His Majesty GRANTS and DISPONES to said Daniel Campbell his heirs and assignies whatsoever during his Majesty's pleasure and until the Grant from her Majesty Queen Anne to the said Synod of Argyle shall be recalled, all and whole the valued teinds due and payable out of the lands and island of Islay and the foresaid yearly feu duty payable furth thereof to his Majesty as come in place of the Bishop and which have been in use "to be uplifted by the Synod of Argyle their ffactors, he paying yearly to each of the three ministers of the said Island the sum of £51: 13: 4d Str. and procuring them manses and Glebes according to law and his majesty does further ratify, approve and confirm all agreement entered into between the said Synod and the said Daniel Campbell for the purposes aforesaid and ordains the same to be carried into execution".

Extensive and convenient Glebes have been accordingly designed for the Ministers far above the legal Standard, but in lieu of Manses till the Proprietor inclines to build them he pays to each minister £10 a year.

The property which Calder had in Jura together with the Forest of Jura was held by him of the Duke of Argyle for a feu duty of £200 Scots, and in 1738 the "Memorialist's Grandfather sold and subfeued the whole excepting one farm called Tarbert to Archibald Campbell of Sandack afterwards designed of Jura Reserving always to his Grace the Duke of Argyle his heirs and Successors and their children full power and liberty of hunting through the said fforest of Jura whensoever they shall think fit and expedient at any time coming.

Reserving likeways to the said Daniel and John Campbells (the Memorialist's Grandfather and Father) their heirs and Successors in the lands and estate of Islay full power and privilege of hunting in and thorrow the said Forest of jura whenever they or their foresaids shall think fit or expedient AS ALSO RESERVING to them and to the feuars, wadsetters, tacksmen, tenants & possessors of the Island of Islay full power liberty and priveledge of transporting and ferrying the Cattle and Bestial of Islay whether horse colt, Goat, sheep or others from the said Island of Islay to the Isle of Jura and of driving the same through the said island of Jura to any Ferry they or the Drovers who purchase the same shall think fit conform to use and wont without paying toll, custom or any other gratuity therefore.

Giving therefore yearly the said Archibald Campbell and his therin mentioned to the said Daniel Campbell in liferent and to the said John Campbell and his heirs mail and of Tailzie succeeding to him in the lands and estate of Islay in ffee 1000 merks Scots at ilk term of Martinmas in name of feuduty and doubling the said feuduty the first year of the entry of each heir to the said lands and relieving them and their heirs and successors of the foresaid Sum of £200 Scots of feuduty payable to the Duke of Argyle yearly out of said lands and to report Discharges thereof from the said Duke his heirs or successors or their factors or Chamberlains at each term of Martinmas yearly in all time coming And also relieving the said Daniel and John Campbells and the said feuduty of 1000 Merks Scots of all Cesses, Taxations Teind duties, Ministers Stipends, Schoolmaster's Salaries and all other public burdens and impositions whatsoever due and payable or that shall be due and payable furth of the said lands in time coming and paying and delivering yearly to the said Daniel and John Campbells and their foresaids four fat Deer out of the Forrest of Jura yearly at their Mansion House in Islay when they shall happen to reside there And being expressly obliged to keep the ferryboat in constant repair with a competent number of Seamen for transporting and ferrying the Cattle and Bestial of Islay and Jura to the continent for payment of a reasonable freight not exceeding eight shillings Scots for each Cow or Bullock and twelve Shilling Scots for each aged horse or mare.

The farm of Tarbert the Memorialists only remaining property in that Island has been also sold to hold of him for a feu-duty of 6000 Oysters to be delivered annually at Islay House from a Salt water loch in that farm famous for producing them.

JURA lies to the North of Islay, they are only separated by a cut of the Western Ocean called the Sounds of Islay about a mile broad and eight long which penetrates to the Channel that divides these islands from the continent, and the reason of transporting the Islay cattle to the Continent through Jura, is because of the narrowness of the Channel a few miles North of Islay where the run from Jura to the Continent of Argyle is so short that travellers or bestial can be transported with great safety in Ferry boats in about an hour, not an accident having happened to either in the memory of man and so little does Dealers or Drovers dread any risk in transportation that they purchase and take delivery of the Cattle in Islay itself without any deduction, for which purpose there is an established Fair in the island held annually about the 20th May so well frequented that the whole of the Cattle are sold and delivered in the Island.

The estate of Islay was entailed by the memorialists Grandfather, but the Entail has never been recorded in terms of the Act 1685: when he made the purchase from Calder the greatest part of the island was under wadsett or tacks for triffing quitt Rents to friends or descendants of that family and the free rent over payment of the feuduty and ministers Stipends is only yet brought to about £6,000 Str. at which rent the memorialist would not hesitate to guarantee it for the avoient leases & might do the same that at the end thereof it will yield at least £10,000 of Rent entirely independant of the Mines the value of which cannot be known without abilities to make a fair trial of them.

The late Shawfield having contracted Debt to a very considerable amount, the memorialist in Spring 1778 applied for and obtained a special Act of parliament empowering the Judges of the Court of Session at the Suit of himself or any of the heirs of Entail to sell the whole or such parts of his estates as shall be sufficient to pay the debts then affecting the same he always reimploying the surplus of such purchase money in the purchasing lands to be laid under the same Entails to which purpose an action was accordingly brought and is now depending.

17 Walter Campbell, 3rd Laird of Shawfield & Islay. Third grandson of Daniel Campbell, 1st Laird. **1768:** Married
(1) Eleanor Kerr (d. 1785); married (2) Mary Nisbet. **1777:** Succeeded his eldest brother Daniel, Yr., 2nd Laird.
1777–84: Completed the Day Book. Photograph by Allan Wright.

State of the Process
of
Declarator and Sale
Walter Campbell, Esq; now of Shawfield
against
The Heirs of Entail, and Creditors of Daniel and Daniel Campbells
of Shawfield, and the Tutor *ad litem* for the children of said Walter
Campbell, Pursuer.
February 28 1781

(The State of Process is among the Kildalton Papers. It is a printed copy of the
documents produced at the application of Walter Campbell for Disentailment
Act and the following Proofs and Rental of Islay and Jura are extracted from it.)

For PROVING the RENTAL of the Pursuer's property in the island of Islay.

Neil M'Gibbon writer in Inverary, factor upon the estatae of Islay and Jura,
depones, That he has been factor for the late and present Mr. Campbell of
Shawfield, since December 1773; and that the first rent he collected was that due
at Martinmas, 1773; and that he is now in the course of collecting the rent that fell
due at Martinmas last 1778. Depones, That when he entered as factor upon the
estate of Islay, there was a rental delivered him by which he was directed to
collect, amounting in the whole, including the rent of the farm of Tarbert in Jura,
and feu-duties payable out of the island of Jura, to the sum of L2756 : 12 : 66/12
Sterling exclusive of the rents and feu-duties payable out of the town of
Bowmore; and that it was by this rental, that the deponent collected since he was
appointed factor upon these estates, subject to such variations in the arrangement
as the management of the business required. Depones, that for crop and Martinmas 1777, there was this variation from the rental delivered him at his entry *to wit*,
a decrease upon some of the lands to the amount of L.98 : 7 : 4 Sterling; and that
the deponent thinks the rental stands much in the same state for crop and
Martinmas 1778. Depones That by a rental made up of rents and feu-duties,
payable out of Bowmore and Ardlarach in the year 1775, the same amounted to
L.105 : 10 : 8 Sterling; but varied yearly according to circumstances. The said Neil
M'Gibbon being further interrogate, depones, That the old leases from which the
foresaid rental was made up, all expired upon the 26th day of this present month
(viz. May 1779); at which time the tenants entered into possession of the lands
upon new leases, most of them to endure for 19 years, some of them for 21, some
for 22, some for 20, some for 23, some for 25, one or two for 14 or 16 years and
one farm for 30 years. And by a rental made up last year of such of these lands as
were then let, the same then amounted to the sum of L5303 : 8 : 4 Sterling of
yearly money rent. Since the making up of which rental, the remaining part of

the estate of Islay, exclusive of what is in the possession of the proprietor and of the lands of Bowmore, Ardlarach and Cruach, has been set in lease, and mounts per particular rental, to the sum of L444 : 9s. Sterling; and the rents and feu-duties payable out of Bowmore, Ardlarach and Cruach, amount to L.101.10s. Sterling, making together L.5849 : 7 : 4 Sterling: That besides the lands so let, the proprietor will have in his own natural possession, upon the 26th curt (*viz*. 26th May 1779) Islay farm, with the lands of Killarow, and part of the old Glebes and Carnaan, valued L.100 Sterling per annum; and at Lammas next, he will have in his own natural possession, the mill of Ealabusa, valued at about L.60 Sterling per annum. Depones, That the rents payable in consequence of the said new set. commence at the said term of Martinmas next; and that besides the money rent above mentioned, the tenants are bound by their leases to pay 1s. Sterling for each pound Sterling of the foresaid rents, in lieu of the court mail-dues and compearance money formerly in use to be paid out of the said lands; and that they are also bound by their leases, to pay four days service of four men and eight horses yearly, for each quarter land, or 1s. Sterling per day each man and two horses: And the number of quarter lands belonging to Shawfield within the island is Islay, is computed at 128 quarter lands; and one fourth of a quarter, and several of the farms last set, are burdened with the payment of some hens and eggs, the exact number the deponent cannot at present condescend upon. Depones further, That the whole tenants of Shawfield's estate of Islay, are bound by their tacks to pay, besides what is already mentioned, at the rate of 3s.4d. each quarter land, towards the support of the minister of the third erection in Islay yearly, and 1s. Sterling yearly for each pound Sterling of valued rent, in the terms of the late Act of Parliament for making and repairing highways and bridges in Argyleshire; and the tenants are also bound to pay the cess and all public burdens affecting the lands. Depones, further, That there is L.55 : 55 : 11 : 11/3 Sterling of feu-duty payable to Mr. Campbell of Shawfield out of the estate of Archibald Campbell of Jura, in the island of Jura; and that there is also payable to him yearly, the sum of L.3.5s. two-thirds of a penny Sterling of feu-duty out of the farm of Torabols in Islay, belonging in property to Sir James Riddle of Ardnamurchan; and that there is likewise payable to him of teinds and feu-duties, out of Robert Campbell's of Sunderland's property in Islay, the sum of L.15.3s.4d. Sterling yearly; and to verify what is above deponed to, the deponent has now exhibited the different rentals. The said Neil M'Gibbon being further interrogate, depones, That the rents above mentioned are exigible from the tenants by written leases or missives of set, a great many of which leases are already subscribed and delivered; and the remaining new leases nearly ready for signing and delivering up. Depones, That there are three established ministers in the island of Islay, to each of whom there is payable by the proprietor L.50 Sterling of money stipend, and L.5. Sterling yearly for communion elements each, besides L.10 Sterling yearly each in lieu of manse, all payable by the proprietor; and that there is also payable L.2.10s. Sterling yearly to the schoolmaster of Bowmore, and L.2.10s. Sterling yearly to the schoolmaster of Skipness, by a mortification made by Daniel Campbell first of Shawfield.

Archibald McQuilken, clerk to the said Neil M'Gibbon, writer in Inverary, depones, That he has been for many years past apprentice and clerk to the said

Neil M'Gibbon, who is factor upon the estates of Islay and Jura, since December 1773, or January 1774 years, and that the first rent he collected was that due at Martinmas 1773: that the rental then given him amounted in whole, including the rent of the farm of Tarbert in Jura, and feu-duties payable out of the islands of Islay and Jura, to the sum of L.2756.12s.6d. six twelfths of a penny Sterling, exclusive of the rents and feu duties payable out of the town of Bowmore: and that it was by that rental Mr. M'Gibbon collected, since he was appointed factor upon these estates, subject to such variations in the arrangement as the management of the business required. Depones, That for crop and Martinmas 1777, there was the variation from the rental delivered to the factor at his entry, viz. a decrease upon some of the lands to the amount of L.135 : 11 : 31/2 Sterling, and an increase upon others of the lands in the said rental to the amount of L98 : 7 : 4 Sterling, and that the deponent thinks the rental stands much in the same state for crop and Martinmas 1773. Depones, That by a rental made up of the rents and feu-duties payable out of Bowmore and Ardlaroch in the year 1775, the same amounted to L.105 : 10 : 8 Sterling, but varied yearly according to circumstances. Depones, That the old leases from which the foresaid rental was made up expired at Whitsunday last 1779. And being further interrogate, depones, That he witnessed and assisted at many of the setts made to the tenants in Islay in the years, 1775, 1776 and 1777, and wrote many of the tacks and missives by Shawfield to the tenants, which were all to commence at the said term of Whitsunday last 1779: That he compared most of these tacks from which he has great reason to believe, that the rentals now marked by him, the Commissioner and Clerk, and deponed to by the said Neil M'Gibbon, are true and just. Depones, That he was informed, many of these tacks have been signed and delivered, and that the tenants entered into possession at Whitsunday last (*viz.* Whitsunday 1779): that the most part of the whole leases of Islay endure for 19 years from their commencement: That by a rental made up last year of such lands as were then set, the same then amounted to the sum of L.5503 : 8 : 4 Sterling of yearly money rent, since the making up of which rental, the remaining part of the estate of Islay, exclusive of what is in the possession of the proprietor, and of the lands of Bowmore, Ardlaroch and Cruach has been set in lease, amounts *per* particular rental to the sum of L.444 : 9s. Sterling making together L.5849 : 7 : 4 Sterling; That besides the lands so set, the proprietor has in his own natural possession Islay farm, with the lands of Killarow and part of the old Glebes and Carnaan, and at Lammas next (Lammas 1779), he will have in own natural possession the mill of Ealabus. Depones, That the rents payable in consequence of the said new sets, commence at the term of Martinmas next (Martinmas 1779) and that besides the money rent above mentioned, the tenants are bound by their leases to pay 1s. Sterling for each pound Sterl. of the foresaid rents in lieu of the court mail dues, and compearance money formerly in use to be paid out of the said lands, and they are also bound by their lease to perform four days service of four men, and eight horses yearly for each quarter land, or one shilling sterling *per* day for each man and two horses, and the number of quarterlands belonging to Shawfield within the island of Islay, is computed at 128 quarter lands, and one fourth of a quarter land, and several of the farms last set are burdened with the payment of some hens and eggs, but the exact number the deponent cannot at present condescend on, Depones. That the whole tenants of Shawfield's estate of Islay, are bound by their tacks to pay, besides what is already mentioned at the rate of 3s.4d. Sterling for each quarter land, towards the support of the minister of the third erection in Islay yearly, and 1s. sterling yearly for each pound Sterling of valued rent in terms of the late act of Parliament for making and repairing highways and bridges in Argyleshire; and the tenants are also bound to pay the cess and all other public burdens affecting the said lands. The said Archibald M'Quilkan being further interrogate, depones, That there are three established ministers in the island of Islay, to whom there is payable by the proprietor L.55 Sterling yearly of money stipend, and L.5 Sterling for communion elements, besides L.10 Sterling yearly to each of the said Ministers in lieu of manses, and that there is also payable L.2.10s. Sterling yearly to the schoolmaster of Bowmore, and L.2.10s. Sterling to the schoolmaster of Skipness, by a mortification made by Daniel Campbell first of Shawfield.

Malcolm M'Neil. tacksman of Ardtalla, depones, That he knows Islay farm, with that part of the Glebes, Carnaan and Killarow added thereto, and that in his opinion, it is well worth L.100 Sterling yearly, but that he does not know the value of the mill of Ealabus.

Archibald Campbell, tacksman of Kintour, depones conform to the preceeding witnesses as to the value of Islay farm with the addition, but cannot exactly say what rent the mill is worth; but he has heard the present miller pays to Doctor Robertson the tacksman 80 bolls of meal, at the rate of 10 stones to the boll yearly out of the said mill.

FROM these Depositions, rental therein referred to and produced, and scheme relative thereto, it appears that the rent of that part of the pursuer's property lands in Islay formerly set, amounts to L.5303 : 8 : 4 Sterling. That the rent of these parts of the lands lately set, amounts to L.404 : 9s. Sterling and which having been added to the rent of the other lands, the whole amounts to L.5747 : 17 : 4 Sterling.

That the lands of Bowmore, Ardlaroch and Cruach, pay yearly of rents and feu-duties, about L.101 : 10s. Sterling. That the lands of Islay farm, Killarow, and part of the old Glebes in Shawfield's natural possession, are valued at L.100 Sterling.

That the mill of Ealabus, also in Shawfield's possession, is valued at L.60 and that the whole foresaids rents of Islay, amount to L.6009 : 7 : 4 Sterling. Besides the foresaids rents, the tenants are bound to pay 1s. Sterling for each L.1 Sterling of the foresaid rent in lieu of the court mail dues and compearance money, formerly in use to be paid out of the said lands, amounting to L.300 : 9 : 4 Sterling.

Item, Four days service of four men and eight horses for each of the 128 quarter lands, and one-fourth of a quarter, or 1s. Sterling *per* day for each man and two horses, being L.25 : 13s. Sterling; and 3s.4d. each quarter land, toward the support of the minister of the third erection in Islay, amounting to L.21 : 6 : 8 Sterling.

Amounting the total gross yearly rent of the said estate of Islay to L.6356 : 16 : 4. From which deduce the feu-duty payable to the pursuer out of the lands of Bowmore, & c. as ascertained by the rental produced by Neil M'Gibbon, being L.20.2.36/12; Sterling. and there remains of rent L.6336 : 14 : 6/12 Sterling.

For Proving the Holding and Deductions from the Rental

From the special retour and recept from the Chancery before produced, it appears that the lands and barony of Islay, comprehending the island and lands of Islay, Rhinds and Middleward of Islay, and Islandtassen, and burgh of barony of Laggan, all formerly united into one barony, hold feu of the Crown, for payment of a yearly feu-duty of 9001 merks Scots, or L.500 : 1 : 1 4/12 Sterling.

And that the tenandry of Losset, part of the said lands of Islay, hold also feu of the Crown, as come in place of the bishop, for payment of 41 merks Scots, or L.2 : 5 : 6 8/12 Sterling.

Item, Certificate by Mr. John Murdoch, minister of the united parishes of Bowmore and Kilmeny in Islay, dated the 5th day of August 1780, bearing that there was paid to him of stipend yearly of money L.50; for communion elements L.5: and of manse money L.10. Amounting in whole to L.65 Sterling.

Item, Certificate by Mr. John McMillan, minister of the parish of Kilchoman, dated the 12th day of August 1780, bearing, that there is payable yearly to him of stipend of money L.50; for communion-elements L.5; and of manse-money L.10 Sterling. Amounting in whole to L.65 Sterling.

Item, Certificate by Mr. John Woodrow, minister of the parish of Kildalton, dated the 9th day of August 1780, bearing, that there is payable yearly to him of stipend money L.50; for communion elements L.5; and of manse-money L.10. Amounting in whole to L.65 Sterling.

Item, Certificate by Neil M'Caffer, parochial schoolmaster of the parish of Kilchoman, dated 10th August 1780, bearing, that there is payable yearly of salary to him, as schoolmaster of said parish, L.5 : 11 : 1 4/12 Sterling.

Item, Certificate by William Currie, parochial schoolmaster of the parish of Kilmeny, dated 8th August 1780, bearing, that there is payable yearly of salary to him, as schoolmaster of said parish, L.5 : 11s : 1 4/12d.

Item, Certificate by Walter Graham, Parochial Schoolmaster of the Parish of Kildalton, dated 8th August 1780, bearing that the yearly salary payable to him, as schoolmaster of said parish, is L5 : 11s : 1 4/12. Amounting these salaries payable to the schoolmasters, to L.16.13s.4d. Sterling.

As one half of these schoolmasters salaries falls to be paid by the tenants, the other half is here stated as a deduction, being L.8.6s.8d. Sterling. And there is produced a certificate by Lauchlan M'Lauchlan, schoolmaster in Bowmore, dated 7th August 1780, bearing, that he receives yearly from the pursuer, as schoolmaster of said parish, a sum mortified by Daniel Campbell first of Shawfield, being L.2.10s. Sterling. Amounting these feu-duties, ministers stipends, and schoolmasters salaries, to L.708 : 3 : 4 Sterling. And being deduced from the foresaid gross rent, there remains of free rent L.5628 : 10s. 86/12d. Sterling.

For Proving the Value

William McDonald, Writer of the Signet, depones, that he has had occasion to be acquainted with the value of lands and superiorities in Argyleshire, and is of the opinion, that the lands belonging to the pursuer in the island of Islay, in said county, are worth, and may give at sale, 23 years purchase of the proven free rent.

Allan M'Dugald, Writer to the Signet, depones and concurs with the immediate preceding witness *in omnibus*. And if the Lords please to value the foresaid free rent at 23 years purchase, in terms of these dispositions, the price will be L.129,456. 6s. 36/12d. Sterling. The feu-duties payable out of the lands of Bowmore, as before, is L.20 : 2 : 36/12.

The feu-duties of Jura is L.55 : 11 : 1 4/12.

The feu-duties of Torrobols, is L.3 : 5 : 0 8/12

Feu-duties of Sunderland's property, is L.15.3s.4d.

Amounting these feu-duties to L.94 : 1 : 9 6/12 Sterling.

For Proving the Value of These Feu-Duties

The said *William M'Donald* and *Allan M'Dugald* depone and concur, That the superiorities of the lands holding of the pursuer in the said Island of Islay and Island of Jura, with the feu-duties payable to him furth thereof, are, in the deponents opinion, worth 20 years purchase of the said feu-duty. And if the Lords please to value these feu-duties at 20 years purchase, according to the foregoing depositions, the price will be L.1881 : 15 : 10. And which being added to the price of the lands of Islay, the total price of these lands, including the feu-duties will be L.131338 : 2 : 1 6/12 Sterling. As to the teinds of the island of Islay, there is produced a gift of the valued teinds thereof by his Majesty King George the Third, in favours of Daniel Campbell late of Shawfield, his heirs and assignees whatsoever, which teinds are therein, and in a decree of valuation thereof valued at L.111 : 2 : 2 2/3 Sterling; and which gift is dated the 29th day of November 1765 written to the Privy Seal, and registered the 19th of December said year.

For Proving the Rental of the Farm of Tarbert in Jura

The said Neil M'Gibbon depones, that the present rent of the farm of Tarbert in Jura is L.44 : 8 : 10 8/12 Sterling.

For Proving the Holding of the said Farm of Tarbert

There is produced a precept of *clare constant* by John Duke of Argyle, in favours of John Campbell of Calder, for infefting him as heir to his father in the lands and estate of Jura, comprehending the said farm of Tarbert, to be holden feu of his Grace for payment of L.200 Scots of feu-duty; and which precept of *clare constant* is dated 11th July 1726.

Item, Extract Disposition, dated 16th July 1726, registered in the books of session the 22nd day of July 1734 by the said John Campbell to Daniel Campbell first of Shawfield, of the said lands and estates of Islay and Jura.

Item, Extract Disposition, dated 1st March, 1738, recorded in the books of Council and Session the 2nd day of the said month and year, by the said month and year, by the said Daniel Campbell first of Shawfield and John Campbell his son, to Archibald campbell of Jura, therein designed of Sandake, and Duncan Campbell his son, of the said Daniel Campbell his whole property in Jura, except the said farm of Tarbert, to be held feu of him the said Daniel Campbell and his successors, and freeing and relieving them of the foresaid feu-duty of L.200 Scots, payable to the Duke of Argyll out of the said lands of Jura. So that there is no deduction on account of the holding, or on account of minister's stipend, or any other burden; especially as the witnesses who depone upon the value fix the price at 40 years purchase of the proven rent, without any of the above reductions.

For Proving the Value

The said *Allan M'Dugald*, writer to the Signet, depones That in his opinion, the farm of Tarbert in Jura, belonging to the pursuer, the proven rent whereof is L.44.8.10 8/12 Sterling, is worth, and may give at sale, 40 years purchase of the proven rent, in respect it has long been under lease at that rent, and to the deponent's knowledge has been low rented; *causa scientiae*, it consists with the deponent's knowledge, that a client of his own offered more for the foresaid farm of Tarbert than the value put on it by the deponent.

Archibald Fletcher, writer in Edinburgh, depones and concurs with the immediate preceeding witness *in omnibus* as to the worth and value of the foresaid farm of Tarbert; *Causa Scientiae*, that he has had occasion to know the value of lands in Argyleshire; and in the present case forms his opinion in part from the other deponent's knowledge as to the farm being low rented, and the price his client offered for it.

And if the Lords please to value the foresaid rent of L.44.8s.108/12d. Sterling at 40 years purchase, conform to these depositions, the price of the foresaid farm of Tarbert will be 1777,15s.68/12d. Sterling.

Proof respecting the Mines of *Islay*

The said *Neil M'Gibbon* depones, that there are no coal-workers or quarries of free-stone in Islay or Jura; but that there are lead mines wrought in Islay by Charles Freebairn, the tacksman of the mines, and his partners: but as the proprietor is paid a dish or certain share of the produce in lieu of tack-duty, the deponent cannot say or ascertain the yearly profit arising to the proprietor, as it entirely depends on the quantity of ore that is turned out.

The said *Archibald M'Quilkan* depones, That there are lead mines wrought in Islay by Charles Freebairn, the tacksman thereof and his partners; but as there is a dish or certain share of the produce paid in lieu of tack-duty, the deponent cannot say or ascertain the yearly profit arising to the proprietor, as that depends on the quantity of ore that is turned out.

Ronald Crawford, Esq; marchant in Glasgow, depones, That he has had occasion to know the progress and produce of the Islay mines, from the 26th day of April 1776 to this date, having during that period advanced almost the whole monies expended upon the mines or works; and received or purchased from Mr. Charles Freebairn the tacksman, down to his death in August last, the rough and driest ore taken out of said mines since April 1776. Depones, That upon the 5th day of July 1777, the deponent by order of Charles Freebairn, paid L.22.1s. Sterling, as Shawfield's proportion or share of a cargo of lead then owing: That upon the 21st October said year, the deponent also paid, by Mr. Freebairn's order, L.24.10s. money foresaid, as Shawfield's proportion or dish of another cargo of lead disposed of that autumn. Depones, That to the best of the deponent's knowledge and belief, there has been no later payment of the proprietor's proportion or dish; but that there is presently owing to him his proportion or fourteenth share or half dish of the proceeds of three cargoes since sold, *viz*. L.10.10s., L.14. and L.13, all amounting to L.37.10s. which or thereabouts, to the best of the deponent's belief, is all that the proprietor has to receive, or is entitled to in terms of his tack and relative agreement with Mr. Freebairn from and since the date of the last payment in October 1777 to this date. Depones, further, That to the best of the deponent's understanding, no just or certain estimate can be hitherto put upon the value of said mines, or the proprietor's interest in the same, or tack thereof. All which is truth, & c.

Isaac Grant, writer to the Signet, depones, That as doer for the late and present Shawfield he got possession of the following papers, which he presently exhibits, *viz*. Principal Tack of the Islay mines, by the deceast Daniel Campbell last of Shawfield, to the also deceast Charles Freebairn, therein designed architect in Edinburgh, dated and subscribed by both parties the 8th day of July 1762, whereby the said Daniel Campbell sets to the said Charles Freebairn, his heirs and assignees, the foresaid mines, for the space 31 years from Martinmas then next, for the payment to the said Daniel Campbell, his heirs or assignees, or to his factors or agents in his name of 1/8th share or dish of all the ore of whatever quality that should be raised or taken out of the aforesaid mines during the first 15 years, and one-seventh share or dish of what should be so raised during the remainder of the lease, and that dressed and made mercantile, and delivered at the bank of the pits or bing-stead where the same should be dressed, free of all charges and expences whatever. *2ndly*, Fitted accounts between the said Daniel Campbell and Charles Freebairn, dated the 9th day of September 1768, bearing Shawfield's proportion of the first dividend to be L.48 : 4 : 6 Sterling. *3dly*, Discharge by said Charles Freebairn, subsuming an agreement betwixt him and the said Daniel Campbell, whereby Mr. Freebairn was to pay L.1000 Sterling of grassum, for the foresaid tack; but on condition, that on every dividend of lead, or sale of lead or other metals, he was to retain the equal half of the said Daniel Campbell's dish or eshare, ay and until he should be refunded and paid of the foresaid sum of L. 1000 and interest: That at striking the first dividend, the said Daniel Campbell's dish or share, came to L96.9s. Sterling; the equal half of which, he hereby acknowledges to have retained in terms of the foresaid agreement; which discharge is dated the 3d September 1768. *4thly*, Fitted account betwixt the said parties, dated 15th January 1770, bearing the equal half of Shawfield's dish and proportion of the next dividend to be L.67 : 11 : 10 1/2 Sterling. *5thly*, Ackowledgement by said Charles Freebairn, of said dish, in terms of the foresaid agreement. *6thly*, fitted account betwixt the said parties, dated 6th January and 20th April 1776, bearing the said Daniel Campbell's half dish or proportion of the next dividend, to be L.174 : 18 : 3 1/2 Sterling. *7thly*, Discharge by said Charles Freebairn, acknowledging to have retained the other half of the said dish towards payment of the foresaid sum of L.1000 and interest, in terms of said agreement; which discharge is also dated the said 20th day of April the said year. Depones and concurs with Ronald Crawford the preceeding witness, as to the payments made by him on the 5th July and 21st October 1777; The same having been received by the deponent on Shawfield's account. And depones, That to the best of his belief or knowledge, there has been no later payment or accounting regarding the proprietor's dish. Depones further, that to the best of his information or knowledge from any accounts he has seen relative to said mines, the gross produce of them has not hitherto been equal to the expence laid out upon them. All which is true & c. N.B. The above accounts and depositions are the accounts and proof referred to in the following depositions.

Andrew Crosbie, Esq; Advocate, being examined and interrogate as to the value of the mines in Islay belonging to the pursuer, and under sale, depones, That from the accounts and proof which has been shown to him, regarding the produce of the said mines, and the return which they have made to the proprietor as his dish or share thereof, from Martinmas 1762, that the present tack, in favours of Mr. Freebairn, commenced at the term of Martinmas last, and the great decrease of the value of the lead in late years, he is of opinion that no separate value can be put upon said mines, but that they ought to follow the lands, and be always considered an appendage thereof, being, if exposed by themselves separate from the lands, in his opinion, not saleable.

George Buchan-Hepburn, Esq; Advocate, depones, and concurs with the immediate preceding witness, as to the mines *in omnibus*, except the *ratio* as to the decrease of the value of lead of late years; as to which, the deponent knows nothing, nor does he in any degree found his opinion on that circumstance.

RENTAL of the LANDS in the Island of Ilay, 1780. From the depositions of Neil M'Gibbon and Archibald M'Quilkan, and rental relative thereto, these lands are possessed by the tenants, and pay the yearly rents following, *viz*.

	Sterling		
William Adair, Duncan Carmichael, Donald McNeil and Archibald McMillan for Ballulive.	L. 45	0	0
Duncan Brown for Bolsay and one half Grobols	35	0	0
Donald Brown, Neil M'William, and Alexander M'Pherson for Carabus	25	0	0

Peter, John, Angus, and Malcolm Browns, and Neil Buchanan for Ballieharvie	44	0	0
Archibald and Donald Bells, Neil M'Lean, Malcolm Gillespie, Alexander Currie, Hector McAllester, Dugald Gillespie, and Archibald M'Niven for Conisby	54	0	0
John Bell and Archibald Bell, junior, for Gortantoide and Dudilbeg	25	0	0
Donald Brown, John M'Arthur, Duncan M'Arthur, John Ferguson, Hugh M'Invin Alexander McKenzie and Margaret M'Lergan for Tormastill	38	0	0
John Brown and Donald M'Inture for Talent	31	17	6
John Campbell in Ardneave for Ardneave Breackachie, Olista, Mergadale, and one half Eoribus	151	0	0
Archibald Campbell in Kintour for Ardnahow, Cove, and Dudilmore, Coultorsa and Braebruick	92	0	0
John Carmichael for Arrichalloch, Balligally, Torra	112	0	0
Dugald Campbell, Angus Campbell Duncan Campbell and Donald M'Intyre for Ardachy	37	0	0
Robert Campbell of Sunderland for Ballichlavan	45	0	0
Colin Campbell of Carnbeg for Balole Leck-Balole, Cairnbeg, Coulton and Craigfinn	169	0	0
Mrs. Campbell of Kilinalian, and Angus Campbell her son for Kilinalian, Rim, Ballimish, Sornasary, Croshvoir, and one half Eoribus	80	0	0
Cuthbert Campbell for one half Ballynaughton More,	20	0	0
Una Campbell for Culabus	20	0	0
John Carmichael, Senior, Duncan Carmichael, Finlay and Hugh M'Phaidens Archibald M'Phaiden, Donald M'Aarthur John M'Lugash, Duncan Clerk, and Colin M'Invine for Kinegary	60	0	0
Mrs. Campbell of Ballinaby, Malcolm Curry, Dugald and Archibald M'Leans John and Donald Leitch for Leck Oshenish	40	0	0
John Carmichael for Loarine-lower	27	0	0
Henry Campbell of Knockamily for Kilchoman, mill of ditto, Upper Greimsa, one half of upper Kilinan, and Goaline	169	0	0
Archibald Campbell for Duisker	30	6	0
Hugh Cameron, Archibald Sinclair, Neil M'Gown, and Donald M'Gown for Grastill	32	0	0
Dugald Campbell, Alexander M'Cowaig, John M'Intaggart, Alexander and Donald Campbells, Malcolm M'Cowaig, and John M'Nab for Gille	46	0	0
Rental of Islay carried	L. 1428	3	6
Duncan Campbell for Proaig, and Island Texa	46	0	0
Alexander Campbell of Ormsary for Kilcharan, Braide, one half of Kilinan	154	0	0

Thomas Calder, George and John M'Core.

Coillabus in Oa	12	0	0
Dugald Carmichael, John Wilkieson, and John M'Diarmid			
for Knockroanistle	45	0	0
Colin Campbell for Kennabus and			
Stromnishbeg	20	0	0
John Carmichael, Duncan M'Aulay, Donald M'Phaiden,			
Alexander Gilles for Lossit in the Rinns	59	0	0
Neil, Duncan, William, Nicol and John Campbells, Andrew			
and Donald M'Nabs, and John Carmichael			
for Lurabus in Oa	34	0	0
John Campbell for Loraine Upper	15	0	0
Duncan Campbell for one half of Laggavuline			
and Mill of ditto	44	10	0
Archibald, Colin, George and John			
Campbells for Mullindrae	43	12	6
John and Alexander Campbells for Mulrish	19	11	6
John Carmichael, Archibald Sinclair, Donald and John			
Johnstons, Donald M'Intyre Neil Carmichael, Hugh			
M'Kay, and Margaret M'Nab for Nearby	36	0	0
James Campbell, Donald Lamont, Charles M'Lean, John			
M'Eachern, John Smith, and Alexander Lamont for			
Portaneillan	53	0	0
John Campbell for Kintour	70	0	0
Coll Campbell for Sanaigmore, one half of Scarabus,			
Upper Stoinsha and Sannaigbeg	123	0	0
Colin Campbell for Scanastile	71	0	0
Thomas Calder, John Campbell, Neil and			
James Camerons, Robert and Duncan M'Kerrols			
James Kerr, Alexander Johnston and William			
Gilchrist for Tighcarmogan	52	0	0
John Campbell for Carnaan	6	0	0
Peter and John Curries for Lyrabus	20	0	0
Angus and John Campbells, Archibald Kelly			
and John M'Queen for Balligillan	42	18	0
Alexander Campbell for one half of Knocklerach	20	0	0
Charles Freebairn for Persabus and Glasgowbeg	36	13	4
Hector, David and Alexander Grahams for Ballivicar	60	0	0
Patrick, John and William Grahams, Hugh M'Arthur,			
Neil M'Gilchrist, Finlay M'Nab, John Carmichael,			
Duncan Callendary Angus M'Bride and Andrew			
M'Gibbon for Ballichatrican	61	0	0
James Duncan and Donald Grahams, John Graham, Senior,			
and John Graham, Junior, Donald and Duncan			
Carmichaels for Cragabus	38	10	0
Archibald Graham for one half Nosebridge, one half Allaly,			
Doudle, Dail and Lower Grimsa	100	0	0

Donald, John, Angus senior, Alexander, Archibald, and Angus junior Gillespies and John M'Callmon for Grunart.	40	0	0
Ronald, William, and Archibald Gilchrist, William Ogilvie, Hugh Hunter, and Alexander M'Donald for Glenegedale	57	0	0
Archibald Gillies, John M'Kay, Duncan Leslie, Malcolm M'Inish, Malcolm Shaw and Donald M'Nab for Kippolsmore	50	0	0
William Graham for Kintraw	26	0	0
Duncan Graham for Machrie	33	0	0
Peter and Archibald Hyamans, Angus M'Indore, Duncan M'Indore, and Archibald M'Dougall for Octavouline	67	0	0
Lauchlin Hunter, Archibald and Gilbert Reids, John M'Intaggart and Dugald M'Gibbon for Lower Killean	22	0	0
Ronald, Alexander and Archibald Johnstons for one half Corrary, one half Courlach	15	0	0
Mr. John Murdoch, minister of Bowmore for Gartbrek and Bunanuisk	24	0	0
John M'Lean for Octofad, Amod, Mill of Octofad and Lower Kilinan	105	0	0
Peter and Archibald M'Queen for Arriguiry	21	0	0
Gilbert and John M'Arthur for Avonvogie	28	6	0
Malcolm M'Neil for Artalla, Claggan, Trudernish	95	0	0
Archibald M'Lauchlan for Ardmore, Admenoch, Kildalton	105	0	0
Duncan M'Intyre and Neil M'Arthur for Ardelister	44	0	0
Angus M'Cowaig for Assabus	15	10	0
Hugh MacKay for Laggan, Duich, Strathnaboddach, Ardimersy, one half Grobals	152	0	0
Donald M'Donald, Samuel and Angus Johnstons and Donald M'Alister for Gartachra	25	0	0
Godfrey M'Neil for Collumkill, Ardbeg, Arinabiest, Solam, Lergavreck, Ballinaughtonbeg	138	0	0
Alexander and Archibald M'Lauchlans for Ballimartine, Stoinsha	50	0	0
Donald, Donald junior, Lauchlan, Duncan, Gilbert and James M'Vurrichs, and Alexander Spence for Lossit in the Harris, and for Ballicrach	62	0	0
Murdoch and Donald McVurrichs for Balliclauch	14	10	0
Lauchlin and Samuel M'Dougalls, Duncan M'Eachern, Mary M'Vurrich, Dougald Campbell and Duncan Reid for Barr	32	10	0
Alexander M'Cowaig, David Torry, Peter Spence, William Robertson and Malcolm Sinclair for Ballitarsin	30	0	0
Hugh M'Dougall for one half Ballinaughtonmore	20	0	0

Hugh, Neil, and Archibald M'Intaggarts,			
and three more for Corspollan	36	0	0
Neil M'William for one half Carrabus	12	10	0
Archibald M'William and Malcolm M'Phaden for Cattadale	18	0	0
John and Neil M'Diarmids for Carn	25	0	0
Malcolm and Neil M'Duffies for Upper Duich	17	0	0
Donald, Malcolm and Charles M'Diarmids			
for Easter Ellister	50	0	0
Godfrey M'Lean for Wester Ellister,			
Island Oversea Gearach	105	0	0
Dugald M'Duffie, and Hugh M'Lellan for Gruline	15	10	0
Alexander M'Ewan for Gortanilvory	14	0	0
Duncan M'Dougal for Gartachossan	30	0	0
Peter and Dugald M'Cowaigs for Upper Glenastile	16	16	0
Dugald, Donald, John and Finlay M'Cowaigs,			
for Lower Glenastile	21	0	0
John M'Vorran for Half Island	10	0	0
Finlay M'Intyre and Angus Taylor for Balligrant and Mill	50	0	0
Donald and Duncan M'Millans, Donald, Archibald,			
and John M'Connels, John and Duncan Leitches			
for Kinadrochit	36	0	0
Rental of Islay brought over	L. 4439	10	10
Martin and Neil M'Alpines, John M'Lellan, Alexander			
M'Pherson, and John Carmichael for Kilneave	36	0	0
Duncan M'Laughlin's heirs for Portaskaig, Ferry of ditto,			
Columkill in the Harris	38	0	0
Neil M'Eachern, Donald M'Millan, Alexander M'Dougall,			
and Malcolm M'Eachern for Kilmeny	40	0	0
Donald, John and Alexander M'Nabs for Kilbranan	18	0	0
John and Ronald M'Dougalls, Neil and Angus M'Inish,			
for Kilbride	23	0	0
Angus M'Duffie for Kilnaughton	30	0	0
Duncan McVurrich, Donald Kerr, Archibald M'Lellan,			
Angus and Neil Curries for Leck Grunert	36	0	0
Hugh M'Donald for one half Laggavullin	22	10	0
Alexander and Hugh M'Dougalls, Duncan and			
Nicol M'Ichans for one half Nosebridge	25	0	0
Peter, Ronald, John and Allan M'Donalds for Nerabus . .	40	0	0
Donald M'Niven and Duncan M'Callman			
for Rosequern	16	17	6
Neil M'Eachern, Alexander M'Neil, Archibald and			
Ronald M'Eacherns, Angus M'Ilvoil, and Archibald			
M'Vurrich for Small Migram, Artornish	60	0	0
Neil, Archibald and John M'Lauchlans Finlay M'Arthur,			
Collin, Duncan and Archibald M'Callums, and			
Donald M'Neil for Shengart	30	0	0
John McEachern, and Martin M'Diarmid for Storkaig . . .	20	0	0

Duncan M'Arthur, Gilbert and Duncan M'Vorran, John and Malcolm M'Math for Stromnishmore	33	0	0
Duncan, Angus, and Neil M'Curries for Torranich	25	10	0
Finlay McDiarmid, Neil M'Vurrich, and Donald Brown for Teorvagan	22	0	0
Duncan M'Arthur, Archibald M'Millan, and William Gilchrist for Tockamill	13	0	0
John senior, John junior, Duncan and Dugald M'Dougalls for Tighandrom	24	0	0
Samuel M'Nicol for Blackrock	6	0	0
Donald M'Indoire for Koilade	6	0	0
Neil M'Intyre, Robert Dallas, senior and junior, for Glassins	60	0	0
Robert Paterson for one third Gartachossan	11	0	0
Donald and Archibald Stewarts, Donald M'Lean, and Patrick M'Queen for Gartloist, Gartmain	27	0	0
David Simson for Toradale, Achnacarnan	48	0	0
James, Angus and Samuel Smiths, John M'Lergan, John Sinclair, John M'Vurrich and Archibald M'Duffie for Eskinish	40	0	0
John Taylor of Skerrols, and Waukmill thereof	39	0	0
Mr. John Woodrow, minister of Kildalton, for Ballyneal Arrivolcallum	40	0	0
John Ross for Kelsoa	34	0	0
Amounting the rent of these Lands to RENTAL of part of the Estate of Ilay set since the foregoing . . . . .L. 5303		8	4
Taynacrock . . . . .L. 15		0	0
Kilslevan	40	0	0
Craigfadd	26	0	0
Ealabus	11	0	0
Mill of Skiba, meal and money	15	2	0
Mill of Oa, ditto, ditto	23	10	0
Mill of Breckachy, ditto, ditto	20	0	0
Lorgabow	28	0	0
Gartfadd	26	0	0
Octomore and Changehouse of Skiba	30	7	0
Lagintraw	7	0	0
One half of Scarabus	22	0	0
Upper Corrary	16	0	0
Upper Killean in Oa	20	0	0
Part of Kilchoman to Mrs. M'Millan	20	0	0
North, east and west lots of Surn	41	0	0
Angus Brown's croft	1	10	0
Robus and Keppolslachan	44	0	0
Eachvernach	38	0	0
Amounting the Rent of these Lands last set to	444	9	0

And which being added to the Rent of the
other lands, the whole amounts to . . . . .L. 5747   17   4
The lands of Bowmore, Ardlaroch,
Gruach pay yearly of rents and feu-duties   101   10   0
The lands of Islay farm, Killarow, and part of the old glebe
in Shawfield's natural possession, valued at   100   0   0
The Mill of Ealabus, also in Shawfield's Possession,
value at   60   0   0
_____

Amounting the whole foresaid Rents of Islay to L.6009   7   4
Besides the foresaid rents, the tenants are bound to pay 1s.
Sterling for each pound Sterling of the foresaid rent, in lieu of
the Court mail dues, and compearance money, formerly in
use to be paid out of the said lands, amounting to   300   9   4
Item, 4 days service of 4 men and 8 horses for each of 128
quarter lands, and one fourth of a quarter, or 1s. Sterling *per*
day for each man and 2 horses, being   25   13   0
And 3s. 4d. each quarter land towards the support of the
Minister of the third erection in Islay, amounting to   21   6   8
_____

Amounting the Total Gross yearly rent of
the Lands in Islay to L.6356   16   4
From which deduce the feu-duty payable out of the lands of
Bowmore, &c. as ascertained by the Rental produced by Niel
M'Gibbon in respect they are separately valued, being
and there remains of gross Rent   20   2 $3\frac{6}{12}$
_____

(Carried forward)   L.6336   14 $0\frac{6}{12}$

For Proving the Holding and Deductions from the Rental

From the special retour and precept from the Chancery
before produced, it appears that the lands and barony of
Islay, comprehending the island and lands of Islay
Rhinds and Middle-ward of Islay, and Islandtassen, and
burgh of barony of Laggan, all formerly united into one
barony, hold feu of the Crown for payment of and yearly
feu-duty of 9001 merks Scots, or   500   1 $1\frac{4}{12}$
And that the tenandry of Losset, part of the said lands
of Islay, hold also feu of the Crown, as come in place of the
Bishop, for payment of 41 merks Scots, or   2   5 $6\frac{8}{12}$
Item, Certificate by Mr. John Murdoch, minister of the united
parishes of Bowmore and Kilmeny in Islay, dated
5th August 1780, bearing, that there was paid to him

of stipend yearly of money L50   0   0
For Communion-element 0   0   0
And of Manse money 10   0   0
Amounting his stipend to   65   0   0
Item, Certificate by Mr. John M'Millan minister of the
parish of Kilchoman dated 18th August, 1780,
bearing, that there is payable yearly of stipend to
him of money L50   0   0
For Communion-element 5   0   0
And of Manse money 10   0   0
Amounting his stipend to   65   0   0
Item, Certificate of Mr. John Woodrow, Minister of the
parish of Kildalton, dated the 9th August,
1780, bearing, that there is payable yearly to him
of stipend money L50   0   0
For Communion-element 5   0   0
And of Manse money 10   0   0
Amounting his stipend to   65   0   0
Item, Certificate by Neil M'Caffer
parochial schoolmaster of the
parish of Kilchoman, dated 18th
August 1780, bearing that there
is payable yearly of salary to
him, as schoolmaster of said
parish . . . .   5. 11 $1\frac{4}{12}$
Carried over   L. $5:11:1\frac{4}{12}$ L.697: 6:8   L6336:14:$0\frac{6}{12}$
Brought over gross rent of Islay   L6336:14:$0\frac{6}{12}$
Brought over feu-duty and ministers
stipend   L.697: 6:8
Brought over from schoolmasters
Salaries   L. $5:11:1\frac{4}{12}$
Item, Certificate by William Currie
parochial schoolmaster of the
parish of Kilmeny, dated 6th August
1780, bearing that the yearly
salary payable to him, as school-
master of said parish   L. $5:11:1\frac{4}{12}$
Item, Certificate by Walter Graham
parochial schoolmasteer of the parish
of Kildalton, dated 8th August 1780
bearing, that the yearly salary payable to him as schoolmaster of the
said parish is   L. $5:11:1\frac{4}{12}$
Amounting these salaries payable
to the schoolmasters etc . . . . . .

L.16 13. 4

As one half of the schoolmasters salaries falls to
be paid by the tenants, the other half is here
stated as a deduction. . . . .   8 : 6 : 8
And there is produced a certificate by
Lauchland McLauchlan Schoolmaster
in Bowmore, dated the 7th August, 1780,
bearing that he received yearly, as
schoolmaster of said parish, a sum mortified by
Daniel Campbell, first of Shawfield, to the
schools of Islay, being . . . .   2 : 10 : 0
Amounting these feu-duties, ministers
stipends, and schoolmasters salaries to   708: 3: 4

And being deducted from the foresaid gross
rent, there remains of free rent . . . .   L.5628:10: $8\frac{6}{12}$

For Proving the Value

William M'Donald, writer to the Signet,
depones, that he has had occasion to be
acquainted with the value of lands and
superiorities in Argyleshire; and is of the
opinion, that the lands belonging to the
pursuer in the island of Islay in said
county, are worth, and may give at a sale,
23 years purchase of the proven free rent.

Allan M'Dugall, writer to the Signet,
depones, and concurs with the immediate
preceeding witness *in omnibus*

And if the said Lords please to value the
foresaid free rent at 23 years
purchase, in terms of these depositions,
the price will be . . . .   L.129,456: 6: $3\frac{6}{12}$
The feu-duties payable out of the lands of
Benmore [Bowmore], is as before . . . .   20. 2. $3\frac{6}{12}$

The feu-duties of Jura is . . . .   55. 11. $1\frac{4}{12}$

The feu-duties of Torrabus is . . . .   3. 5. $0\frac{8}{12}$

Teinds and feu-duties of Sunderland's
property is 15. 3. 4

Amounting the feu-duties to . . . . L.94. 1. $9\frac{6}{12}$

For Proving the Value of these Feu-duties.

The said William and Allan M'Dugall,
depone and concur, That the superiorities of
the lands holding of the pursuer in the said
island of Islay and island of Jura, with the
feu-duties payable worth 20 years purchase of
said feu-duty. And if the Lords please to value
these feu-duties at 20 years purchase, according
to the foregoing depositions,
the price will be 1881:15:10

And which being added to the price of the
lands of Islay, the total price of these lands,
including the feu-duties, will be . . . .   L.131,338: 2: $1\frac{6}{12}$

As to the teinds of the island of Islay, there is
produced a gift of the valued teinds thereof by
his Majesty King George III in favours of
Daniel Campbell, late of Shawfield, his heirs
and assignees whatsoever, during his Majesty's
pleasure: and until the grant thereof from her
majesty Queen Ann to the Synod of Argyll,
shall be recalled.

And which teinds are therein, and in a decree
of valuation thereof, valued at L.111.2.2$\frac{2}{3}$
Sterling, besides an annual feu-duty of
L.22.5.6$\frac{2}{3}$ Sterling, payable by said Daniel
Campbell to his Majesty as come in place of
the bishop of Argyle: Which gift is dated the
29th November 1765; written to the
Privy Seal, and registered 19th December
said year.

The Free Yearly RENT of the Lands and others before is

Free yearly rent of the lands of Woodhall,			
including the coal	L.330.	8.	6. 2/12
of the lands of Greenside	143.	13.	3. 4/12
of the lands of Crew-woods,			
part of Greenside	43.	16.	4.
of the lands and barony of Shawfield	318.	11.	7. 10/12
of the lands in the Island of Islay	5628.	10.	8. 6/12
Feu-duties of Bowmore, & c.	94.	1.	9. 6
Rent of lands in Tarbert in Jura	44.	8.	10. 8/12
Rent of lodging in Edinburgh	25.	0.	0.
Surplus rent on the Estate of Kilsyth	586.	0.	8. 4/12
Feu-duty on Auchindavie, & c.	1.	3.	3. 8/12

Amountint the free yearly produce of the foresaid subjects to	L.7615.	15.	2.
The amount of the debts, as before, is	L.88871.	3.	0. 8/12
The yearly interest whereof is	4443.	11.	1.

Which being deduced from the free rent,
there remains of surplus yearly rent,
over paying the interest of the debts . . . . . .   L.3172.   4.   1.

The price of the lands of Woodhall, as before, is	L.15629.	15.	9. 10/12
The price of the lands of Greenside	3304.	5.	4. 8/12
The price of the lands of Crew-woods	1007.	15.	8.
The price of the woods on these lands	2000.	0.	0.
The price of the lands and barony of Shawfield	7327.	8.	10. 2/12
The price of the lands in the Island of Islay	L.129456.	6.	3. 6/12
The price of the feu-duties of Bowmore . . .	1881.	15.	10.
The price of the lands in Tarbert in Jura . . .	1777.	15.	6. 8/12
The price of the lodging in Edinburgh	200.	0.	0.
The price of the tack of Kilsyth	10000.	0.	0.
The price of the feu-duties of the lands of Auchindavie, & c.	24.	9.	5.

The total price of the whole of the foresaid subjects, ...	L.172609.	12	9. 10/12
The debts, as before, is	88871.	3.	0. 8/12

And being deduced from the total price, there
remains over payment of the debts 83738.   9.   9. 2/12
This is the Scheme referred to in the state of
Shawfield's Sale.

ROBERT M'QUEEN.

PAYMENTS
to acct of
PRICE OF SUNDERLAND
1787–1791
and
RENTAL of the
ESTATE OF SUNDERLAND
for CROPT & MARTs 1790

(The originals are among the Kildalton Papers. The first is written on a half sheet of foolscap and the second, is a particularly fine script, on a single sheet of foolscap.)

Payments to accot of price of Sundl

				£	Sh	d
1781	Dec 24	Paid to Mr. Campbell of Ormsary to accot of his debt		£100	—	—
1788	Mar 10	Paid to Mrs. Campbell of Kilinallain		20	—	—
	19	do		20	—	—
1789	Sept 2	Paid the Royal Bank in full of Princ & Interest		547	11	1
1791	Jany 14	Paid A. Young in full of the debt due to Al McCausland Princ and Interest		103	—	4

RENTAL of the ESTATE OF SUNDERLAND for MARTs
1790 years

SUNDARLAND		£.	Sh.	d.
	John McLergan Malcolm Ferguson, Neil Curry, Aulay McAulay and John Ferguson	52.	10.	—.
PARK OF Do.	Archibald Anderson, Arch. McLergan Donald Clark & John McIntyre	31.	10.	—.
FORELAND Coul, Machary and Coulerach	Charles Fraser	175.	—.	—.
CLADDICH	Lachlan McLean	28.	—.	—.
BALLIMEANOCH And part of Duire	John McLean	30.	—.	—.
CLADAVIL	John Carmichael	120.	—.	—.
PORTNAHAVEN Set in 5 difft Lots	Archd McAlister & others	44.	10.	—.
		£431.	10.	—.

RENTAL OF ISLAY
for the year from WHITSUNDAY, 1798 to WHITSUNDAY, 1799, payable at MARTs, 1798 and WHITs, 1799.

Farms	Tenants	£.	s.	d.
Knock and Ardelister	Malcolm MacNeill, silver rent	120.	—.	—.
Ardtalla	Duncan MacIntyre and John Johnstone	84.	—.	—.
Proaig & Island Texa	Dr. Samuel Crawford	71.	—.	—.
Kenture, Stoine	Archibald MacDuffie	90.	—.	—.
Ardmore, Ardmenoch, Kildalton	Arch. Campbell	130.	5.	—.
Claigin, Trudernish and Craigfin	Donald Campbell	100.	—.	—.
Balinaughtonmore	Hugh MacDougall, John Campbell	60.	—.	—.
Calumkill, Balinaughtonveg milne Laggavulline	Godfrey MacNeill during pleasure	100.	—.	—.
Ardbeg, Arinabiest, and 1/2 Laggavuline	Duncan MacDougall Burdened with a proportion of Miln, Croft & Grass upon his half of Lagavulline	100.	—.	—.
Laggavulline	John Johnstone Burdened with a proportion of Miln, Croft & Grass	30.	—.	—.
Solam	Coll. Campbell	80.	—.	—.
Achnacarnan	Arch. Robertson during pleasure	11.	—.	—.
Ballyneal	Neil MacArthur & Others	63.	—.	—.
Toradill	Donald Johnstone & others	60.	—.	—.
Taycarmogan	Robert McKerrol & Others	68.	—.	—.
Tayindrom	Arch. Carmichael, John & Allan McDougall The tenants to Accomodate Alexr. McDougall with a house & cows grass at a Moderate rate	32.	—.	—.
Kilnaughton, Carrabus Frachtilt, upper Leorine	John MacDuffie	90.	—.	—.
Kenabus, Stremnishbeg, Milne of Oa	George Campbell	55.	—.	—.
Kilbride	Ronald MacDougall & others	50.	—.	—.
Tockamill	Duncan McArthur Neil & Malcolm McMillan	16.	—.	—.
Stremnishmore	Hugh McArthur & others	40.	—.	—.
Ballivicar	Alex. Graham & Others	60.	—.	—.
Assabus	Angus, Peter, William McCuaig	20.	—.	—.
Ballichatrigan	Peter Graham & others	80.	—.	—.
Cragabus	Duncan McCuaig & others	50.	—.	—.
Lyrabus & Oa	. . . Campbell & others	45.	—.	—.
Geill	John Campbell & others	65.	—.	—.
Grastil, exclusive of Frachtil	Alex. MacDougall & others	30.	—.	—.
Upper Glenastil	Duncan MacCouaig and others	23.	—.	—.
Lower Glenastil	Dugal McCuaig and Donald McNab	31.	10.	—.
Ardeenistle	Duncan MacDougall incl. Int. of Houses	20.	—.	—.
Lower Laorine	James Campbell	40.	—.	—.
Coillibus	Finlay MacCowaig and others	20.	—.	—.

Farms	Tenants	£.	s.	d.
Lower Killean	John MacIntaggart and others. During pleasure	30.	—.	—.
Kintra & Machary	Duncan Taylor	90.	—.	—.
Gleneigdale	Ronald Gilchrist and others	70.	—.	—.
Laggan, Duich and Ar	Alexander McKay. No claim of grazing on Knock & Ardelister	175.	—.	—.
Island	John MacVorran	16.	—.	—.
Upper Corrary and part of Lower do.	Archibald Adair	20.	—.	—.
Lower Corrary	John Johnstone	10.	10.	—.
Courlach	John MacNiven and Allan MacQueen	14.	—.	—.
Gartbreck	Mrs. Murdoch	33.	—.	—.
Ardlaroch	Mrs. Woodrow	17.	—.	—.
Gartmain	David Simson	20.	—.	—.
Arighuiry	Colin McFaiden and others N.B. Gortaninurish excluded at a proportion of the rent which is fixed at £6 str. – to Mr. McGibbon so that the tenants pay	24.	—.	—.
Avinlussa & Avonvogie with Glenmolachan.	Arch. McArthur & others	45.	—.	—.
Nereby	John Johnstone & others	50.	—.	—.
Gartloist	John Stewart & others exclusive of Craiganinpenin	20.	—.	—.
Part of Gartachossan excl. of Shawfield's pt.	Donald McEachern. Do. for the small park at the River side	17.	17.	—.
		4.	—.	—.
Part of Ditto	Archibald McViccar	9.	—.	—.
Part of Ditto	James Livingstone, Mason	5.	10.	—.
Part of Ditto	Neil Campbell, Weaver	3.	—.	—.
Part of Do.	Duncan Anderson	2.	10.	—.
Part of Do.	Malcolm McEvoy	2.	—.	—.
Part of Do.	. . . Currie	2.	5.	—.
Part of Do.	Alex. Campbell & Livingstone	4.	4.	—.
Part of Do.	Finlay McArthur's widow	11.	15.	—.
Cragininfinin	Malcolm McNeil	2.	10.	—.
Drumduich	Arch. McNab	4.	—.	—.
Gortanilivory part.	Ivor McEwan & Neil McKeechan	15.	—.	—.
Cattidill	Alex. McMillan & others	25.	—.	—.
Tallant	Donald Johnstone & others	44.	—.	—.
Daill	Donald McEachern & sons	75.	—.	—.
Kinegary	Duncan Carmichael & others	70.	—.	—.
Nosebridge of Allaly	John McEwan & others	52.	13.	4.
Allaly & pendicle of Nosebridge	Dugal McNiven	6.	—.	—.
Part of Ballitarsin	Alexr., Robertson . . . £10.10 Charles McEwan and others . . . £31. —	41.	10.	—.
Part of Loagine	Angus & John Campbell	34.	—.	—.
Balligillan	John McQueen and others Old Rent. N.B. This Tack expires Whitsunday 1799	22.	12.	2.
Kilbranan, exclusive of the Wood park	John McNab & others	32.	—.	—.
Mulindry	John Campbell & others N.B. Arch. Campbell to have	70.	—.	—.

Farms	Tenants	£.	s.	d.
Esknish	Dugal McLellan & others	67.	12.	—.
Storkaig	Donald McDermind & others	26.	12.	—.
	N.B. The shore is taken off			
	at an adequate rent, which has			
	been fixed at £6 to Dr. Crawford			
Kilmeny	John Campbell & others	70.	—.	—.
Part of Do.	John Campbell . . . £7.			
Part of Slate Houses	John McDougall . . . £5.	12.	—.	—.
Grobolls & Torra	Duncan & Archibald Brown	40.	—.	—.
Rosquern	Duncan Campbell, Peter McQueen	24.	—.	—.
	and Malcolm Currie			
Balligrant	Arch. Campbell, Mercht	46.	3.	—.
	for part . . . £12.			
	Ardnahow for part . . . £6.			
	William Carrick " . . . £3.3.			
	Arch. McGilvra . . . £21.			
	John McDougall for			
	the first year . . . £4.			
	and for every after year . . . £6.			
Miln of Do.	Arch. Campbell, Mercht.	60.	—.	—.
Tirvagan	Hugh McKay & others. The rent of	23.	—.	—.
	this farm after Whit 1799 is £32.			
Balole, Leek, Duisker, two				
Stoinshas and $\frac{2}{3}$				
Eallibus	Dr. Samuel Crawford . . . £209.10.			
Miln of Glenguy	Silver rent of Miln . . . 12. —.	$221\frac{1}{2}$	10.	—.
	Besides this rent the miln pays 70 bolls of			
	meal short weight			
Barr	Angus McFaden & others	45.	—.	—.
Portaskaig, Keill Persebus,	John Hill	100.	—.	—.
and Ballachroy				
Mulriesh	Alex. Campbell & others	35.	—.	—.
Ardnahow, Cove, Robolls,	Archd. Campbell	137.	—.	—.
Bolsa & Peter Brown's croft				
Scanlastill	Captain John Campbells part . . . £58. 1. 8.	74.	18.	6.
	Alexr. Curry's part. 16. 16. 10.			
	N.B. Shawfield has in his own possession			
	part of this farm called			
Portaneilan	Donald Lamont & others	70.	—.	—.
Kilslevan	John Campbell & others	68.	—.	—.
Carnbeg	Archd. Campbell, Merchant	38.	—.	—.
Killichlaven	Colin and Charles Campbell and Donald	66.	—.	—.
	McEachern			
Balliharvie	Donald Brown & others	60.	—.	—.
Ballimartine	Donald Campbell, Ormsary	55.	—.	—.
Kepolsmore	John McKay & others	70.	—.	—.
Lossit, Ballicrach Balliclach,	Mr. MacGibbon £175			
Eachvernock, Arivrun,				
Gartaninuisk, part of	Do. for Gortaninunisk £6	181.	—.	—.
Ariguary				
Torabolls	Dugal Campbell Feuduty to the Minr. of	2.	18.	4.
	the 3 Erections			
Scarabus	Duncan Currie & others	70.	—.	—.
Lower Kilinan	Donald McIntyre & others	31.	10.	—.

Farms	Tenants	£.	s.	d.
Taynaknock, pendicle of Leek,	Alex. Ogilvye . . . . . . £15. 15. 10.			
Do. of Octovoulin	Alex. Oguilvye . . . . . . 2. 10 . — .	18.	5.	10.
Shenegart	Arch. McLauchlin & others The Set of this farm expires at Whit. 1802	31.	13.	4.
Octovulline	John Currie & others	80.	—.	—.
Upper Kilinan	John McDougall, Neil Darroch & others	34.	—.	—.
Eoribus	Donald Baxter & others	53.	—.	—.
Carabus	Rodger Brown & others. Exclusive of Knockdon, the Loch & Heath to be enclosed therewith	34.	—.	—.
Coulade	Donald McIndoer	8.	—.	—.
Uiskintuie as marked out with part of Lyrabus Muir	Archd. McLean	8.	—.	—.
Conisby	Arch. Bell & others . . . . . . £90. Deduce for land possessed by McAlisters widow as the keep possession at the old rent till the Lease expires at Whits. 1801. . . £2. 15.	87.	18.	7.
Culabyus, Lyrabus & Balivogie as marked	Mrs. Currie, exclusive of what is added to Uiskintuie of the Black Rock grazings	63.	—.	—.
Corsapolls, exclusive of Balivogie.	John McNiven and others, the tenants burdened with a house & Cows grass to Neil McIntaggart	80.	—.	—.
Kilinalen & Crosshmoir	Alexr. Campbell	105.	—.	—.
Octofad, Amod, Gortantoide & Dudilbeg	John McLean, the old rent during his life £84. 5. — 40. —. —.	124.	5.	—.
Ardnave, Breckachy, & Margadale with Kelp Shores	Duncan Campbell	130.	—.	—.
Miln of Kilneave, grass & acres	John McIndoer	21.	—.	—.
Leckosnish	John McEachern & others	24.	—.	—.
Carndonachy	Arch. & Dugal MacLargans & others	32.	—.	—.
Sannaigmore	Coll Campbell	85.	—.	—.
Gruinart	Neill Currie & others	65.	—.	—.
Kenadrochit	John Leitch & others	65.	—.	—.
Smaill, Migrim Part of Ardtornish	Dugald Campbell, Balinaby Subject to the Marches with Ballinaby being fixed and to thirlage to Shawfield's Miln	100.	—.	—.
Kilchoman & Milne, & upper & Lower Greamsay	Henry Campbell, Exclusive of what is possessed by Mr. McLeask, Minister	235.	—.	—.
Kilnave	Martin McAlpine & others. Exclusive of the Miln & Croft	63.	—.	—.
Part of Kilchoman	Mr. John McLeish, during pleasure	20.	10.	10.
Cairn	Neil McDermind & others	40.	—.	—.
Easter & Wester Ellister, Island Oversa & ½ Dudilmore	Neil McNeil	167.	18.	7.
Gruilinbeg	Neil MacLellan & others	22.	—.	—.
Nerebolls	Malcolm McEachern & others	63.	—.	—.
Kelsay and ½ Olista	John Ross	71.	—.	—.
½ Olista	Neil McCaffer	21.	—.	—.
Gearach	Mrs. McLean (late Ellister) during pleasure	58.	—.	—.
Coultorsay	Hector & William Simson, they are to pay for what may be added to Gart besides what is here stated	42.	—.	—.

J

Farms	Tenants	£.	s.	d.
Glashans	Arch. Sinclair & others	88.	—.	—.
Gartcharra	Alex. McDonald & others	38.	—.	—.
Arichallich, Balimony &	Hector McNeill	290.	—.	—.
Balligaly and Cladavill				
Tormistle	John McArthur & others	68.	—.	—.
Kilchirian & Braid	Neil McEachern & others, formerly tenants	200.	—.	—.
	in Small			
Craigfad	John & Arch. James & others	34.	—.	—.
Lorgbaw, lower half	A. McFaiden & John Gillespie & Son	21.	—.	—.
Upper half of Do.	Duncan, George & Robert Campbell	18.	—.	—.
Gartfad & Lagintra	John Montgomery & others	46.	—.	—.
Octomore Mid Division		36.	—.	—.
Miln of Skilba	Duncan Jamieson	15.	17.	1½
Changehouse of Skilba	Arch. Gillis	7.	14.	4.
Feu Dutys of Jura	Arch. Campbell	55.	—.	—.
Coul, Coulerach, Foreland,	John Campbell	327.	10.	—.
Coultoune Park of				
Sunderland, Sannaigbeg,				
Buninuilt Corygortan				
& Dudilmore				
Lower Sunderland	Neil Currie & others	52.	10.	—.
Cladich	Lauchlane McLean, during pleasure	28.	—.	—.
Ballimeanich and part Duire	Donald McNab	32.	—.	—.
Portnahaven				
No. 1.	Arch. McAlister & McArthurs £12. 12.			
No. 2.	A. McIntyre & John Ferguson £12.			
No. 3.	Arch. & John McPhaill £10.			
No. 4.	Js. McNiven & Gilbert McAulay £8			
No. 5.	Dn Campbell Changehouse £12.	54.	12.	—.
Part of Grobolls	Mr. McIntosh, Minister	18.	—.	—.
Part of Cruach	Chas. McArthur	3.	3.	—.
Part of Do.	John McKiachan	8.	8.	—.
Bunanuisk	Chas. McGilvra £10. Jas. Ferguson £2. 2.	12.	2.	—.
Fishing of Lagan, & Logan's	George Kilpatrick	8.	—.	—.
House				
Claigincarrach	Neil McEachern	8.	—.	—.
Carnaan	John Campbell	2.	—.	—.
Croft of Robolls	Archd. McLauchlan	2.	10.	—.
Muir of Knocklaeroch	Donald McDuffie	4.	—.	—.
Part of Gartanloist	George Shanks & James Campbell N.B.	5.	10.	—.
	the 12/– in the above lot No. of 1			
	Portnahaven is added to the last page of this			
	Rental			
Baluilve	William Adair & others	47.	8.	10.
	N.B. the old set expires at Whits. 1800			
	& set now at £72.			
Skerrols Waulk Miln	Alexr. Taylor The old set expires at	46.	7.	—.
& Lenimore	Whit. 1802			
Leck Gruinart	Peter McDonald & others	37.	19.	4.
	The old set expires Whit. 1802			
Torronich	George Campbell & others. The old set	26.	17.	—.
	expires Whit, 1800 Let to McLelan			
	& sons at £35.			

Farms	Tenants	£	s.	d.
Lossit in Rinns	John Carmichael & others. The present tenants have renounced the old Lease which did not expire till Whit. 1804 and agreed to pay £84. yearly from Whit. 1799. The following farms are in Shawfield's own hands and are only stated at the old rent.	62.	—.	—.
Upper Dluich		£15.	—.	—.
Part of Gartahasan		18.	—.	—.
Gortenloist		8.	8.	—.
Part of Gortinilivory		5.	—.	—.
Ardachy		39.	4.	—.
Pt. of Scanlastill		24.	—.	—.
Knocklaeroch		42.	3.	4.
Glasgowbeg		5.	5.	5.
Lintmiln & Croft		5.	5.	—.
North lot of Surn		10.	10.	—.
East lot of Do.		15.	15.	10.
South lot of Do.		16.	16.	10.
A lot formerly possessed by Angus Brown taken from Carabus (supposed)		2.	2.	5.
Knockdon		5.	—.	—.
North Parks of Daill				
Robolls & Baligrant (supposed)		10.	—.	—.
Knockans etc.		158.	5.	11.	380.	13.	11.
Gartintra Houses				
Gardens & Grazing	Mrs. Grahame	£7.	7.	0.
	Donald McDermined	7.	7.	0.
	Arch. McFaden	3.	10.	0.
	Donald Shaw	3.	10.	0.
	John McDonald	3.	10.	0.
	Angus Clark	3.	10.	0.
	Duncan McAlister	3.	10.	0.
	Arch. McIver	3.	10.	0.
	James Livingstone	3.	10.	0.
	John Carrick	2.	0.	0.
	John Gillies	2.	0.	0.
	Archd. McLellan	2.	0.	0.
	John Smith	3.	10.	0.
Bowmore	Donald McLellan	3.	10.	0.	52.	4.	—.
John Sinclair Rent				
The heirs of John McIntyre, Shoemaker, Feuduty		2.	10.	—.
Peter McIntyre Feuduty		2.	9.	8.
Robert McKay Feuduty		2.	9.	2.
William Mitchel Feuduty 12/ Acres £2. 8.		3.	—.	—.
Captain S. Stewart House & acres		8.	8.	—.
D. Simson for McCuaig's Acres £2. 10. a lot of land £1. 1. to Feuduty 7/6		3.	18.	6.
George Douglas house & garden 10/ of acres £3. 5.		3.	15.	—.
Hugh McCrillin (?)				
John Jamieson Feuduty		2.	16.	3.
Robert McAlpine's widow Feuduty		2.	16.	3.
Donald McEachern, Mason		1.	10.	—.

Farms	Tenants	£	s.	d.
Donald & Ard Adair		5.	10.	—.
William Simson		10.	—.	—.
Robert Douglas including feuduty		4.	12.	—.
Dugal McAlpines widow garden 7/6 acres 21/–		1.	8.	6.
John Douglas house & part garden 10/ acres 30/		2.	—.	—.
Duncan McEwan house & garden 10/ acres 25/		1.	15.	—.
Duncan Taylor Machary house rent 7/6 Acres 20/		1.	7.	6.
Mr. McKay Laggan for a piece ground along the road from the Church of Bowmore to Corrary				
Dn McCarmaig & Malcolm McMillan		1.	—.	—.
Duncan McMillan Acres		1.	10.	—.
Dn McCormaig House garden 10/ acres £2		2.	10.	—.
Malcolm McMillan House & garden 5/ Acres £2. 5.		2.	10.	—.
Archd C. (?) Campbell		2.	—.	—.
Donald . . . (?) Campbell		3.	15.	—.
Duncan Campbell Mason, Hse & garden 5/ Acres £2		2.	5.	—.
Mrs. Currie Cullibus for the half of A. Curries acres 30/ Feuduty of her house 7/		1.	17.	—.
John McVorran Feuduty		2.	14.	1½.
Mrs. McKay Laggan Acres		2.	—.	—.
Feuduty of McAlisters house and store houses				
John Thomson Sadler House & Gardens £5.5. Acres 30/		6.	15.	—.
John Campbell Ronachmore		3.	5.	—.
James McNicol Acres		1.	—.	—.
Duncan McGilvra House & garden 5/ Acres 22/		1.	7.	—.
Hugh Currie House & Garden 5/ Acres 20/		1.	5.	—.
John Campbell Herd Acres			15.	—.
Mrs. McLauchlane Ballimartine Hse & garden £4 Acres 21/		5.	1.	—.
Alexr Douglas House & garden		1.	10.	—.
Widow McColman A poor object		—.	—.	—.
Miss Lily Simson Public House & acres & garden		12.	—.	—.
Ard Adair Feu duty of house & garden		1.	—.	—.
Houses & Gardens without Acres.				
John Morrison			5.	—.
Peter Smith			5.	—.
Rt, Keith			5.	—.
Duncan McNiven			5.	—.
Mary McCuaig			7.	6.
Wm. Semple			10.	—.
Dn. Gilchrist			12.	—.
D. McLugash			10.	—.
Dn. Taylor Stocking Weaver		1.	5.	—.
Ard. Gillies Shoemaker for Loft of said house.			15.	—.
Hector Beaton			7.	6.
Dn. Cameron			12.	—.
Mrs. A. McLean			7.	6.
Tom Spaden & Neil McIntosh Smith		3.	—.	—.
Dugal Carmichael feuduty		1.	—.	—.
		132.	1.	7½.
		2.	4.	3

Farms	Tenants	£	s.	d.
Deductions				
Talent	The widow of D. McIntyre only pays the old rent for 4d. land of this farm till Whits. 1800 so that the difference falls to be deducted from the rental being	£1.	14.	7½
Mulrish	The one half of the rise on the Farm for this year paid to Agnes Campbell for giving up his lease of it and of this half of Loagine being	7.	3.	8.
Balliclach	The Tack of this farm does not expire till Whit 1800 tho Mr. McGibbon purchased the Lease from the tenants so that it only falls to pay the old rent of £17. 2. 11. for 2 years the difference therefore between the old rent and the new rent which is £25 Stg. falls to be deduced being	7.	17.	1.
Gruinart	The Augmentation of 10d. land of this form kept possession of by the Tenants at the old rent till Whit. 1799 falls to be deduced being	7.	2.	7.
		23.	17.	11.
Portnahaven	Page II Lot No. 1. The 12/ omitted to be added to this page.			
		£9149.	—.	—.

Appendix

Missives and Tacks of Farms 1769–1802

Missive Tack of Storgag 1769

and

Tenants of Storgaig & Balliclach
To Shawfield 1779 Wrote
N 30 no kelp Kilmeny

and

Note anent Storkaig 1776

and

Tack

and

Walter Campbell of
Shawfield Esqr
To
McVurrichs & Others
1777
Compd
Storkaig & Balliclach
N 30
£34.10

Isla House   19th Septemr 1769

Sir,

Whereas by an Obligatory Missive of this date you have agreed to grant us a tack of the Eighteen part Land of Storgag for Nine years from and after the term of Whitsunday next Therefore wee hereby oblige us our Heirs and Successors to pay to you or your ffactors A yearly Rent of Twenty pound Str during the currency of said Nine years and that under the penalty of Ten pounds Str

his

To Daniel Campbell
of Shawfield Esqr   Murdoch   McVurrich

mark

(signed)   DUNCAN MCAT[HUR]

his

Charles   McAlister

mark

(signed)   MARTIN MCDEARMID

Woodhall   6th Feb: 1773

Sir,

Whereas by your Missive of this date agreeing to give us a Twenty One years Tack of the Eighteen part Land of Storgaig and of the Eighteen part Land of

Balliclach Therefore Wee Duncan McCarter and Dond McVurrich Tenants in
Storgaig and taking burden for our two brothers Neil McCarter and Murdoch
McVurich Do herby oblige us to pay you a Rent of Thirty four pounds Ten
Shillings Sterl for each year of the said twenty one from and after Whitsunday
1779 Also to pay the publicks payle out of the said Lands in order and proportion
with the Tennants of Isla who obtained Tack in 1769 Also obliges us to pay you
a Grassum of Fifty pound Sterl at Whitsunday next or to pay the Same with
Interest at or before Whitsunday 1778 The which last if wee fail in then you are at
freedom to dispose of the Lands as you find proper and all these wee oblige
ourselves under the penalty of Seventy pound Sterl payle by us to you In Witness
whereof we have signed this Missive wrote by Gilbert McCulloch Servt to
Shawfield and before these witnesses Daniel Sinclair Sert to Shawfield and the sd
Gilbert McCulloch not only as wittnesses to our signing this missive but as
specially called to witness the meaning of parties

                                        (signed)   DUNCAN MA[cARTHUR]
                          his
        Dond   McVurrich
                          mark

To Daniel Campbell of
Shawfield Esqr   (signed)   GILBR MCULLOCH witness
                                                   DANiel SINCLAIR witness

Martin McDiarmid in the Tack comes in place of Neil McArthur & John
McEachern in Kilmeny comes in place of Duncan McArthur now Deceasd
                                                   Signed   N MG
Islay House 26th Oct 1776

        N 30
The TACK for the Eighteen part land of STORKAIG and the Eighteen part land
of BALLICLACH for TWENTY ONE years from Whitsunday 1779 for
a RENT of £34.10 Sterling was compiled in 1777 and signed on the 6th October
1778 by
                                        Wa: CAMPBELL
                                        JOHN MCEACHARN
                                        MARTIN MCDEARMID
        "At the special command of the above designed Murdoch and Donald
        McVurrichs who declare they cannot write and have severally touched our
        Penns We Neil McGibbon and Angus Taylor Notarys Public and Co,
        Notarys in the premises for them subscribe
                                        (signed)   NEIL MACGIBBON N.P.
                                                   ANGUS TAYLOR N.P.
Before these Witnesses
        COLIN CAMPBELL Tacksman of Carn beg
        LACHLAN MCLACHLAN Preacher of the Gospel in Isla
        ALEXR FFRASER Officer of the Customs
        CUTHBERT CAMPBELL Ground Officer in Isla

Missive
Alex. McCheckeran
Alex McNeil & others
to
Shawfield
for the Rent and Grassum
of Smail and Migrim
1777 Wrote
No. 17

(The original is in the Islay Estate Papers)

Woodhall   9th ffeb: 1773

Sir,

Whereas by your Missive to us of this date agreeing that wee Neil McCheckeran now in Grunard Alexr McNeil in Corrary Archd McCheckeran in Grunard Angus McIlvile there and Ronald McVurrich there are to have Twenty two years Tack of the lands of Small and Migram in Isla from and after Whitsunday 1779 that is one third of the same to the said Neil McCheckeran and the other two thirds equally divided betwixt the other four. Therefore, We hereby oblige us to Grant you a Grassum of One hundred and Eighty pound Stirlg for the same at the term of Whitsunday next and to pay you a Rent of Sixty pound Sterlg for each year of the said twenty two years also to pay the whole annual publicks payle out of the said lands in rate & proportion with the Tenants of Isla who obtained Tacks in 1769 and we hereby agree that if we do not pay the said Grassum at Whitsunday 1778 Then we are not to expect the above mentioned Tack and you are at freedom to dispose of the said Lands as you see proper and these conditions we enter into under the penalty of one hundred pounds money aforsaid payle by us to you.

(signed)   NEIL McEAUCHIRN
           ALEXR McNIALE
           his
Angus   McIlvile
           mark

To Daniel Campbell of
   Shawfield

TACK No. 17.

To   NEIL MacEACHERN 1/3
     ARCHIBALD MacEACHERN, ALEXANDER MacNEILL
     ANGUS MacILVOIL and RONALD MacVURRICH 2/3
     equally betwixt them. . . .

STANDARD TACK.
SPECIAL CLAUSE: "Reserving there from the seaware for Kelp which is to be
        at the disposal of the Proprietor.
DURATION: 22 Years from Whitsunday 1779.
RENT: £60 Sterling.
"In witness whereof these presents consisting of this and the three preceeding
pages of Stamped Paper wrote by Archie MacGibbon Clerk to Neill MacGibbon
Writer in Inveraray are subscribed by the said parties as follows vizt by the said
Walter Campbell at Islay House the 14th day of October One thousand Seven
Hundred and Seventy Eight years before these Witnesses the said Neil McGibbon
and Donald Bell his Servitor."

Missive
Curry & Others
To
Shawfield
Part of Lickosnich
1778
2 Tacks to be extended on this
(signed) A. MQ.

(2 Tacks, one for each portion of Leckoshnish were drawn out to commence at
Whitsunday 1779.)
    The first Tack, dated 31. 8. 1779, is signed by Walter Campbell, witnessed by
Saml Crawford, Surgeon in Islay, Gilbert Curry, Ground Officer there, William
Pearson at Islay House, Neil MacGibbon, and Donald Bell his servitor. Malcolm
Curry alias McVastan Dugald & Archibald MacLeans who declare they cannot
write "touch our pense, Mr. Neil MacGibbon & Angus Taylor Notarys Publick
& Co-notarys in the premisses Do not subscribe for them."
    The second Tack in favour of Mrs. Campbell of Ballinaby, John & Donald
Leitches, is only signed by Walter Campbell and the copy has not been delivered.
    (All originals are in the Islay Estate Papers.)

                                        Islay House   5th October 1778
Sir,
    As By your Missive to us of this date you have agreed to Grant us Malcolm
Curry alias McVastan in Lick Dugald & Archd McLeans now in Foreland
nineteen years lease of that part of Leckosnish lying on the Grulin side of Liog (the
burn running out of Loch Corr into Loch Gorm) & to us Donald & John Leitches
the one half on that part of Lickosnish lying upon the Lick side of Leog & on

which the houses of Lick stand, & that exclusive of Gartaholl, Mrs. Campbell of Balinaby & us the said Dond & John Leitches having Liberty of Grasing our yeald Cattle & Sheep in common with the said McVastan & McLeans on the Gruline side of Lick except in the end of Harvest when the yeald Cattle & Sheep are brought to the Stubble, at which time the Cattle of each must grase on their own stubble and that also for Nineteen years. Therefore we the saids Malcolm Curry & Dugald & Archd McLeans oblige us to pay the sum of £25 pounds Str money of yearly rent & Twenty four Hens & Twenty four dozen of Eggs yearly for that part of Lick on the Gruline side with the Burden of grasing above mentioned And we the said Donald & John Leitches for ourselves and Mrs. Campbell of Balinaby oblige us to pay Fifteen Pounds Sterling money of yearly rent for that part of Lickosnish on the Lick side of Leog with the Liberty of grasing above mentd & we the said Leitches oblige us to pay four hens and four dozen eggs each yearly, and the whole of us oblige us to Implement the other Conditions of the Tacks of Islay and to Implement this Missive under penalty of Thirty pounds Sterl & we are

Your Hnrs Servts
his   their
John   Leitch   Malcolm   Curry
mark   his
Dond   Leitch   Dugd   McLean
mark
Angs   McLean
marks

To Walter Campbell of
Shawfield Esqr   Neil MacGibbon   Witness

N   16
Quarter Land of
CONOSBY
This TACK, compiled in 1777, was granted to
ARCHIBALD BELL
DONALD BELL
MALCOLM & DUGALD MACGILESPIES
NEIL MACLEAN
ALEXANDER CURRY
HECTOR MACALESTER
ARCHIBALD MACNIVEN
at a yearly Rent of £54 sterling for TWENTY TWO years from WHITSUN-DAY 1779. The conditions are the same as the other Tacks of this date.
The Tack was signed on the 3rd October 1778 at Islay House by
Walter Campbell
Malcolm Gillespy
Archibald Niven
Archibald Bell
Neill McLean

"At the special command of Alexr McVurrich, Donald Bell, Hector McAlester & Dugald Gillespy above designed who declared they cannot write and have severally touched our Penns We Neil MacGibbon & Angus Taylor Notaries Public and Co, Notaries in the premissed for them subscribe

(signed)   Neil MacGibbon N.P.
Angus Taylor N.P.

Before these Witnesses Coll Campbell, Tacksman of Sannaig Duncan McLellan Ground Officer in Islay, James McNab at Kilbranan

MISSIVE
SHAWFIELD
to
RONd JOHNSTONE
1773

(The original is among the Kildalton Papers.)

Isla House   3d Septe 1773

Sir,

WHEREAS BY your missive to me of this date you have obliged yourself to pay me a Rent of Fifteen pounds sterling money yearly for the Space of Nineteen years from & after Whity Seventeen Hundred and Seventy Nine years ALSO to pay the whole public Burdens affecting the same Lands Ministers Stipends Schoolmaster & Surgeons Sallery Pacquet money and others payts out of the said Lands and that in Rate and proportion with other Tenants in Isla who have obtained Tacks from me this year AS ALSO to pay you a Grassum of Twenty five pounds Sterling money with Interest on or before Whity Seventeen Hundred and Seventy Eight years agreeing if you fail in this last condition that you are not to expect a Tack from me – Therefore I hereby promise that how soon you make payt of the said Grassum Principal and Interest I am to grant you a Tack of the 12/– land of the half of Corrary & Couralach for the space of nineteen years from and after Whity Seventeen hundred and Seventy nine years – UNDER the penalty of Thirty pounds Sterling money – And am

Yours & c
(signed)   D. Campbell

The half of Corrary and Courlach in Rond Johnstones Possession as the Land above Sett.

(signed)   D. Campbell

To Ronald Johnstone
Tenant in Corrary

TACK

WALTER CAMPBELL of

SHAWFIELD ESQr

to

JOHNSTONES

1777

Compd

1/2 CORRARY & COURAALOCH

N21

£15. Stg.

(The original is among the Kildalton Papers)

IT IS CONTRACTED AGREED AND FINALLY ENDED betwixt the parties following TO WITT Walter Campbell of Shawfield Esquire Heretable proprietor of the Lands and others underwritten ON THE ONE PART, and Ronald Johnstone, Alexander Johnstone and Archibald Johnstone ON THE OTHER PART, THAT IS TO SAY the said Walter Campbell has Sett and in Tack and Assedation Letts and by these presents for payment of the Tack duty and performance of the whole other Conditions and prestations after mentioned SETTS to the said Ronald, Alexander, Archibald Johnstones their heirs and successors expressly secluding and debarring Assignees and Subtenants ALL and WHOLE the one equal half of the Lands of Corrary and Couraloch being Twelve Shilling Land with the houses, Biggings, Yards, Mosses, mures, meadows, Grazings, Sheildings, parts, pendicles, and pertinents thereof as the same is presently possessed Lying within the Parish of Kildalton, Island of Islay and Sherriffdom of Argyle AND THAT for the space and term of NINETEEN full and compleat years and Cropts from and after their entry thereto which is hereby declared to begin and Commence as to the House, Grass and Pasturage of said Lands at the term of Whitsunday Jaivyc and Seventy nine years and to the Arrable Land at the separation of the Cropt from the Grounds the said year AND TO BE from thence furth peaceably possessed and enjoyed by the saids Ronald, Alexander and Archibald Johnstone's and their foresaids during this Tack WHICH TACK the said Walter Campbell BINDS and OBLIGED him his heirs and successors in his Lands and Estate of Islay to warrant to the said tenants and their foresaids at all hands and against all deadly as Law will FOR THE WHICH CAUSES AND ON THE OTHER PART the saids Ronald, Alexander and Archibald Johnstone's BIND AND OBLIGE them their heirs Executors and Successors and Intromitters with their goods and gear whotsoever Thankfully to Content and pay to the said Walter Campbell his heirs or assignees or to his or their ffactors or Chamberlains in his or their names the sum of Fifteen pounds Sterling money yearly in the name of Silver Tack duty and Tiends formerly in use to be paid out of the said Lands, beginning the first terms payment thereof at the term of Martinmas Jaivyc and Seventy nine years and so furth to continue the punctual payment of the said Silver Tack duty at the term of Martinmass yearly thereafter during this Tack with one fifth part more of Liquidate penalty and expences incase of Failzie and Annualrent of the said Tack duty from and after the term of payment during the not payment AND the said tenants BIND and OBLIGE them and their foresaids to make payment to the said Walter Campbell or his above written of the sum of Fifteen Shillings Sterling yearly in lieu of the Court Maill dues and Compearance money formerly in use to be paid out of the said Lands AS ALSO to make payment at the said terms of Martinmas yearly of the proportion effiering to the Lands hereby sett of the sum of three Shillings and fourpence Sterling the Quarter Land toward the support of the Minister of the third erection in Islay, and to join with the other Tenants of Islay in carrying materials for Building and Repairing the Churches and Manses when necessary AND FURTHER the said Tenants BIND and OBLIGE them and their foresaids to bring their whole grindable Corns of whatever kind growing upon the said Lands to be Ground at the Miln used and wont and to pay the Accustomed Multure therefore, and to perform their proportions of the

(signed)   Wa: CAMPBELL
Ronald Johnstone
(very indistinct)

Service necessary for keeping in proper the miln dam and Lead and bringing Milnstones thereto AND that they shall bring their whole Iron work to the Common Smiddy and pay the ordinary dues and Services therefor AS ALSO that they shall bring the whole flax to be Raised by them on the said Lands to be dressed at either of the flax Milns of Skerrols or Lagavulline and to pay the accustomed dues therefore AND that they shall bring the whole woolen Cloth which they shall Manufacture in Ilay to be waulked and dressed at the Walk Miln of Skerrols for payment of the accustomed duties AND FURTHER the said tenants BIND and OBLIGE them and their foresaid to make payment of the equal proportion with the other tenants of Islay of the Schoolmasters and Surgeons Sallarys and of one Shilling in the Pound of Valued Rent of Road-money in terms of the Act of Parliament past in the [ ] of his present Majesty, AND that they shall also make regular payment of Cess and other publick burdens and Impositions Imposed or to be Imposed upon the said Lands during this Tack And that they shall Cutt and Cause Cutt their peats yearly in a regular and proper manner as they shall be directed by the Bailie of Islay for the time being or to pay Six pounds Scots toties Quoties for each Irregular Cutt and they FURTHER OBLIGED them and their foresaids to give proper suit and presence to the Baillie Courts of Islay so often as they shall be Called thereto and to obtemper and fulfill the whole acts Statutes and regulations thereof otherwise be subject and Liable to the pains and penalties to be imposed on Transgressors for contumacy or other: wise AND as it is highly material for the Improvement and Good order of the Country that marches be Straightened and proper march Dykes built betwixt the different farms the said tenants oblige them and their foresaids when required by the said Walter Campbell or his above written NOT ONLY to Straighten Marches BUT ALSO to exchange pieces of Ground with the neighbouring farms and if such exchange Cannot Conveniently be made to give of such pieces of ground as the propreitor or his factor shall Judge necessary to be added to any adjoining farm the tenants being allowed in this last case a proportional abatement of their Rent as the same shall be ascertained by one person to be named by the proprietor or his ffactor and another to be named by the tenants with power to the said persons in Case of Variance to choose an Oversman to determine the difference AND FURTHER the said Tenants OBLIGE them and their foresaids to take in and Cultivate from heathy mossy or Coarse pasture Ground a proportion effeiring to four acres in the Quarter Land yearly to be manured Lime sand or marle AS ALSO that they shall plant their potatoes in new ground which never bore a Grain Cropt and whatever extent of new Ground is so planted with potatoes shall be Considered as part of the above four Acres in the Quaterland and failing of their so doing the said tenants their foresaids shall be subject and Liable in payment to the proprietor of ten Shillings Sterling yearly for each acre they shall be short of the said number or Rate of four acres in the Quarter Land to be applied as he may think proper and the said Tenants LIKEWISE BIND and OBLIGE them and their foresaids that they shall not plough up any of the meadow Grounds of the said Lands at any time during the five last years of this Tack nor over Cropt nor Run out the arrable Lands but that they shall keep the same in Good Heart and tilth

(signed)   Wa: Campbell
Ronald Johnstone

and that they shall have a third of their Wintertown Lee yearly during this Tack and leave one full third thereof Lee the year of their Removal under the penalty of forefeiting the one third of the Wintertown Cropt to the Interent tenant AND the said tenants FURTHER OBLIGE them and their foresaids to perform four days Service of four men and Eight horses yearly for each Quarter Land and so on in proportion for a greater or a lesser extent it being always optional to the said Walter Campbell or his foresaids either to exact the said Service or in lieu thereof one Shilling Sterling per diem for each man and two horses AND the said tenants FURTHER OBLIGE them and their foresaids that they shall not at any time Carry or use fire arms or kill Game of any kind, and they shall not with Nets Rods or spears Slay or kill Black fish or use bleezes on any of the waters or Burns within the Island of Islay, and that they shall not keep Setting dogs greyhound or other dogs that may be destructive to the Game otherwise if they be detected they shall forefiet and pay to the proprietor Twenty Shillings Sterling for the first offence, forty Shillings Sterling for the Second and in Case of a third offence they shall forfeit this Tack AND IT IS HEREBY EXPRESSLY PROVIDED AND DECLARED THAT the said tenants or their foresaid shall not at any time during this Tack keep Changehouses Tipling Houses or Malt Kilns on the said Lands that they shall not import buy or Sell any foreign spirits nor vend in wholesale or retail malt or Spiritous Liquors of any kind without having a Special License for that purpose under the penalty of forty Shillings Sterling for the first offence and doubling that sum for every after offence AND IT IS FURTHER EXPRESSLY PROVIDED AND DECLARED that the said Walter Campbell or his foresaids shall have the Liberty at any time during this Tack to Inclose and use any Wood Grounds on the said Lands that he may think necessary and sell and manufacture the same woods, and that they shall also have Liberty to work any mines of Lead Silver or Copper that may be found on the said Lands and to carry away the same or dispose of such mines as they may think proper during this Tack, they allways paying to the tenants the damages they may sustain thereby as the same shall be Ascertained by two honest men to be Mutually Chosen AND the said tenants FURTHER BIND and OBLIGE them and their foresaids to build their proportion of march dykes with their neighbours when required and that they shall uphold and keep inproper Repair the whole Houses and Biggings on the said lands during this Tack and leave the same in a Sufficient tenantable Condition at their Removall, they being allways at Liberty to claim payment from the Interant tenants of the price of the timber of the said Houses according to the custom of the country of Islay to Carry Sand Limestone and Marle from the said Lands they paying the Damage the Corn and Grass may sustain hereby at the sight of two sworn Birleymen BUT DECLARING THAT no marle is to be Carried off the Lands without the proprietors consent had and obtained in writing AND the said tenants ALSO OBLIGE them and their foresaids that they shall flitt and Remove from the Lands hereby sett at the Expiration of this Tack without the necessity of a warning or other process of Law for that purpose AND IT IS HEREBY FURTHER EXPRESSLY PROVIDED AND DECLARED that NOT ONLY in the rent of one years Tack duty Running in to the second

(signed)   Wa: CAMPBELL
RONALD JOHNSTONE

Unpaid BUT ALSO upon the said tenants and their foresaids their failure in performance of any of the Conditions above mentioned THEN and IN THAT CASE this present Tack shall become ipso Facto void and Null AND it shall be Lawfull to the said Walter Campbell or his foresaids to sett use and dispose of the said Lands as if this present Tack and agreement had never been entered into and that without any Declarator or Process of Law whatever AND LASTLY BOTH PARTIES BIND AND OBLIGE them and their foresaids to perform their respective parts of the premises to each other under the penalty of FIFTEEN pounds Sterling to be paid by the party failling to the party observor or willing to observe the same by and attour performance AND THEY CONSENT to the Registration hereof in the Books of Council and Session or others Competent that Letters of Horning on Six days Charge and all other Execution necessary may pass and be directed hereon in form as Effiers and for that Effect THEY CONSTITUTE THEIR PRORS & ca in witness thereof these presents consisting of this and the three preceeding pages of Stamped paper wrote by Archibald McGibbon Clerk to Neil MacGibbon writer in Inverary ARE SUBSCRIBED by the said parties at Islay House the fifth day of October One thousand Seven hundred and Seventy Eight years before these Witnesses the said Neil MacGibbon above designed and Donald Bell his Servitor the place and date of signing and Witnesses names and designations being Insert by the said Neil MacGibbon above designed Alexr and Archd Johnston being now dead

(signed)	NEIL MACGIBBON Witness	Wa: Campbell
	DONO BELL Witness	Ronald Johnston

MISSIVES AND SUMMARIES OF TACKS
EXTRACTS From RENT ROLLS – 1773 to 1802
Clagen – original among Kildalton Papers
Talant
Upper and Lower Corrary
Courloch
Torodale
Lagavulline
Ardtalla

<u>(originals among the Islay Estate Papers)</u>

Missive for Talant

Woodhall   27th January 1773

Sir,
WHEREAS by your Missive of this date you have agreed to grant us a Tack
of the Twenty Shilling Land of Talant for Twentyone years from and after
Whitsunday 1779 Therefore we hereby oblige us to pay you a Rent of Thirty
One Pounds Seventeen Shillings and Sixpence Str. for each year of said twentyone years also oblige us to pay the whole Publics payle out of the said Lands and
that in rate and proportion with the Tenants of Islay who obtained Tacks in 1769
as also obliges us to pay you a Grassum of Thirty one pounds Stl at the term of
Whitsunday next or with interest from the said term of Whitsunday to any term
or period at or before Lammas 1778 wee oblige us to make good otherwise you
shall be at full Liberty to sett use or dispose of the said Lands at your pleasure and
all these under the penalty of Fifty pounds Stl In witness whereof we have signed
this Missive wrote by Gilbert MacCulloch Servant to Shawfield and the said
Gilbert MacCulloch not only as witnesses to our signing this Missive but as
witnesses specially called to the meaning of parties.

				his	
		John			Brown
				mark	
To Daniel Campbell of					
Shawfield				his	
Gilbert MacCulloch		Witness	Dond		McIntyre
Daniel Sinclair		Witness		mark	

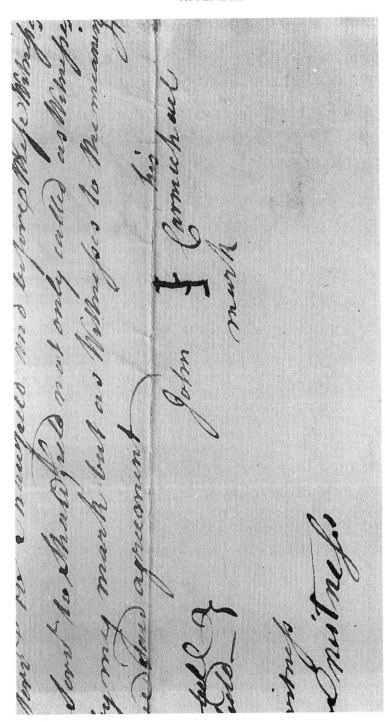

18 Extract from Missive for Tack of the Eighteen Part Land of Claggan, Kildalton, 1773, signed by the Mark of John Carmichael, whose direct descendants live in Canada. Kildalton Papers. *Photograph by Fraser MacArthur.*

Two Copies of Lease and Missive

TACK	FARM	TENANT	TENURE	RENT
No. 66	Talant	John Brown	from	£31:17:6 st
	20/– land	Donald McIntyre	Whitsund	
		as possessed by	1779	
		them and others		
			1777	
			compd	

STANDARD LEASE

"subsribed at Islay House the 14th day of October, One thousand seven hundred and seventy eight years before these Witness Neil MacGibbon, Writer in Inveraray, and Donald Bell, his Clerk.

(signed)   Wa: CAMPBELL
                                              not signed by the Tenants

Copy Delivered

TACK	FARM	TENANTS	TENURE	RENT
	Talant	Donald Johnstone	19 years	£47.1. 8
		John Johnstone	from	
		Duncan Brown	Whitsun	
		Neil Brown	1802	
		Hugh McDougall		

STANDARD LEASE

"written upon this and the three preceeding pages of stamped Paper by Robert Maxwell Apprentice to Neil MacGibbon Writer in Inveraray are subscribed by the said parties at Islay House the ffirst day of October eighteen hundred and four years before these witnesses Samuel Crawford, Surgeon in Islay and the said Neil MacGibbon before designed. The name *Neil* in place of *John* Brown being insert by the said Neil MacGibbon before signing and the place and date of signing and Witnesses names and designation being filled up by him Declaring that this proportion of the farm occupied by Duncan Johnstone is reserved from this Tack to be disposed of as the proprietor pleases.

(signed)   Wa: CAMPBELL
                                                   DONALD JOHNSTONE
                                                      JOHN JOHNSTONE
Neil MacGibbon Witness   DUNn BROWN
Samuel Crawford Witness   NEIL BROWN
                                                   HUGH MACDOUGALL

Copy Delivered

TACK	FARM	TENANT	TENURE	RENT
	Upper Corrary	Archd Adair	19 years from Whitsun 1802	£21. 8. Ost.

STANDARD LEASE

Signed in Islay House the 18th day of October one thousand eight hundred and four years before these witnesses Samuel Crawford, Surgeon in Islay and Neil MacGibbon, Writer in Inverary

WA: CAMPBELL
(signed)   ARCHd ADAIR
    Samuel Crawford
    Neil MacGibbon

Copy Delivered

TACK	TENANTS	FARM	TENURE	RENT
	John McQueen Duncan McKerrel as presently possessed by them	Courloch	19 years from Whitsun 1802	£14. 19. 6. St.

STANDARD LEASE

"written upon this and the three preceeding pages of stamped paper by Robert Maxwell Apprentice to Neil MacGibbon, Writer in Inveraray., are subscribed by the said parties in Islay the twelfth day of September one thousand eight hundred and five years before these Witnesses the said Neil MacGibbon and Samuel Crawford, Surgeon in Islay, being concerted and agreed upon before Signing that John Johnston in Lower Corrary shall be a party to this lease for the land he possesses, for which he is to pay yearly £11. 4. 8. sterling at the Term before mentioned and to implement and perform the whole other conditions prestable by the Tenants of Couraloch and himself and contained in the foresaid Lease in proportion to the extent of Land each of them occupy. The place, date of signing and Witnesses names and designations with this addition being all insert by the said Samuel Crawford before signing

(signed)   WA: CAMPBELL
NEIL MACGIBBON Witness   JOHN McQUEEN
SAMUEL CRAWFORD Witness   DUNCAN McKERROL
                                             JOHN JOHNSON
      [not the same signature for ARDTALL[n] or TALLANT]

Copy Delivered

TACK	FARM	TENANTS	TENURE	RENT
	Torodale	Donald Johnston	19 years	£64. 4. 0. st.
		Alexr McQuilkan	from	
		Dunn McQuilkan	Whitsun	
		Alexr MacDougall	1802	
		Dunn MacDougall		
		Dugald Carmichael		
		Donald McDiarmid		
		all tenants in		
		Torodale		

STANDARD LEASE

SPECIAL CLAUSE Reserving Kelp to the Proprietor. "subscribed by the said parties in Islay the sixth day of October one thousand eight hundred and four years before these Witnesses Samuel Crawford, Surgeon in Islay, and Neil MacGibbon, Writer in Inveraray, written by Donald Bell, Clerk to said Neil MacGibbon."

(signed)
SAMUEL CRAWFORD Witness
NEIL MACGIBBON Witness

WA: CAMPBELL
DONALD JOHNSTONE
ALEXANDER MCQUILKAN
DUNCAN McQUILKAN
DUNCAN McDOUGALL
for self & brother Alex
DUGALD CARMICHAEL
DONALD MCDIARMID

Copy Returned

TACK	FARM	TENANT	TENURE	RENT
	1/2 Ardtalla	John Johnstone	19 years	£77. 0. 9.
	1/2 Laggavuline	in Lagavuline	from	
			Whitsun	
			1802	
			(compd)	

STANDARD LEASE

SPECIAL CLAUSE Kelp reserved to the Proprietor "written upon this and the two preceeding pages of Stamped Paper by Donald Bell Clerk to Neil MacGibbon, Writer in Inverary, are subscribed by the said parties as follows viz. by the said Walter Campbell at Bridgend in Islay House the 7th day of October one thousand eight hundred and two years before these Witnesses Lachlan Currie residing in Daill and the said Donald Bell and by the said John Johnston also at

Bridgend the nineteenth day of the said month of October and year foresaid before these witnesses the saids Lachlan Currie and Donald Bell

(signed)
Lachlan Currie Witness
Dond Bell Witness   Wa: CAMPBELL
Lachlan Currie Witness
Dond Bell Witness   JOHN JOHNSTON
                                            (not the same signature as at Talant)

MISSIVE LETTER
The Tennants of
BARR
To
SHAWFIELD
1775
Tack Extended
1777
No. 47

Islay House   23rd Octr 1775

Sir,
    WHEREAS by your Missive to me of this date you have bound and obliged yourself to Grant us a Tack of the Quarter Land of Barr for Space of Nineteen Years from Whitsunday one thousand Seven hundred and Seventy nine years and that within Twelve Months from and after this date Therefore we hereby Bind and Oblige us Conly and Seally to make Payment to you, your heirs or ffactor's in Your Name of the Sum of Thirty two pounds ten Shillings St. money of Yearly Rent for the said Quarter Land of Barr during the said Space ALSO to make payment of the whole Publick Burdens affecting the said Lands during the mentioned and that in Rate and proportion with other Tenants in Islay who have obtained a Tack from you in Summer One thousand Seven hundred & Seventy three – all which Conditions we Bind and Oblige us Conly and Seally to Stand by and abide at under the Penalty of Thirty-two pounds St. Money and we are Sir

Your Most obedt. humle Servants

his

<table>
<tr><td></td><td>Duncan</td><td>McEachearn</td><td>8 shilling</td></tr>
</table>

To   Daniel   Campbell

Esq

of Shawfield

mark
her

<table>
<tr><td>Mary</td><td>McVurrich</td><td>4 Do</td></tr>
</table>

mark

<table>
<tr><td>(signed)</td><td>LACHLAN McDUGALD</td><td>6 Do</td></tr>
<tr><td>(signed)</td><td>SAMUEL MACDOUGALL</td><td>4 Do</td></tr>
<tr><td>(signed)</td><td>DUGALD CAMPBELL</td><td>4 Do</td></tr>
</table>

his

<table>
<tr><td>Duncan Reid</td><td>6 Do</td></tr>
</table>

mark

Quarter Land of
BARR

The TACK, compiled in 1777 and on the same terms as others of this date, was granted to

<table>
<tr><td>DUNCAN MACEACHERN</td><td>eight shilling land thereof</td></tr>
<tr><td>MARY McVURRICH</td><td></td></tr>
<tr><td>SAMUEL MACDOUGALL</td><td>four shilling land thereof each</td></tr>
<tr><td>DUGd CAMPBELL</td><td></td></tr>
<tr><td>DUNCAN REID</td><td></td></tr>
<tr><td>LACHLAN MACDOUGALL</td><td>six shilling land thereof each</td></tr>
</table>

It was signed by Walter Campbell at Islay House on the 31st August 1779 Neil MacGibbon, Writer in Inverary, and Donald Bell his Servitor. The Tenants have not signed and the copy has not been delivered.

MISSIVE
The Tenants of
TIGHCARMOGAN
To
DANIEL CAMPBELL
OF SHAWFIELD Esq.
1776
TIGHCARMOGAN
£52 Str
Kildalton
1777 Wrote
N 24

(The original is among the Kildalton Papers.)

Islay House   9th Oct. 1776

Sir,
        Whereas by your Missive to us of this date you have bound and obliged
yourself to grant us a Tack of the Quarter Land of Tighcarmogane for the Spce of
Nineteen years from Whitsunday One Thousand Seven Hundred and Seventy
nine years according to the Division following To witt Robert MacKerrol Eight
Shilling land, Duncan MacKerrol four shilling, James Kerr two shilling, Neil
& James Cameron four Shilling, Wm Gilchrist two Sh: and Alexr Johnstone four
Sh: and that to be delivered you within ffifteen months from and after this date
Therefore we Bind and Oblige us to make payment to you your Heirs or ffactors
in your name of the Sum of fifty two pounds Sterling money of yearly rent
during this Tack as Also to make payment of the whole publick Burdens affecting
the said Lands and that in rate and proportion with other Tenants in Islay who
have obtained Tacks from you in Summer One thousand Seven hundred and
Seventy three Excepting from the Lands above mentioned the House of Gayskeir
with the Croft thereto belonging and the Grass of two Cows and One Horse and
that with the horses and Cows of Tighcarmogane which is to be given to the said
Neil Cameron besides the above possession the rent of which to be paid by him to
us in proportion to the rent above mentioned as the same shall be ascertained by
two judicious men to be mutually Chosen and we hereby oblige us to allow the
Tenants of Tighandrome liberty of Carrying sea ware for Manure from the shore
of the said Lands They paying the Damage the Grass and Corn may Sustain
thereby, all which Conditions we Bind and Oblige us to implement under the
penalty of Fifty two pounds Sterling money ----- and we are

Sir
Your most Obedt Servts

To Daniel Campbell of   (signed) Robt MacKerrol
Shawfield Esque   Dunc McKerall
                                                              James Kerr
                                                              James Cameron
                                                              Thomas Calder
                                                              John Campbell
                                                            Alexander Johnstone
                                                              Neil Cameron
          Thomas Calder for William Gilchrist

MISSIVE
DANIEL CAMPBELL
of SHAWFIELD
Esqr
to
The TENANTS of
TIGHCARMOGANE
1776
TIGHCARMOGANE

Islay House   9th October 1776
Sirs,
     Whereas by your Missive to me you have Bound and obliged yourselves to
make payment to me my Heirs or ffactors in my name of the Sum of Fifty two
pounds Str money of yearly rent for the Space of Nineteen years from Whitsunday one thousand Seven hundred and Seventy nine years and that for the quarter
Land of Tighcarmogane according to the division following To witt Robert
MacKerrol Eight Shilling land, Duncan MacKerrol four Shilling James Kerr two
Shilling and James Cameron four Shilling William Gilchrist two Shilling,
Thomas Calder four shilling, John Campbell four Shilling and *Alexander Johnstone* four Shilling AS ALSO to make payment of the whole publick burdens
affecting the said Lands and that in rate and proportion with other Tenants in
Islay who have obtained tacks from me in Summer One thousand Seven hundred
and Seventy three years. Therefore I oblige myself to Grant you a Tack of the said
Quarter Land of Tighcarmogane for the Space Of Nineteen years from Whitsunday One thousand Seven Hundred and Seventy nine years and that to be
delivered to you within ffifteen months from and after this date, Excepting from
the lands above mentioned the house of Gayskeir with the Croft thereto belonging and the Grass of two Cows and one Horse and that with the horses and Cows

of Tighcarmogane which the said Neil Cameron is to have over and above the above possession the rent of which to be paid by him to you in proportion to the rent above mentioned as the same shall be ascertained by two judicious men to be mutually Chosen with Liberty to the Tenants of Tighandrom to Carry sea ware from the Shore of the said Lands for Manure They paying the Damage the Corn and Grass may sustain thereby, all which Conditions I oblige me to implement under the penalty of Fifty two pounds Str money And am

Yours & c

(signed)   D. CAMPBELL

To
Robert MacKerrol in Torodale
Duncan MacKerrol in Kentraw
James Kerr James Cameron
Wm Gilchrist Thomas Calder
John Campbell *Alexdr Johnstone*
All Tenants in Tighcarmogane and
Neil Cameron in Lagavuline

TACK
WALTER CAMPBELL of
SHAWFIELD Esqr
To
MacKERROLLS & OTHERS
1777
TIGHCARMOGANE
N 24

£52
Copy Delivered
£2. 8.–

(The original is among the Kildalton Papers.)

IT IS CONTRACTED AGREED and FINALY ENDED betwixt the parties following TO WITT Walter Campbell of Shawfield Esqr heretable proprietor of the Lands and others under written ON THE ONE PART and Robert MacKerrol, Duncan MacKerroll, John Kerr, Neil Cameron, James Cameron, William Gilchrist, Thomas Calder, John Campbell and *Alexander Johnstone* ON THE OTHER PART THAT IS TO SAY the said Walter Campbell has SETT and in Tack and Assidation LETTS and by these presents for payment of the Tack duty and performance of the whole other Conditions and prestations after mentioned Setts to the saids Robert and Duncan MacKerrolls, John Kerr, Neil and James Camerons, William Gilchrist, Thomas Calder, John Campbell and Alexander Johnstone their heirs and Successors (expressly secluding and debarring assignees and subtenants) ALL and WHOLE the one Quarter Land of Tighcarmogan by the proportions following Vizt to the said Robert McKerroll an Eight Shilling land thereof, to the said Duncan MacKerroll a four shilling land thereof, to the said John Kerr a two Shilling Land thereof, to the said William Gilchrist a two Shilling Land thereof, to the said Thomas Calder a four Shilling land thereof, to the said John Campbell a four Shilling land thereof, and to the said Alexander Johnstone a four Shilling land thereof, with the houses, Biggings, mosses, muirs, meadows, grazings, Shieldings, parts, pendicles, and pertinents thereof, as the same is presently possessed, Lying within the Parish of Kildalton, Island of Islay and Sherriffdom of Argyle, Excepting and Reserving from the said Lands the House of Gayskeir with the Croft thereto belonging and the Grass of two Cows and one Horse and that with the horses and Cows of Tighcarmogan which is to be given to the said Neil Cameron besides the above possession the Rent of which to be paid by him to the other Tenants and that in Rate and proportion to the Rent of the said Lands as the same shall be ascertained by two Judicious men to be mutually Chosen Excepting also and Reserving therefrom full power and Liberty to the tenants of Tighandrom of Carrying what sea ware may be necessary for manuring their Lands from the shore of Tighcarmogan they paying the damages the Corn and Grass may sustain thereby, as also excepting and reserving therefrom the sea ware for Kelp which is to be at the disposal of the Proprietor AND THAT for the Space and term of Nineteen full and Compleat years and from and after their entry thereto which is hereby declared to begin and Commence as to the house Grass and pasturage of said Lands at the term of Whitsunday Haivyc and Seventy Nine years and to the arrable land at the separation of the Cropt from the ground the said year AND TO BE from thence furth peacably possessed and Enjoyed by the saids Robert and Duncan MacKerrolls, James Kerr, Neil and James Camerons, William Gilchrist, Thomas Calder, John Campbell, and Alexander Johnstone and their foresaid during this Tack WHICH TACK the said Walter Campbell BINDS and OBLIGES him his heirs and Successors in his Lands and Estate of Islay to warrant to the said Tenants and their foresaids at all hands and against all deadly as Law will FOR THE WHICH CAUSES and on the other part the said Robert and Duncan MacKerrolls, John Kerr, Neil and James Camerons, William Gilchrist, Thomas Calder, John Campbell and *Alexander Johnstone* Bind and OBLIGE themselves their heirs Executors and Successors and Intromitters with their Goods and gear whatsoever thankfully to Content and pay to the said Walter Campbell his heirs or assignees or to his or their ffactors or Chamberlains in his or their names the sum of FIFTY TWO pounds Sterling money yearly in the name of Silver Tack duty and tiends formerly in use to be paid out of the said Lands beginning the first terms payment thereof at the term of MARTINMASS Jaivyc and Seventy Nine years and so forth to Continue the punctuall payment of the said Silver tack duty at the term of Martinmas yearly thereafter during this Tack with one fifth part more of Liquidate penalty and expences in Case of Failzie and annualrent of the said Tack duty from and

after the term of payment during the not payment AND the said tenants BIND
and OBLIGE them

(signed)   Wa: CAMPBELL
DUNCAN MCKERRAL
JOHN CARR
NEIL CAMERON
JAMES CAMERON
THOMAS CALDER
JOHN CAMPBELL

NEIL MACGIBBON N P

and their foresaids to make payment to the said Walter Campbell or his above
written of the sum of Two pound twelve Shilling Sterling yearly in lieu of the
court Maill dues and Compearance money formerly in use to be paid out of the
said Lands AS ALSO to make payment at the said term of Martinmas yearly of
the proportion effiering to the Lands hereby Sett of the sum of three Shillings and
fourpence Sterling the Quarter Land towards the Support of the Minister of the
third Erection in Islay and to join with the other tenants of Islay in Carrying
materials for Building and Repairing the Churches and Manses when necessary
AND FURTHER the said tenants BIND and OBLIGE them and their foresaids
to bring their whole Grindable Corns of whatever kind growing upon the said
Lands to be ground at the Miln used and wont and to pay the accustomed
multures therefore and to perform their proportion of the Service necessary for
keeping in proper repair Miln Miln dam and Lead and bringing in Milnstones
thereto AND that they shall bring their whole Iron work to the Common
Smithy and pay the ordinary dues and Services therefore AS ALSO that they
shall bring the whole fflax to be raised by them on the said lands to be dressed at
either of the fflax Milns of Skerrolls or Lagavulline and to pay the Accustomed
dues therefor AND that they shall bring the whole woolen Cloath which they
shall manufacture in Islay to be waulked and dressed at the Waulk Miln of
Skerrols for payment of the Accustomed duties and FURTHER the said tenants
BIND and OBLIGE them and their foresaids to make payment of an equal
proportion with the other tenants of Islay of the Schoolmasters and Surgeons
Sallaries and of one Shilling in the pound of Valued Rent of Road money in
terms of the Act of Parliament past in the year of the Reign of his present Majesty
and that they shall also make regular payments of the Cess and other publick
burdens and Impositions imposed or to be imposed upon the said Lands during
this Tack AND that they shall Cutt and cause Cutt their peats yearly in a regular
and proper manner as they shall be directed by the Bailie of Islay for the time
being or to pay Six pounds Scots Toties Quoties for each irregular cutt And
further oblige them and their foresaids to give proper suit and presence to the
Bailie Courts of Islay so often as they shall be Called thereto and to obtemper and
fulfill the whole Acts Statutes and Regulations thereof otherwise be Subject and
liable to the Pains and penalties to be imposed on Transgressor for Contumacy or
otherwise AND as it is highly material for the Improvement and Good order of
the Country that marches be straightened and proper March Dykes built betwixt
the different farms the said tenants oblige them and their foresaids when required

by the said Walter Campbell or his above written NOT ONLY to straighten Marches BUT ALSO to exchange pieces of Ground with the neighbouring farms and if such exchange cannot Conveniently be made, to give off such pieces of grounds as the proprietor or his ffactor Judge necessary to be added to any adjoining farm the tenants being allowed in this last Case a proportionall abatement of their Rent as the same shall be ascertained by one person to be named by the proprietor or his ffactor and another to be named by the tenants with power to the said persons in Case of Variance to Choose an oversman to determine the difference AND FURTHER the said Tenants OBLIGE them and their foresaids to take in and Cultivate from heathy mossy or coarse pasture Ground a proportion Effiering to four acres in the Quarter land yearly to be manured with Lime sand or Marle as also that they shall plant their potatoes yearly in new Ground which never bore a grain Cropt and whatever Extent of new Ground is so planted with new potatoes shall be considered as part of the above four acres in the Quarterland and failing of their doing so the said tenants and their foresaids shall be subject and liable in payment to the proprietor of ten shillings Sterling yearly for each acre they shall be short of the said number or Rate of four acres in the Quarter land to be applied as he may think proper AND the said tenants LIKEWISE BIND and OBLIGE them and their foresaids that they shall not plough up any of the meadow Grounds of the said Lands at any time during the five last years of this Tack nor over Cropt nor Run out the Arrable lands but that they shall keep the same in good heart and tilth and that they shall have a third of their wintertoun lee yearly during this tack and leave one full third thereof lee the year of their Removal under penalty of forfeiting the one third of the wintertown cropt to the Interant tenants AND the said tenants FURTHER OBLIGE them and their foresaids to perform four days Service of four men and Eight horses yearly for each Quarterland and so on for a Greater or Lesser Extent it being allways optionall to the said Walter Campbell or his foresaids either to exact the said Services or in lieu thereof one Shilling Sterling per diem for each man and two horses AND the said tenants further oblige them and their foresaids that they shall not at any time carry or use fire arms or kill Game of any kind and that they shall not with Nets Rods or Spears slay or kill Black Fish or use bleezes on any of the waters or burns within the Island of Islay and that they shall not keep Setting dogs Greyhounds or other dogs that may be destructive to the Game otherwise if they be detected that shall forfeit and pay to the proprietor Twenty shilling Sterling for the first offence ffourty Shillings Sterling for the Second and in case of a third offence they shall forfeit this Tack AND IT IS HEREBY EXPRESSLY PROVIDED and DECLARED that the said tenants or their forsaids shall not at any time during this Tack keep Changehouses Tiplinghouses or Malt Kilns on the said Lands and that they shall not import buy or sell any foreign Spirits nor Vend in wholesale or retail malt or spiritous Liquers of any kind without having a Special License for that purpose under the penalty of ffourty Shillings Sterling for the first offence and doubling that sum for every after offence AND IT IS FURTHER EXPRESSLY PRO-VIDED AND DECLARED that the said Walter Campbell or his foresaids shall have liberty at any time during this Tack to Inclose and use any wood Grounds on the said Lands that he may think necessary and Sell and manufacture the said

woods and that they shall also have Liberty to work any mine of Lead Silver or
Copper that may be found on the said Lands and to Carry away the same and
dispose of such mines as they may think proper during this Tack they always
paying to the tenants the damages they may sustain thereby as the same shall be
ascertained by two honest men to be mutually Chosen AND the said tenants
FURTHER BIND AND OBLIGE them and their foresaids to build their
proportion of March dykes with their neighbours when required and that they
shall uphold and keep in proper Repair the whole houses and Biggings on the said
Lands during this tack and leave the same in a sufficient tenantable Condition at
their Removall they being allways at Liberty to Claim payment from the
Interant tenants of the price of the timber of the said houses according to the
ancient Custom of the Country of Islay AND FURTHER they OBLIGE them
and their foresaids to allow any of the tenants of Islay to Carry Sand

<pre>
                                        (signed)   Wa: CAMPBELL
                                                 DUNCAN MCKERAL
                                                      JOHN CARR
NEIL MACGIBBON N P   NEIL CAMERON
                                                  JAMES CAMERON
                                                 THOMAS CALDER

JOHN CAMPBELL
</pre>

limestone and Marle from the said Lands they paying the damages the Corn and
Grasses may Sustain there by at the sight of two sworn Birleymen BUT
DECLARING that no marle is to be carried off the Lands without the propri-
etors consent had and obtained in writing AND the said tenants ALSO OBLIGE
them and their foresaids that they shall flitt and remove from the Lands hereby
Sett at the Expiration of this Tack without the necessity of warning or other
process of Law for that purpose AND IT IS HEREBY FURTHER EXPRESS-
LY PROVIDED and DECLARED that NOT ONLY in the event of one years
Tack duty running into the Second unpaid BUT ALSO UPON the said tenants
and their foresaids their failure in performance of any of the Conditions above
mentioned THEN and IN THAT CASE this present Tack shall become ipso
facto Void and null AND it shall be Lawfull to the said Walter Campbell or his
foresaids to sett use and dispose of the said Lands as if this present Tack and
Agreement had never been entered into and that without any Declarator or
process of Law whatsoever AND LASTLY BOTH PARTIES BIND and
OBLIGE them and their foresaids to perform their respective parts of the
premisses to each others under the Penalty of FIFTY TWO pounds Sterling to be
paid by the party failing to the party observer or willing to observe the same by
an attour performance AND THEY CONSENT to the Registration hereof in
the Books of Council and Session or other Competent that Letters of horning on
Six days Charge and all other Execution necessary may pass and be directed
thereon in form as Effiers and for that effect THEY CONSTITUTE THEIR
PRORS & c In witness whereof these presents consisting of this and the
preceeding pàges of stamped paper wrote by Archibald MacGibbon Clerk to
Neil MacGibbon writer in Inverary ARE SUBSCRIBED by the said parties as

follows VIZt by the said Walter Campbell at Islay House the Thirty first day of August One thousand Seven hundred and Seventy Nine years before these witnesses the said Neil MacGibbon and Donald Bell his Servitor and by the said Tenants also at Islay House the fifteenth day of November and year foresaid before these witnesses Samuel Crawford Surgeon in Islay Mr. John WODROW Minister of Kildalton Gilbert Curry Ground Officer in Islay and the said Donald Bell the place and date of signing with the witnesses names and assignations being Insert by Donald Bell

(signed)
NEIL MACGIBBON   Witness Wa: CAMPBELL
DONd BELL   Witness DUNCAN MACKEROL
JOHN WODROW   Witness JOHN CARR
SAMI CRAWFORD   Witness NEIL CAMERON
GILBERT CURRY   Witness JAMES CAMERON
DONd BELL   Witness THOMAS CALDER
                                          JOHN CALDER
At the Special Command of the above named & designed ROBERT McKERROLL & WILLIAM GILCHRIST who declare they cannot write they having touched my pen I Neil MacGibbon Notary Publick do subscribe for them
                              NEIL MACGIBBON N P

MISSIVE
DONALD CAMPBELL
of BALLINABY
To
D. CAMPBELL of
SHAWFIELD Esqr
1776
Leck–oshnish Cultoon Sannaig beg
and the Miln and Changehouse of Breckachy
177 Tack Extended No. 69

(The original is among Islay Estate Papers.)

Islay House   1st Nov. 1776

Sir,

WHEREAS by your Missive to me of this date you have obliged yourself within ffifteen months from this date to grant me a Tack of the one quarter one penny one third land of Leckoshnish, the one quarter one penny one third land of CULTOON the Sixteen Shilling two third land of Sannaig beg, the miln of Breakachy with the Changehouse acres and Grazing on the Lands of Kilneave with which the Tenants thereof are Burthened for the space of Nineteen years from Whitsunday one Thousand Seven hundred and Seventy nine years and that the Lands after mentioned shall be thirled to the said Miln VIZt, the Lands of Smail Leckoshnish Menadrochaid Grulinbeg Sannaigbeg, Sannaig more Ardneave Breakachy Kilneave Leckgrunart, Grunart Corsabols Buninnuilt Corrygortan Kilenailen Rimm Dudle beg Dudle more Bolsa & Cove Ballenish Gortantoid with all other lands formerly in use to be Sucken'd to the said miln THEREFORE I hereby Oblige me to make payment to you your heirs ffactors or Chamberlainds in your name of the sum of One hundred Pounds Stl. money of yearly rent for the Space and from the Term above mentioned for the lands Miln Change house Croft and Grazings above Specified AS ALSO to make payment of the Cess and other publick Burdens affecting the said Lands and that in rate and proportion with others in Islay who have obtained Setts and Tacks of Lands from you in harvest One Thousand Seven Hundred Seventy five years and to obtemper and fullfill the whole acts statutes and regulations thereof anent the improvement of Lands preservation of the game ffishing & c – all which conditions I bind & oblige me to implement under the penalty of One Hundred Pounds Sterling money and I am

Sir
Your Most Obedt. Servt
(signed) DONd CAMPBELL
[of Balinaby]

To Daniel Campbell of Shawfield
Esqr

TACK
WALTER CAMPBELL of
SHAWFIELD Esqr
To
BALINABY
1777
Compd
LECKOSHNISH & c
No 69
£100

(The original is among the Kildalton Papers.)

TACK	TENANT	FARM	TENURE	RENT
No 69	Donald Campbell of Ballinaby	1 qtr Ld. 1/3 land of Leckoshish ditto Cultoon 16 2/3 land of Sannaigbeg Miln of Breckachy, Changehouse acres & grazing on lands of Kilneave.	19 years from Whitsun 1779	£100. St

Special Clause: . . . "Thirlage to the said Miln of the lands after mentioned VIZt The Lands of Smail, Leckoshinish, Kenadrochaid, Grulinbeg, Sannaigbeg, Sannaigmore, Ardneave, Breckachy, Kilneave, Leckgrunart, Grunart, Corsabolls, Bunanuilt Corrygortan, Kilnalen, Rimm, Balinish Gortantoid, Dudelbeg Dudlemore, Bolsa and Cove.

Standard Lease.
The two copies of the Lease are unsigned. At the Meeting of the Stent Committee on the 8th October 1778 it is stated that the Committee (Colin Campbell of Ardnahow and Donald Campbell of Balinaby) formerly appointed for Contracting with Carnbeg as Contractor for the Pacquet have left this Kingdom. . . . . "

ARTICLES of
AGREEMENT
Betwixt
NEIL MACGIBBON
and
JOHN HILL and
NEIL BROWN
1780
Portaskaig, ffery &
1/2 Keills.

(The original is among the Islay Estate Papers written on four pages of a double
foolscap. Very frail)

ARTICLES OF AGREEMENT Betwixt
Neil MacGibbon Factor of Islay and
John Hill at Keills, Knapdale

The said Neil MacGibbon as having power from and as taking burden upon him
for Walter Campbell of Shawfield Esquire Proprietor of the Lands aftermentioned hereby Setts to the said John Hill and Neill Brown at Keills in Knapdale
Jointly, All and whole the Change House of Portaskaig fferrie acres and grazings
thereto belonging as the same are presently possessed As Also that half of the
ffarm of Keilcolmkill commonly called Keils, Lying next to Portaskaig as the
same shall be divided and separated from the other half of Keills by two skilfull
persons, And that for the Space of Eighteen years from and after the term of
Whitsunday next one thousand seven hundred and Eighty years. Therefore the
said John Hill for himself and as taking burden in and upon him for the said Neil
Brown his father-in-law, hereby bind and oblige them their Heirs Executors and
Successors to make payment to the said Walter Campbell and heirs or ffactors in
their name of the sum of Ten pound Sterling money of yearly Rent for the lands
of Portaskaig, acres and ffery, and the sum of Fifteen pounds Sterling of yearly
rent for the said half of Keills, extending together to Twenty five Pounds St.
money yearly beginning the first terms payment thereof at Martinmas next
Jaivyc and Eighty years as also that they shall

(signed)   NEILL MACGIBBON
JON HILL

shall make payment yearly of one shilling in the pound of the said rent in lieu of
the Court mail dues & Compearance money formerly in due to be paid out of the
said Lands and to make payment of the Cess & Contingencies Minrs Stipends
road money and other publick Burdens Imposed or to be Imposed upon the said
Lands during the said space And further that they shall at their Entry make
payment of the Comprisement of the houses on the said Lands, to the outgoing
tenants conform to the practice in Islay and for the Encouragement of the said

L

John Hill and Neil Brown to put the houses in proper order and to assist them in paying the said Comprisement the said Neil MacGibbon hereby engages that Shawfield shall lend them Twenty pounds Str. at the term of Whitsunday next for the space of one or two years from that date upon their granting their joint security for payment thereof with the legal Interest from the date of advance till payment and in regard an excambion is proposed betwixt the possessor of Persabus and Shawfield for having part of the farm of Keills added to Persabus in lieu of the Change House & Croft of Ballochroy which is not included in the tack of Persabus. Therefore in the event of such Excambion taking place, the saids John Hill and Neil Brown will have Ballachroy & Croft thrown in their share of Keills in lieu of what may be added to Persabus and if the one is reckoned better than the other the difference to be paid or received as the same shall be ascertained by Skilfull persons, and the said John Hill and Neil Brown Bind and oblige them and their foresaids to keep good ffery boats at the said ffery of Portaskaig fit for fferying passengers, Cattle and Horses, well manned & rigged and that they shall keep a good stable ffurnished with Corn & hay for Gentlemen's horses, and Park for Grazing Gentlemen's Horses in Summer, and that they shall also keep good clean Bedds for Gentlemen and Servants, and the house of Portaskaig always well stocked with provisions Liquors and other necessaries for the accommodation of Strangers and of the people of the Country, when they come there, and they are also to take out a License annually for Brewing and retailing from the Lessee of the Excise of Islay, and further the said John Hill for himself and Neil Brown oblige them to keep the whole houses on the Lands hereby sett in a Tenantable Condition during the whole years above mentd and to leave them so at their removal, they being entitled to claim Comprisement from the interant tenants conform to the custom of the country of Islay, and upon the above considerations the said Neil MacGibbon Engages that Shawfield shall grant them a tack of the foresaid subjects when required containing the ordinary Clauses and obligements respecting the Improvements of the lands and police of the country contained in the other

(signed)   NEIL MACGIBBON
JNO HILL

other Leases of Islay granted by the said Walter Campbell extended in ample form on Stamped paper AND LASTLY both parties oblige them to perform their parts of the premises under the penalty of Twenty pounds Str ATTOUR performance In witness whereof the said Neil MacGibbon as having power for the said Walter Campbell and the said John Hill as taking burden upon him for the said Neil Brown have subscribed these articles Wrote upon this and the three preeceding pages by Archibald MacQuilkan Writer in Inverary. At Inverary the Ninth day of ffebruary one thousand seven hundred & eighty years before these Witnesses the said Archibald MacQuilkan & Archd MacKay Writer in Inverary
(signed) ARCHD MCKAY Witness   NEIL MACGIBBON
          ARCHD MACQUILKIN Witness   JNO HILL

Payments of Debts and Interest on Bonds

(The following List of Payments of Debts and Interest on Bonds is among the Kildalton Paper.)

LIST made out from Mr. Grant's Books 6 June 1791

Sums bearing Interest at 5p. cent and payable yearly	Price	Interest
Miss. Drummond	1000 — —	50 — —
Interest paid to Whity 1791		
Eliza Fraser, formerly Udny.	600 — —	30 — —
Interest paid up to do		
Robertson of Kindeace	1000 — —	50 — —
do		
Dr. Laings Widow	1000 — —	30 — —
Intr paid up to 13 March 91		
Miss. Scott	3000 — —	150 — —
Intr paid up to 3 December 90		
ditto	5000 — —	250 — —
Intr paid to 1 March 1790		
Miss. Sandilands	200 — —	10 — —
Intr paid to Cands 1791		
Lord Sackville	20000 — —	1000 — —
Intr paid to Marts 1790		
John Gordon W.S.	1000 — —	50 — —
Intr paid to Marts 1790		
Archd. Grant p Bill	1000 — —	50 — —
Interest paid to 8 June 1790		
David Forbes	500 — —	25 — —
Interest paid to 1 August 1790		
Ditto Bond to John Lumsdane		
for £1000 whereof Carradell	300 — —	25 — —
is due one half		
Intr paid to 27 Nov 1790		
Lady Aberdeen	600 — —	30 — —
Intr paid up to Marts 1790		
Mrs. Bell widow of John Bell		
Intr paid to Marts 1790	500 — —	25 — —
William Moubray	2000 — —	100 — —
Interest paid to Marts 1790		
George Miller	1500 — —	75 — —
Intr paid of 11 Aug 1790		
Mrs. Wood and Daughters	720 — —	36 — —

Sums bearing Interest at 5p. cent and payable yearly	Price	Interest
Intr paid up to Aug 1790		
Heirs of Captain McCulloch	2000 — —	100 — —
Intr paid to Whity		
Lady Mary Hays Trustees	2000 — —	100 — —
Intr paid to Whity 1790		
Phineas McIntosh	1000 — —	100 — —
Intr paid to 27 Nov 1789		
	£46120 — —	£2306 — —

Sums bearing Interest at 5 p Ct but payable once in two years	Price	Interest
Lady Campbell	500 — —	5 — —
Intr paid to Whity 1791		
Archd Hebburn	1000 — —	50 — —
Intr paid to Whity 1791		
James Miller Bentend	500 — —	25 — —
Intr paid to March 1790		
Miss. Flemings	150 — —	7 10 —
Intr paid to 8 Aug 1790		
Mathew Haldanes Trustees	300 — —	15 — —
Intr paid to 23 May 1790		
Dalyel of Lingo	200 — —	10 — —
Intr to Whity 1790		
	£2650 — —	£132 10 —

Sums bearing Interest at $4\frac{1}{2}$ p Cent	Price	Interest
Mr. David Beatson	500 — —	28 18 —
Intr paid to Why 1791		
Lady Campbell	1800 — —	81 — —
Intr due from May 1791		
Mrs. Skene and family/$\frac{1}{2}$ Yearly	1200 — —	54 — —
Intr paid to Whity 1791		
Mr. James Walker Minr	1200 — —	54 — —
Intr paid to Whity 1791		
Alexr Forbes W. S.	4000 — —	180 — —
Intr paid to Whity 1791		
Sir Michl Malcolm	7000 — —	315 — —
Interest from 16 May 1791		
Wm Robertson	1000 — —	45 — —
Intr from 30 Dec 1790		
A. Robertson for D. Ross's Trustees	1100 — —	49 10 —
Intr from 30 Dec 1790		
Miss. Durhams	200 — —	9 — —

Sums bearing Interest at 5p. cent and payable yearly	Price	Interest
Intr paid to 27 June 1790		
Baron Moncrieffe's Trustees	6000 — —	270 — —
Intr paid to Marts 1790		
George Malley	209 — —	9 8 1
Intr paid to 2 July 1790		
	£24209 — —	£1089 8 1

ABSTRACT

	Price	Interest
Sums at 5 p Ct payable yearly	£46120 — —	£2306 — —
ditto @ do payle once in 2 years	2650 — —	132 10 —
ditto @ 4½ p Cent	24209 — —	1089 — —
	£72979 — —	£3527 13 —

Glossary

Arage and Cairage	Loading and cartage.
Bear, Bere	Barley with six or four rows in its ear.
Birleyman	Officer appointed to settle agricultural disputes.
Bleezes	Blazes; torches used for night fishing.
Boll	Measure of grain etc., varied from district to district. Finalized: 5 Scots Bushels = 6 Imperial.
Changehouse	Inn, where horses could be changed for fresh ones.
Cherurgeon	Surgeon.
Effiers	To pertain to.
Entail	Settlement of heritable property on a specified line of heirs.
Evest	Nearest.
Failizie	Failure.
Feu, few	Feudal tenure of land, perpetual lease with a nominal annual rent.
Gressum	Premium paid to the Superior on entering into a new Lease.
Groatland	Land measurement = 4/– Scots or 4d. sterling
Herezeld	A feudal payment of the best beast on a farm if the tenant died during the term of his Lease.
Heritor	Proprietor of heritable property liable to payment of public burdens connected with the parish.
Knaveship, Kneaveship	The quantity of corn or meal due to be paid to the Miller's servant.
Jajvyc	Used in dates, meaning Seventeen Hundreds.
Leorhas, Learhess	8 Horsegang or 10/– land.
Mail	Rent: Court Mail = Rent collected by the Bailie Court.
Marle	Soil consisting of unconsolidated Clay and Carbonate of Lime, useful as a manure.
Merk	13/4 Scots: payment for a Merkland.
Merkland	A division of land, varying in size, usually 480–560 acres, according to quality. Should maintain 14 cows and 4 horses.
Multer, Multour	Proportion of meal or grain payable to the Proprietor or Tenant of a Mill.

Nolt	Cattle, particularly young beasts.
Quarterland	1/4 of a Merkland, usually 120–140 acres, according to quality.
Shilling-land	A small-holding equivalent to 1/– Scots or 1d. Sterling; sometimes referred to as a Penny-land.
Soumes	Fixed number of animals to be kept on land occupied by more than one Tenant.
Sucken	The duty and liability of Tenants within a district, astricted to a Mill.
Tack	Lease of land from a principal landowner, usually to a kinsman.
Tacksman	A chief tenant, often a relative of the landowner, who leased land directly from him and sublet it to lesser tenants.
Teinds	Church Tithes = 1/10th of the harvest.
Umquhile	The Late, i.e. deceased.
Wadset	Form of land mortgage, a loan from tenant to landowner – if not redeemed, tenant gains the land.
Writer	to the Signet (W.S.): senior solicitor, Edinburgh.

Bibliography

Papers

Islay Estate Papers: in the possession of Lord Margadale.
Kildalton Papers: in the possession of the Editor.
Teinds of Islay: Minutes of the Presbytery of Kintyre, 1763. Minutes of the Synod of Argyle 1747/62/69. Gift of the Revenues of the Bishoprick of Argyll and the Isles to the Synod of Argyll 1705. Gift of the Valued Teinds of Islay (1634) to Daniel Campbell of Shawfield and Islay, 1765. Printed record in the possession of the Editor.
The Process of Declarator & Sale: Shawfield Papers 1781. Printed record in the possession of the Editor.
Ms. History of the Campbells of Shawfield: J. F. Campbell: in the possession of Lord Margadale.
Ms. Pedigree of the Campbells of Shawfield: J. F. Campbell: in the possession of Lord Margadale.
Ms. Day Book of Daniel Campbell: in the possession of the Editor.

Books

Donaldson, Prof. Gordon: Scottish Historical Documents (Scottish Academic Press 1974).
Howell's State Trials – Vol. 19. 1753–1770.
Lamont, W. D.: Early History of Islay. Old & New Extent in Islay. Islay: A.D. 500–1615.
Lindsay, Ian G. and Mary Cosh: Inveraray and the Dukes of Argyll. (Edinburgh O. P. 1973).
McKay, Dr. Margaret M.: The Rev. Dr. John Walker's Report on the Hebrides, 1764.
MacKenzie, History of the Camerons.
Pennants Tour in Scotland, 1769. London 1777.
Ramsay, Lucy: The Stent Book of Islay, Privately printed in Edinburgh, 1895.
Shaw, Francis: The Northern & Western Isles of Scotland.
Smith, G. Gregory: Editor. The Book of Islay. Privately printed Edinburgh, 1895.
Walker, Rev. Dr. John: An Economical History of the Hebrides and Highlands of Scotland.

General Index

Tenants Listed in Rentals

Adair, Alexander
1733 Persabolls [Persabus], Kilmeny, 15
Adair, Andrew
1741 Kilcolmkill [Keils], Kilmeny, 41
Adair, Archibald
1799 Upper Corrary and part lower Corrary, Kilarow, 207
1804 Upper Corrary, Kilarow, 227
Adair, Archibald
1799 Bowmore, Kilarow, 212
Adair, Donald
1799 Bowmore, Kilarow, 212
Adair, William
1780–99 Ballulive, Kilmeny, 194, 210
Agey, Colin
1741 Changehouse in Balochroy, Kilmeny, 41
Anderson, Archibald
1790 Park of Sunderland, Kilchoman, 205
Anderson, Duncan
1799 Gartachossan, Kilarow, 207
Arnot, Donald
1733 Town of Kilarow, 17

Baxter, Donald
1799 Eorabus, Kilarow, 209
Beaton, Hector
1799 Bowmore, Kilarow, 212
Bell, Archibald, Jr
1780 Gortantoide and Dudilbeg, Kilmeny, 194
Bell, Archibald
1777–78–79–80 Conisby, Kilchoman, 108, 194, 209, 218
Bell, Donald
1777–78–79–80 Conisby, Kilchoman, 194, 218

Bell, John
1780 Gortantoide and Dudilbeg, Kilmeny, 108, 194
Brown, Angus
1780 Ballieharvie and croft, Kilmeny, 194, 199, 208
Brown, Angus
1799 Carabus, Kilarow, 211
Brown, Archibald
1799 Groballs & Torra, Kilarow and Kildalton, 207
Brown, Donald
1741 Groballs, Kilarow, 40
Brown, Donald
1780 Teorvagan [Tirvaigain], Kilmeny, 199
Brown, Donald
1780 Carabus, Kilarow, 194
Brown, Donald
1780 Tormastil [Tormastell], Kilchoman, 195
Brown, Donald
1799 Ballieharvie, Kilmeny, 208
Brown, Duncan
1779 half Grobolls, 108
1779–80–99 Bolsay and Grobolls, Kilmeny and Kilarow, 194
1799 Grobolls and Torra, Kilarow and Kildalton, 194
Brown, Duncan
1799–1804 Talent, Kilarow, 226
Brown, John
1773–80 Talent, Kilarow, 108, 195, 224, 226
Brown, John
1780 Ballieharvie, Kilmeny, 195
Brown, Malcolm
1780 Ballieharvie, Kilmeny, 195

Brown, Margaret
　1733 Craigfin, Kildalton, 9
Brown, Mary
　1733 Kilarow, 17
Brown, Mary
　1733 Gartloisk, Kilarow, 13
Brown, Mary
　1741 Groballs, Kilarow, 40
Brown, Neil, ferryman
　1780 Keils in Knapdale, 123, 133, 137,
　241, 242
Brown, Neil
　1799–1804 Talent, Kilarow, 226
Brown, Peter
　1780 Ballieharvie, Kilarow, 195
Brown, Roger
　1733 Gartloisk, 13
Brown, Roger
　1799 Carabus, Kilarow, 209
Brown, Rory
　1741 Groballs, Kilarow, 40
Buchanan, Neil
　1780 Ballieharvie, Kilmeny, 195

Calder, Donald
　1733 Balychatrigan, the Oa, 11
Calder, James
　1733 Stremnishmore, the Oa, 11
Calder, James
　1741 Tycarmagan, the Oa, 38
Calder, John
　1741 Balichristan [Balichatrichan], the
　Oa, 38
Calder, Thomas
　1741 Balichristan [Balichatrichan], the
　Oa, 38
Calder,, Thomas
　1780 Koillabus [Culabus] [Coilabus],
　the Oa, 38, 196
Calder, Thomas
　1776–79–80 Tighcarmagan, Kildalton,
　196, 232, 233, 234, 235, 238
Calder, William
　1733 Lyrabolls [Lurabus], the Oa, 11
Calder, William
　1741 Balichristan [Balichatrichan], the
　Oa, 38
Calder, William
　1741 Tycarmagan [Tighcarmagan],
　Kildalton, 38
Callendary, Duncan
　1780, Balychatrigan, the Oa, 196

Cameron, Duncan
　1799 Bowmore, Kilarow, 212
Cameron, Hugh
　1780 Grastill, the Oa, 195
Cameron, James
　1741 Upper and Nether Gartahossen,
　Kilarow, 40
Cameron, James
　1776–79–80 Tighcarmogan, Kildalton,
　196, 232, 233, 238
Cameron, John
　1733 Nether Dunuvig, Kildalton, 10
Cameron, Neil
　1776–79–80 Tighcarmogan, Kildalton,
　196, 232, 233, 234, 235, 238
Cameron, William
　1733 Gartloisk [Gartlosk], Kilarow,
　13
Cameron, William
　1741 Gartahossen, Upper and Nether,
　Kilarow, 40

CAMPBELL

Campbell, Agnes
　1799 Mulrish, Kilmeny, 213
Campbell, Alexander of Ardmore,
　Kildalton
　　1733 Ardmore, Ardmeanoch,
　　Kildalton, 9
　　1741 Craigfin, Trudernish, Ardmoir,
　　Ardmenish, Kildalton, 37
Campbell, Alexander
　1733 Ardochy, Kilmeny, 14
Campbell, Alexander
　1733–41 Ballieharvie, Kilmeny, 15, 42
Campbell, Alexander
　1780 Cnoclerach [half], Kilmeny, 196
Campbell, Alexander
　1741 Gartahar, Kilchoman, 43
Campbell, Alexander
　1780 Giol, the Oa, 195
Campbell, Alexander
　1799 Raw of Gartahossan, Kilarow,
　207
Campbell, Alexander of Kilinalen
　1733 Rim, Balynis, Gortanted,
　Kilinalen, Ardnahow, Bolsa, Dudil,
　Cove, Small, Migrim, Crulin and
　Ardtornish, Kilmeny, 16, 19
　1741 Kilinalen, Corsabolls, Bolsa, Rim
　Balinish, Gortanted, Migrim, Smail,
　Crulin and Ardtornish, Leck
　Grunart, Kilmeny, 42, 44, 103

Campbell, Alexander
1799 Kilinalen and Crosshmoir,
Kilmeny, 209
Campbell, Alexander
1741 Konigsbay [Conisby], Kilchoman,
43
Campbell, Alexander
1780–99 Mulrish, Kilmeny, 196, 208
Campbell, Alexander
1733 Nether Dunuvig, Kildalton, 10
Campbell, Alexander of Octomore,
Kilchoman
1741 Octomore, Grimsey, Coultersay
and Lergba Dudellmoir, Gylyne,
Kilchoman Change-house, Malt-kiln
and Miln of Skibo, Kilchoman,
43
Campbell, Alexander of Ormsary
1780 tacksman of Kilchirian, Braide
and half Kilinan, Kilchoman and
Kilarow, 195
Campbell, Alexander
1741 Upper and Nether Leurin,
Kildalton, 38
Campbell, Alexander
1733 Talent, Kilarow, 14
Campbell, Angus
1733 Ardochy, Kilmeny, 14
Campbell, Angus
1780 Ardachy, Kilmeny, 195
Campbell, Angus
1733 Balychillen, Kilmeny, 15
Campbell, Angus
1780 Ballygillin, Kilmeny, 196
Campbell, Angus
1733 Barr, Kilmeny, 14
Campbell, Angus
1733 Carabolls, Kilarow, 16
Campbell, Angus
1741 Kilarow, 42
Campbell, Angus
1733 Town of Kilarow, 17
Campbell, Angus
1741 Kilcolmkill, Kilmeny, 41
Campbell, Angus of Kilinalen, Kilmeny,
and mother
1780 tack of Kilinalen, Rim, Ballinish,
Sornusary, Crosshvoir and half
Eoribus, Kilmeny and Kilarow, 195
Campbell, Angus
1741 Knock Clerock [Cnoclerach],
Kilmeny, 41, 196

Campbell, Angus
1799 Loagine, Kilarow, 207
Campbell, Angus
1799 Mulrish, Kilmeny, 208
Campbell, Ann
1733 Kilarow, 17
Campbell, Archibald
1799 Bowmore, Kilarow, 212
Campbell, Archibald of Arderignish
1741 Ardimissy, Ardnebeist, Balnach-
tanmoir, Balnachtanbeg, half Solam,
Largybreckt, Upper Dunuvig, Miln,
Nether Dunuvig, Kildalton, 37
Campbell, Archibald
1733 Arihalloch, Kilchoman, 18
Campbell, Archibald of Ardmore
1798–99 tacksman of Ardmore, Ardmenoch and Kildalton, Kildalton,
206
Campbell, Archibald of Ardnahow
1774–80 Kintour, Miln of Oa,
Kildalton and Oa, 109
1780 tacksman of Ardnahow, Cove,
Dudilmore, Kilmeny, Coultorsa and
Braebruich, Kilchoman, 195
1799 part Balligrant, Robolls, Bolsa,
208
Campbell, Archibald
1733 Arras and Kintour, Kildalton, 9
Campbell, Archibald
1733 Ardimersay, Ardnabist, Ballinachtan More, Ballinachtan Beg, half
Solam, Largybrecht, Kildalton, 4, 9
Campbell, Archibald, tacksman of
Duisker
1774 Duisker, Kilmeny, 108
Campbell, Archibald
1780 Duisker, Kilmeny, 132, 133, 195
Campbell, Archibald
1733 Earobols, Kilarow, 15
Campbell, Archibald
1741 Eorobolls, Kilarow, 42
Campbell, Archibald Baan
1733–41 Eorobols, Kilarow, 15, 42
Campbell, Archibald, Baillie of Jura
1733 Kames, Jura, 20
Campbell, Archibald
1799 Few dutys of Jura, 210
Campbell, Archibald
1741 Lossit, Kilmeny, 44
Campbell, Archibald
1733–41 Lyrabus, the Oa, 11, 38

Campbell, Donald, wadsett
1741 Lossett, Kilmeny, 42
Campbell, Donald of Ormsary, in
Knapdale,
1799 Ballimartine, Kilmeny, 208
Campbell, Donald
1733 half Solam, Largybrecht,
Kildalton, 10
Campbell, Donald of Trudernish
1798–99 tacksman of Trudernish,
Claigin, Craigfin, Kildalton, 206
Campbell, Dugald
1780 Ardachy, Kilmeny, 195
Campbell, Dugald
1799 Smail, Migrim, Ardtornish,
Kilchoman, 209
Campbell, Dougald
1775–77–79–80 Barr, Kilmeny, 197,
230
Campbell, Dugald
1780 Giol, the Oa, 195
Campbell, Dugald
1733 Nether Dunuvig, Kildalton, 10
Campbell, Dugald
1733 Nether Stoinsha, Kilmeny, 15
Campbell, Dugal
1799 Torabolls [Torrabus], Kilmeny,
208
Campbell, Duncan
1780 Ardachy, Kilmeny, 195
Campbell, Duncan, Baillie
1774–79 tacksman of Ardmore, etc,
Kildalton, 108
Campbell, Duncan
1799 tacksman of Ardnave, Brechachy,
Kilchoman, and Mergadale,
Kilmeny, 209
Campbell, Duncan
1733 Balychillen, Kilmeny, 15
Campbell, Duncan
1733–41 Balole and Leek, Kilmeny, 16,
42
Campbell, Duncan, mason
1799 Bowmore, Kilarow, 212
Campbell, Duncan
1733 Esknish, Kilmeny, 15
Campbell, Duncan
1741 Esknish, Kilmeny, 42
Campbell, Duncan
1733–41 Gill [Giol], the Oa, 11, 39
Campbell, Duncan, son of Rev Mr John
Campbell [q.v. 1733 Kilenan, Upper

and Nether]
1741 Kilcarnen [Kilenan], Upper and
Nather, 40
Campbell, Duncan
1741 Kinnibolls [Kinabus], with miln
and changehouse, the Oa, 39
Campbell, Duncan
1780 Tenant of half Lagavulin and
mill, Kildalton, 196
Campbell, Duncan
1799 upper half Lorgbaw, Kilchoman,
210
Campbell, Duncan
1741 Lyrobolls [Lurabus], the Oa, 38
Campbell, Duncan
1780–99 Lurabus, the Oa, 196
Campbell, Duncan
1733 Nether Dunuvig, Kildalton, 10
Campbell, Duncan
1799 Portnahaven, Kilchoman, 210
Campbell, Duncan
1780 Proaig and Texa Island,
Kildalton, 195
Campbell, Duncan
1799 Rosequern, Kilarow, 207
Campbell, Duncan
1741 Stromnishbeg, the Oa, 38
Campbell, Duncan of Sunderland,
Kilchoman
1733 half of Kilhomen [Kilchoman],
19
Campbell, Duncan of Sunderline,
fewduty
1741 Sunderline etc. half Kilchoman,
half miln of Kilchoman, 44
Campbell, Duncan more
1733 Killean, miln of Killlean,
changehouse of Killean [Kileyan],
the Oa, 11
Campbell, Farquhar
1741 Kenabolls, Kilarow, 42
Campbell, Farquhard
1741 Laggan and Torra, Kilarow and
Kildalton, 39
Campbell, Ferquhard
1741 Ammond [Almond], Kilchoman, 43
Campbell, Ferquhard
1733 Lagan and Torra, Tokemiln
[Tuckmiln], Kilarow and Kildalton,
12
Campbell, George
1733 Arras and Keantour, Kildalton, 9

Campbell, John
  1774 Esknish, Kilmeny, 109
Campbell, John
  1780–99 Geill, the Oa, 206
Campbell, John, Baillie of Jura
  1733 Kames, Jura, 20
Campbell, John
  1741 Kepolsmoir, Kilmeny, 41
Campbell, John
  1733 Kilcolumkill [Kiels], Kilmeny,
    15
Campbell, John
  1733 Kilcolumkill, Largybrecht,
    Kildalton, 10
Campbell, John
  1799 Kilmeny, 207
Campbell, John
  1799 Kilslevan, Kilmeny, 208
Campbell, John of Kintour
  1780 tacksman of Kintour, Kildalton,
    196
Campbell, John of Laganlochan
  1733 Ardlaroch, Kilarow, 13
Campbell, John, son of Archibald
  1733 Largybrecht, Kildalton, 10
Campbell, John
  1799 Loagine, Kilmeny, 207
Campbell, John
  1780 Lurabus, the Oa, 196
Campbell, John
  1733 Losset, Kilmeny, 16
Campbell, John
  1733 Lyrabus, 11
Campbell, John Jr
  1741 Lyrobolls, 38
Campbell, John
  1741 Mulendra, Kilarow, 40
Campbell, John
  1780–99 Mulindrae, Kilarow, 196, 207
Campbell, John
  1733 Mulindra, Kilarow, 13
Campbell, John, son of Arch Campbell,
    Upper Stoinsha,
  1733 Milreesh, Kilmeny, 15
Campbell, John
  1780 Mulrish, Kilmeny, 108, 196
Campbell, Rev. John
  1733 Nether and Upper Killenan,
    Kilarow, 14
Campbell, John
  1780 Upper Loraine, Kildalton, 108,
    196

Campbell, John
  1733 Sanaigmore, Keandrochead,
    Kilchoman, 19
Campbell, John
  1733 Scanlaston, Island Taxel [Texa],
    Kildalton, 12, 15
Campbell, John, Captain
  1799 Scanlastill, Kilmeny, 208
Campbell, John
  1779 tacksman of Trudernish;
    Kildalton, 108
Campbell, John, Rev. Mr
  1741 Duock [Duich], Stranabodauch
    [Strathnabodach], Kilarow, 39
Campbell, John, Rev Mr
  1741 Killcarnen, Upper and Nether, 40
Campbell, John Rev Mr
  1733 half Kilhomen, half miln of
    Kilhomen [Kilchoman], 18, 44
Campbell, John
  1741 half Tycarmagan [Tighcarmagan],
    Kildalton, 38
Campbell, John
  1776–79–80 Tighcarmagan, Kildalton,
    196, 232, 233, 234, 235
Campbell, Lachlan
  1733 Upper and Nather Leorin,
    changehouse of Lyrabolls, Kildalton
    and Oa, 10, 11
Campbell, Malcolm
  1733 Ardochy, Kilmeny, 14
Campbell, Malcolm
  1741 Balitarsen, Kilmeny, 40
Campbell, Malcolm
  1741 Knock Clerock [Knocleroch],
    Kilmeny, 41
Campbell, Margaret
  1733 Balyharvie, Kilmeny, 15
Campbell, Mrs of Kilinalen, with son
    Angus
  1780 tack of Kilinalen, Rim, Ballinish,
    Sornusary, Crosshvoir and half
    Eoribus, Kilmeny and Kilarow, 195,
    201
Campbell, Mr
  1781 Ormsary, 205
Campbell, Mrs
  1741 Kilarow, 42
Campbell, Neil
  1733 Craigfin, Kildalton, 9
Campbell, Neil, weaver,
  1799 Gartachossan, Kilarow, 207

Carmichael, Duncan
  1741 Gill [Giol] the Oa, 39
Carmichael, Duncan
  1780–99 Kinegary, Kilarow, 195, 207
Carmichael, Hugh
  1733 Clagnagarroch [Claggan], 9
Carmichael, John
  1741 Arras and Kintour, Kildalton,
  37
Carmichael, John
  1780 Tacksman, Arrichalloch,
  Kilchoman, Ballygally and Torra,
  Kildalton, 195
Carmichael, John
  1780 Balychatrigan, the Oa, 196
Carmichael, John
  1790 Cladavil, Kilchoman, Kilneave,
  205
Carmichael, John
  1733 Clagnagaroch [Claggan],
  Kildalton, 9
Carmichael, John
  1779 Clagingarroch [Claggan],
  Kildalton, 108
Carmichael, John
  1780 Kilnave, Kilchoman, 198
Carmichael, John, Sr
  1780 Kinegary, Kilarow, 195
Carmichael, John
  1780–99 Lossit in the Rinns,
  Kilchoman, 196, 211
Carmichael, John
  1780 Lower Loarine, Kildalton, 195
Carmichael, John
  1780 Lurabus [Lyrabus], the Oa, 196
Carmichael, John
  1780 Neriby, Kilarow, 196
Carmichael, Kathrin
  1741 Cornubolls [Cornabus] and
  Killnachtan, Kildalton, 38
Carmichael, Margaret
  1733 Kinegarry, Kilarow, 14
Carmichael, Margaret
  1733 Rosequern, Kilarow, 13
Carmichael, Neil
  1780 Neriby, Kilarow, 196
Carr—see Kerr
Carrick, John
  1799 Gartintra, Kilarow, 211
Carrick, William
  1799 Balligrant, Kilmeny, 207

Catoch, David
  1733 Town of Kilarow, 17
Clark, Angus
  1799 Gartintra, Kilarow, 211
Clark, Donald
  1790 Park of Sunderland, Kilchoman,
  205
Clark, Duncan
  1780 Kinegary, Kilarow, 195
Clark, Kenneth
  1733–41 Gerrich, Kilchoman, 18, 44
Clark, Neil
  1733 Changehouse of Kilnachtan, the
  Oa, 11
Crawford, Ronald, Esq
  1780 Persabus, Kilmeny, Merchant in
  Glasgow, 193
Crawford, Dr Samuel, Chirurgeon of
  Islay
  1798–99 Proaig, Island Texa, Kildalton
  Balole, Leek, Duisker, two
  Stoinshas, Kilmeny, Ealabus,
  Kilarow, Miln of Glenguy,
  Kilchoman, 206, 207
Crichton, Thomas
  1733 New Park, Kinnabus, Kilarow, 16
  house and gorten [field], Town of
  Kilarow, 17
CURRY, CURRIE, McVURRICH
Curry, Alexander
  1799 Scanlastil, Kilmeny, 208
Currie, Alexander
  1778–1780 Conisby, Kilchoman, 195,
  218, 219
Currie, Angus
  1780 Leck Grunart, Kilchoman, 199
Currie, Angus
  1780 Torronich, Kilchoman, 199
Currie, Duncan
  1779 Leck Grunard, Kilchoman, 108
Currie, Duncan
  1780 Torronich, Kilchoman, 198
Currie, Duncan
  1779 Scarabus, Kilarow, 208
Currie, Hugh
  1799 Bowmore, Kilarow, 212
Currie, John
  1780 Lyrabus [Lurabus], Kilarow,
  196
Currie, John
  1799 Octovulline, Kilarow, 209

Gilchrist, Archibald
    1780 Glenegedale, Kildalton, 197
Gilchrist, Duncan
    1799 Bowmore, Kilarow, 212
[Mac]Gilchrist, Duncan Jr
    1733–41 Glenegedale, Kildalton, 39
[Mac]Gilchrist, Duncan Sr
    1733–41 Glenegedale, Kildalton, 39
[Mac]Gilchrist, John
    1733 Balychatrican, the Oa, 12
[Mac]Gilchrist, Neil
    1733 Machrie, Kildalton, 12
Gilchrist, Ronald
    1780–99 Glenegedale, Kildalton, 197,
    206
[Mac]Gilchrist, Ronald
    1733 Machrie, Kildalton, 12
Gilchrist, William
    1780 Glenegedale, Kildalton, 197
Gilchrist, William
    1776–79–80 Tighcarmogan
    [Tycarmogan], Kildalton, 196, 232,
    233, 238
Gilchrist, William
    1780 Tockamall [Tockmall], the Oa,
    199
Gilles, Alexander
    1780 Lossit in the Rinns, Kilchoman,
    196
Gilles, Archibald
    1780 Kippolsmore, Kilmeny, 197
Gillespie, Alexander
    1780 Grunart, Kilchoman, 197
Gillespie, Angus Jr
    1780 Gruinart, Kilchoman, 197
Gillespie, Angus Sr
    1780 Gruinart, Kilchoman, 197
Gillespie, Archibald
    1780 Gruinart, Kilchoman, 197
Gillespie, Donald
    1780 Grunart, Kilchoman, 108, 197
Gillespie, John
    1799 Lorgbaw, Kilchoman, 210
Gillespie, John
    1780 Grunart, Kilchoman, 197
Gillespie, Malcolm
    1777–78–80 Conisby, Kilchoman, 195,
    218
Gillespy, Dugald
    1777–78–80 Conisby, Kilchoman, 195,
    218, 219
Gillies, Alexander

1733 Almond [Ammond], Kilchoman,
    18
Gillies, Archibald
    1799 Bowmore, Kilarow, 212
Gillies, John
    1799 Gartintra [Gartnatra], Kilarow,
    211
Gillis, Archibald
    1799 Changehouse of Skiba,
    Kilchoman, 210
Graham, Alexander
    1733 Ballyvicar, Kildalton, 10
Graham, Alexander
    1741 Balivicar, Kildalton, 38
Graham, Alexander
    1780–99 Ballivicar, Kildalton, 196, 206
Graham, Alexander
    1733 Ballychatrican, the Oa, 11
Graham, Alexander
    1741 Koilibolls [Cullabus], the Oa, 38
Graham, Alexander
    1733 Lyrabus [Lurabus], the Oa, 11
Graham, Archibald
    1733 Ballyvicar, Kildalton, 10
Graham, Archibald
    1741 Balivicar, Kildalton, 38
Graham, Archibald
    1733 Balychatrican, the Oa, 11
Graham, Archibald
    1780 Nosebridge [half], half Allaly,
    Doudle, Dail, and Grimsa Lower,
    Kilarow and Kilmeny, 196
Graham, David
    1780 Ballivicar, Kildalton, 196
Graham, Donald
    1780 Cragabus, the Oa, 196
Graham, Duncan
    1780 Cragabus, the Oa, 196
Graham, Duncan
    1780 Machrie, Kildalton, 197
Graham, Hector
    1780 Ballivicar, Kildalton, 196
Graham, James
    1733 Balyvicar, Kildalton, 10
Graham, James
    1780 Cragabus, the Oa, 196
Graham, John Jr
    1780 Cragabus, the Oa, 196
Graham, John Sr
    1780 Cragabus, the Oa, 196
Graham, John
    1780 Ballichatrigan, the Oa, 196

M

Kerr, Donald
  1780 Leck Grunart, Kilchoman, 198
Kerr, James [Carr]
  1776–79–80 Tighcarmogan, Kildalton,
    196, 232, 233, 234, 235
Kerr, John [Carr]
  1779 Tighcarmogan, Kildalton, 234,
    235, 238
Kilpatrick, George
  1799 Lagan, Kilarow, 210

Lamont, Alexander
  1780 Portaneilan, Kilmeny, 196
Lamont, Donald
  1780–99 Portaneilan, Kilmeny, 196,
    208
Leitch, Donald
  1733–80 Leck Oshenish, Kilchoman,
    195, 217, 218
Leitch, Duncan
  1780 Kinadrochit, Kilchoman, 198
Leitch, John
  1780–99 Kinadrochit, Kilchoman, 198,
    209, 217, 218
Leslie, Duncan
  1780 Kippolsmore, Kilmeny, 197
Livingston, Duncan
  1733 Ariguary, Kilmeny, 14
Livingston, James
  1799 Gartintra, Kilarow, 211
Livingstone, James, mason
  1799 part Gartachossan, Kilarow, 207
Livingstone
  1799 part of Gartachossan, Kilarow,
    207

MacAlister, Archibald
  1790–99 Portnahaven, Kilchoman, 205,
    210
MacAlister, Charles
  1733 Balychillen, Kilmeny, 15
MacAlister, Charles of Tarbert, N
    Kintyre
  1733–41 Balyneil, Arvolhalm, Proaig,
    Storgag, Kilmeny, 9, 10, 14, 37, 214
MacAlister, Coll, Baillie
  1733 Stoin, Portnellan, Knockan
  1741 Stoin, half Ballegillan, Portnellan,
    Eolobolls, Miln of Kilarow,
    Knockens, Kilarow, 4, 9, 15, 16, 37,
    41

McAlister, Donald
  1780 Gartachra, Kilchoman, 197
MacAlister, Donald
  1733 Stremnishmore, the Oa, 11
McAlister, Duncan
  1799 Gartintra, Kilarow, 211
MacAlister, Mrs [widow]
  1799 Conisby, Kilchoman, 209
McAlister
  1799 Bowmore, Kilarow, 212
McAllister, Charles
  1769 Storkaig and Balliclach, Kilmeny,
    214
McAllister, Coll
  1733 Skerrols and Avinogy, Kilarow,
    16
McAllester, Hector
  1780–99 Conisby, Kilchoman, 195,
    218, 219
McAlpin, Essy
  1733 Machrie, Kildalton, 12
McAlpine, Donald
  1741 Conisby, Kilchoman, 43
McAlpine, Dugald
  1741 Konigsbay [Conisby], Kilchoman,
    43
McAlpine, Mrs Dugal [widow]
  1799 Bowmore, Kilarow, 212
McAlpine, Martin
  1774–80–99 Kilnave, Kilchoman, 109,
    198, 209
McAlpine, Neil
  1780 Kilnave, Kilchoman, 198
McAlpine, Mrs Robert [widow]
  1799 Bowmore, Kilarow, 211
McArthur, Archibald
  1799 Avinlussa and Avinvogy,
    Kilarow, 207
McArthur, Charles
  1799 part Cruach, Kilarow, 210
McArthur, Charles
  1741 Nerebolls [Nerebus], Kilarow,
    43
McArthur, Donald
  1780 Kinegary, Kilarow, 195
McArthur, Duncan
  1733 Glenegedale, Kildalton, 12
McArthur, Duncan [McCarter: McCat]
  1769 Storkaig and Balliclach, Kilmeny,
    214, 215
MacArthur, Duncan
  1733 Stremnishbeg, the Oa, 11

McArthur, Duncan
1780–99 Stremnishmore, the Oa, 199
McArthur, Duncan
1780–99 Tockamall, the Oa, 199, 206
McArthur, Duncan
1780 Tormastil, Kildalton, 195
McArthur, Finlay
1780 Shengart, Kilmeny, 198
McArthur, Mrs Finlay [widow]
1799 Raw of Gartachossan, Kilarow,
207
McArthur, Gilbert
1744 Avonlussa, Kilarow, 108
1780 Avonvogie, Kilarow, 197
McArthur, Gilbert
1733 Stremnishbeg, the Oa, 11
McArthur, Gilbert
1741 Stremnishmore, the Oa, 38
McArthur, Hugh
1780 Ballichatrigan, the Oa, 196
MacArthur, Hugh
1799 Stremnishmore, the Oa, 206
McArthur, John
1780 Avonvogie, Kilarow, 197
McArthur, John
1733 Kilnave, Kilchoman, 19
McArthur, John
1733 Knockcroch [Knockleroch],
Kilmeny, 14
McArthur, John
1741 Nerebolls [Nerebus], Kilarow,
43
McArthur, John
1774–80–99 Tormastil, Kilchoman,
109, 195, 210
McArthur, Neil
1780 Ardelister [Ardelistry], Kildalton,
197
MacArthur, Neil
1778–79 Ballyneal, Kilmeny, 206
McArthur, Neil [MacCarter]
1773 Storkaig [Storakaig], Kilmeny,
215
MacArthur, Patrick
1733 Stremnishmore, the Oa, 11
McArthur, Patrick
1741 Stromnishbeg, the Oa, 38
McArthurs
1799 Portnahaven, Kilchoman, 210
MacAulay, Aulay
1790 Sunderland, Kilchoman, 205

McAulay, Duncan
1774–79–80 Lossit in the Rinns
[Rhinns], Kilchoman, 109, 196
McAulay, Gilbert
1799 Portnahaven, Kilchoman, 210
McBride, Angus
1780 Balychatrigan, the Oa, 196
McCaffer, Neil
1799 Olista, Kilchoman, 209
McCallum, Archibald
1780 Shengart, Kilmeny, 198
McCallum, Collin
1780 Shengart, Kilmeny, 198
McCallum, Duncan
1780 Shengart, Kilmeny, 108, 198
McCallum, Duncan
1741 Talent, Kilarow, 40
McCallman, Donald
1774 Gartacher, Kilarow, 108, 125
McCallman, Donald
1779 Shengart, Kilmeny, 108
McCalman, Duncan
1780 Rosquern, Kilarow, 133, 198
McCalman, Nicholl
1733 Craigfad, Kilchoman, 18
McCalmon, John
1780 Grunart, Kilchoman, 197
McCarmaig, Duncan
1799 Bowmore, Kilarow, 212
McChristan, Alexander
1733 town of Kilarow, 17
McColman, widow
1799 Bowmore, Kilarow, 212
McConnel, Archibald
1780 Kinadrochit, Kilchoman, 198
McConnel, Donald
1780 Kinadrochit, Kilchoman, 198
McConnel, John
1780 Kinadrochit, Kilchoman, 198
McCore, George
1780 Coillabus, the Oa, 196
McCore, Neil
1779 Torronich, Kilchoman, 108
McCormaig, Duncan
1799 Bowmore, Kilarow, 212
MacCormig, Duncan
1733–41 Ballitarsin, Kilmeny, 13, 40
McCOWAIG, McCOWIG, McCUAIG
McCowaig, Alexander
1774–80 Ballitarsin, Kilmeny, 109,
197

McCowaig, Alexander
1780 Giol, the Oa, 195
McCowaig, Angus
1780–99 Assabus, the Oa, 197, 206
McCowaig, Donald
1780 Lower Glenastile, the Oa, 198
McCowaig, Donald
1733–41 Upper Glenastile, the Oa, 11,
39
McCowaig, Dugald
1780–99 Lower Glenastile, the Oa, 198
McCowaig, Dugald
178–99 Upper Glenastile, the Oa, 198,
206
McCowaig, Duncan
1799 Upper Glenastill, the Oa, 206
McCowaig, Edmund
1733–41 Gill, the Oa, 11, 39
McCowaig, Finlay
1799 Coilabus, the Oa, 206
McCowaig, Finlay
1780 lower Glenastile, the Oa, 198
McCowaig, John
1780 Lower Glenastile, the Oa, 198
McCowaig, John
1733 Nether Glenastle, the Oa, 11
McCowaig, John
1733–41 Upper Glenastill, the Oa, 11
McCowaig, Malcolm
1780 Giol, the Oa, 195
McCowaig, Mary
1733 Machrie, Kildalton, 12
McCowaig, Patrick
1733 Island, Kilarow, 12
McCowaig, Peter
1780 Upper Glenastile, the Oa, 198
McCowig, Angus
1733 Cragabolls [Cragabus], the Oa,
11
McCowig, Donald
1733 Cragabolls, the Oa, 11
McCowig, Donald
1733 Machrie, Kildalton, 12
McCowig, Duncan
1733–41 Cragebolls, the Oa, 11, 39
McCowig, Henry
1733–41 Cragebolls, the Oa, 11, 39
McCowig, John
1733 Ardochy, Kilmeny, 14
McCowig, William
1733 Cragebolls, the Oa, 11

McCuaig, Donald
1741 Cragebolls, the Oa, 11
McCuaig, Duncan
1799 Cragabus, the Oa, 206
McCuaig, Duncan Sr
1741 Cragebolls, the Oa, 39
McCuaig, Hugh
1741 Gill, the Oa, 39
McCuaig, John
1741 Lyrobolls, the Oa, 38
McCuaig, John
1741 Nether Glenastill, the Oa, 39
McCuaig, Mary
1799 Bowmore, Kilarow, 212
McCuaig, Patrick [officer]
1741 Assibolls, the Oa, 38
McCuaig, Peter
1798 Assabus, the Oa, 206
McCuaig, William
1798 Assabus, the Oa, 206
McCuaig, William
1741 Cragabolls, the Oa, 39
McCrillan, Hugh
1799 Bowmore, Kilarow, 211
McCrison, Margaret
1741 Kilarow, 42
McCristan, Hugh
1733 town of Kilarow, 17
McCulleam, Donald
1741 Kepolsmoir, Kilmeny, 41
McCurich [McCurrie], Archibald
1741 Konigsbay, Kilchoman, 43
McCurrie, Donald
1733 Craigfad, Kilchoman, 18
McDermed, Archibald
1733 Leckgrunart, Kilchoman, 19
MacDermid, Donald
1799 Storkaig, Kilmeny, 207
McDermined, Donald
1799 Gartintra [Gartnatra], Kilarow,
211
McDiarmid, Charles
1780 Easter Ellister, Kilchoman,
198
McDiarmid, Donald
1804 Torodale, Kildalton, 228
McDiarmid, Donald
1780 Easter Ellister, Kilchoman, 108,
198
McDiarmid, Finlay
1780 Tyrvagan, Kilmeny, 108, 199

McDiarmid, John
1780 Carn [Carn Glassens], Kilchoman, 198
McDiarmid, John
1780 Knockroanistle, Kildalton, 196
McDiarmid, Malcolm
1780 Easter Ellister, Kilchoman, 198
McDiarmid, Martin
1769–78–80 Storakaig, Kilmeny, 198, 214, 215
McDiarmid, Neil
1780–99 Carn [Carn Glassens], Kilmeny, 198, 209
McDonald, Alexander
1799 Gartacharra, Kilarow, 210
McDonald, Alexander
1780 Glenegedale, Kildalton, 197
McDonald, Alexander
1733 Lowdown ferry to Ireland, 12
MacDonald, Alexander
1733 Tycarmagan [Tighcarmagan] Kildalton, 10
McDonald, Allan
1780 Nerabus, Kilarow, 198
McDonald, Donald
1780 Gartachara, Kilarow, 124, 197
McDonald, Donald
1741 Nerabolls [Nerabus], Kilarow, 43
McDonald, Donald
1741 Tycarmagan [Tighcarmagan], Kildalton, 38
McDonald, Duncan
1741 Nerebolls [Nerabus], Kilarow, 43
McDonald, Hugh
1780 Lagavulin, Kildalton, 198
McDonald, Hugh
1741 Nerebolls [Nerabus], Kilarow, 43
McDonald, John
1799 Gartintra [Gartnatra], Kilarow, 211
McDonald, John
1780 Nerabus, Kilarow, 198
McDonald, Neil
1741 Nerebolls [Nerabus], Kilarow, 43
McDonald, Peter
1799 Leck Grunart, Kilchoman, 210
McDonald, Peter
1774–80 Nerabus, Kilchoman, 109, 198
McDonald, Ronald
1780 Nerabus, Kilchoman, 198
McDonald, Ronald

1733 Tycarmagan [Tighcarmagan], Kildalton, 10
MacDOUGAL, MacDOUGALD, Mac-DOUGALL, MacDUGALD
MacDougal, Alexander
1733–41 Noseberg, Kilarow, 13, 40
McDougal, Duncan
1780 Gartachossan, Kilarow, 198
McDougald, Alexander
1733 Carabolls, Kilarow, 16
MacDougald, Alexander
1733 Stremnishbeg, the Oa, 11
MacDougald, Allan
1733 Cattadill, Kilmeny, 14
MacDougald, Allan
1733 Machrie, Kildalton, 12
MacDougald, Archibald
1733 Barr, Kilmeny, 14
MacDougald, Archibald Ban
1733 Barr, Kilmeny, 14
McDougald, Duncan
1733 Carabolls, Kilarow, 16
McDougald, Duncan
1733 Nether Dunuvig, Kildalton, 10
MacDougald, Hugh
1733–41 Barr, Kilmeny, 14, 40
McDougald, Hugh
1741 Naseberg, Kilarow, 40
MacDougall, Alexander
1799 Grastil, the Oa, 206
McDougall, Alexander
1780 Kilmeny, 198
MacDougall, Alexander
1780 Nosebridge, Kilarow, 198
MacDougall, Alexander
198–99 Tayindrome, Kildalton, 198, 206
MacDougall, Alexander
1804 Torodale, Kildalton, 228
MacDougall, Alexander
1733 Upper Dunuvig, Kildalton, 10
MacDougall, Allan
1733 Esknish, Kilmeny, 15
McDougall, Allan
1798–99 Tayindrome, Kildalton, 206
MacDougall, Archibald, Baan
1741 Barr, Kilmeny, 40
McDougall, Archibald
1780 Octavoulin, Kilarow, 197
MacDougall, Dougald
1780 Tighandrom, Kildalton, 199

MacDougall, Duncan
1798–99 Ardbeg, Arinabeist, half Lagavulin, Kildalton, 206

MacDougall, Duncan
1799 Ardenistle, Kildalton, 206

MacDougall, Duncan
1733 Balychatrican, the Oa, 11

McDougall, Duncan
1741 Balichristan [Balichatrigan], the
Oa, 38

MacDougall, Duncan
1733 Tyndrom, Kildalton, 10

MacDougall, Duncan
1780 Tighandrom, Kildalton, 199

MacDougall, Duncan
1802 Torodale, Kildalton, 228

McDougall, Hugh
1780–98–99 Balinaughtonmore, Kildalton, 197, 206

MacDougall, Hugh
1780 Nosebridge, Kilarow, 198

McDougall, Hugh
1804 Talent, Kilarow, 226

MacDougall, John
1799 Balligrant, Kilmeny, 207

McDougall, John
1741 Carabolls, Kilarow, 42

McDougall, John
1741 Kilbride, Kildalton, 38

McDougall, John
1780 Kilbride, Kildalton, 198

MacDougall, John
1799 Upper Kilinan, Kilarow, 209

McDougall, John
1741 Koilibolls, the Oa, 38

MacDougall, John
1799 Slate Houses, Kilarow, 207

McDougall, John
1741 Tyndrom, Kildalton, 38

MacDougall, John
1798–99 Tayindrome, Kildalton, 206

MacDougall, John Jr
1780 Tighandrom, Kildalton, 199

MacDougall, John Sr
1780 Tighandrom, Kildalton, 199

McDougall, Lauchlan
1775–77–79–80 Barr, Kilmeny, 197,
230

McDougall, Ronald
1780 Kilbride, Kildalton, 198

MacDougall, Ronald
1799 Kilbride, Kildalton, 206

McDougall, Samuel
1775–77–79–80 Barr, Kilmeny, 197,
230

MacDugald, Angus
1733 Kilbride, Kildalton, 10

MacDugald, Margaret
1733 Kilbride, Kildalton, 10

McDuff, Archibald
1741 Glassansy, Kilchoman, 43

McDuffie [McPhee], Angus
1780 Kilnaughton, the Oa, 198

McDuffie [McPhee], Archibald
1780 Esknish, Kilmeny, 199

MacDuffie, Archibald
1798–99 Kinture and Stoin, Kildalton,
206

McDuffie, Donald
1799 Muir of Knockleroch, Kilmeny,
210

McDuffie, Dugald
1780 Gruline, Kilchoman, 108, 198

MacDuffie, John
1799 Kilnaughton, Carrabus, Frachtilt,
Upper Leorine, Kildalton, 206

McDuffie, Malcolm
1780 Upper Duich, Kilarow, 198

McDuffie, Neil
1780 Upper Duich, Kilarow, 198

McEachern, Alexander
1774 Portaneilan, Kilmeny, 109

MacEachern, Archibald
1774–79 Buninuilt, Kilarow, 108

McEachern, Archibald [McCheckeran,
McEucheran]
1733 Grunart, Kilchoman, 12
1780 Smaull, Kilchoman, 198, 216

McEachern, Donald, [mason]
1799 Bowmore, Kilmeny, 211

MacEachern, Donald
1799 Gartachossan, Dail, Kilarow,
207

McEachern, Donald
1799 Killichlaven, 208

McEachern, Duncan
1780 Barr, Kilarow, 197, 230

MacEachern, John
1799 Leckoshenish, Kilchoman, 209

McEachern, John
1780 Portaneilan, Kilmeny, 196

McEachern, John
1776 Kilmeny, 215
1780 Storakaig, Kilmeny, 198

McEachern, Malcolm
1780 Kilmeny, 198
McEachern, Malcolm
1799 Nerebolls, Kilchoman, 209
McEachern, Neil
1799 Claigingarrach, Kildalton, 210
McEachern, Neil
1741 Gerrich, Kilchoman, 44
McEachern, Neil
1780 Kilmeny, 198
McEachern, Neil [McEauchirn or
McCheckeran], from Gruinart, 1780
Smaull, 198
1799 Kilchirian and Braid, Kilchoman,
210
McEachern, Ronald
1780 Smaull, Kilchoman, 198
McEcheran, Alexander
1733 Grunart, Kilchoman, 12
1780 Smaull, Kilchoman, 108
McEilmichael, Neil
1741 Nerebie, Kilarow, 40
MacEvoy, Malcolm
1799 Gartahossan, Kilarow, 207
McEuan, Archibald,
1741 Delouach [Dluich], Kilarow, 40
McEwan, Alexander
1774–80 Gortanilivory, 109, 198
MacEwan, Archibald
1733 Balygrand[t], Kilmeny, 14
McEwan, Archibald
1733 Craigfad, Kilchoman, 18
McEwan, Archibald
1741 Craigfad, Kilchoman, 43
MacEwan, Charles
1799 Ballitarsin, Kilarow, 207
McEwan, Duncan
1799 Bowmore, Kilarow, 212
McEwen, Hugh
1733 Nerebolls, Kilchoman, 18
MacEwan, Ivor
1799 Gortanilivory, Kilarow, 207
MacEwan, John
1799 Nosebridge and Allaly, Kilarow,
207
MacEwan, Malcolm
1733–41 Delouach [Dluich], Kilarow,
13, 40
McEwan, Malcolm
1733 Keppolsmore, Kilmeny, 15

MacEwan, Neil
1733 Delouach [Dluich], Kilarow,
13
MacEwan, Neil
1733 Kinegarry, Kilarow, 14
McEwan, Neil
1733 Nerebolls, Kilchoman, 18
McEwan, Patrick
1733 Nerebolls, Kilchoman, 18
MacFaden, Angus
1799 Barr, Kilarow, 203
McFaden, Archibald
1799 Gartintra, 211
McFaiden, A
1799 Lorgbaw, Kilchoman, 210
McFaiden, Colin
1799 Arighuary, Kilmeny, 207
McFadzen, Angus
1741 Kinegarie, Kilarow, 40
McFadzen, Finlay
1741 Kinegarie, Kilarow, 40
Mcffadzen, Malcolm
1779 Cattadill, Kilarow, 108
McFarlane, Malcolm
1733–41 Leckgrunart, Kilchoman, 19,
44
MacGibbon, Andrew
1733 Balychatrigan, the Oa, 11, 196
McGibbon, Dougald
1780 Lower Killean, the Oa, 197
McGibbon, Duncan
1741 Balichristan [Balichatrigan], the
Oa, 38
McGibbon, Hector
1741 Balichristan [Balichatrigan], the
Oa, 38
McGibbon, Mr
1799 Baliclach, Kilmeny, 213
MacGibbon, Neil
1799 Gortanivrish, Kilmeny
1799 Lossit, Ballicrach, Balliclach,
Eachvernock, Arivrun, Gartaninuisk,
part Ariguary, Kilmeny, 208
McGilchrist, John
1733–41 Balichristan [Balichatrigan],
the Oa, 11, 38
McGilchrist, Neil
1780 Balichatrigan, the Oa, 196
McGillespigh, Archibald
1741 Konigsbay, Kilchoman, 43

McGillespigh, Dugald
  1741 Konigsbay, Kilchoman, 43
McGillevrey, Alexander
  1741 Kepolsmoir, Kilmeny, 41
McGilevray, Donald
  1741 Kinegarie, Kilarow, 40
McGillevorigh, John
  1741 Kepolsmoir, Kilmeny, 41
MacGilvra, Archibald
  1799 Ballygrant, Kilmeny, 207
McGilvra, Charles
  1799 Bunanuisk, Kilarow, 210
McGilvra, Duncan
  1799 Bowmore, Kilarow, 212
McGowan, Donald
  1741 Killean, the Oa, 38
McGown, Donald
  1780 Grastil, the Oa, 195
McGown, Neil
  1780 Grastil, the Oa, 195
McIchan, Duncan
  1741 Kepolsmore, Kilmeny, 41
MacIchan, Duncan
  1733 Keppolsmore, Kilmeny, 15
McIlbowie, Mary
  1733 Machrie, Kildalton, 12
MacIlbra, Donald
  1733 Kinegary, Kilarow, 14
McIlbride, John
  1741 Killean, the Oa, 38
MacIlbryde, Duncan
  1733–41 Gill, the Oa, 11, 39
MacIlbryde, Margaret
  1733 Balychatrigan, the Oa, 11
McIlchonel, James
  1733 Changehouse of Keantour, Kildalton, 9
McIlchonil, Duncan
  1733 Nerebolls, Kilmeny, 18
McIlchrist, Janet
  1741 Glenegedill, Kildalton, 39
McIleur, Angus
  1733 Kilnave, Kilmeny, 19
McIlivoil, Angus
  1733 Gerrich, Kilchoman, 18
McIlivorie, John
  1733 Octovulin, Kilarow, 16
MacIlroy, Gilbert
  1733–41 Gill, the Oa, 11, 39
McIlvoil, Angus

1773 Gruinart, Kilchoman, 216
1780 Smaull, Kilchoman, 198
McInchan, Duncan
  1780 Nosebridge, Kilarow, 198
McInchan, Nicol
  1780 Nosebridge, Kilarow, 198
McInclerie, John
  1733 Kilarow, 17
MacIndoer, John
  1799 Miln of Kilneave, Kilchoman, 209
McIndoire, Donald
  1780–99 Koilade [Coulade], Kilarow, 199, 209
McIndore, Angus
  1780 Octavoulin, Kilarow, 197
McIndore, Duncan
  1733 town of Kilarow, 17
McIndore, Duncan
  1780 Octavoulin, Kilarow, 197
McIndore, John
  1733 Balychillen, Kilmeny, 15
McIndore, John
  1741 Carabolls, Kilarow, 42
McInish, Angus
  1780 Kilbride, Kildalton, 198
McInish, Neil
  1780 Kilbride, Kildalton, 198
McInish, Malcolm
  1780 Kippolsmore, Kilmeny, 197
McInnish [McInnes], Angus
  1741 Kilbride, Kildalton, 38
McInnish, John
  1741 Kilbride, Kildalton, 38
McInnish, Malcolm
  1741 Kilbride, Kildalton, 38
McIntagart, John
  1780–99 Lower Killean, the Oa, 197, 206
MacIntaggart, Archibald
  1780 Corspollan, Kilarow, 198
McIntaggart, Duncan
  1733 Gill [Giol], the Oa, 11
McIntaggart, Hugh
  1780 Corspollan, Kilarow, 198
McIntaggart, John
  1780 Giol, the Oa, 195
McIntaggart, Neil
  1780–99 Corspollan, Kilarow, 198, 209
McIntosh, Neil [smith]
  1799 Bowmore, Kilarow, 212

McIntosh, Rev [minister]
1799 part Grobolls, Kilarow, 210
McInture, Donal
1773–79–80 Talent, Kilarow, 195
McInturner, Duncan
1733 Tormistell, Kilchoman, 18
McInturner, John
1733 Tormistell, Kilchoman, 18
McIntyre, A
1799 Portnahaven, Kilchoman, 210
MacIntyre, Alexander
1733 Balytarsen, Kilmeny, 13
McIntyre, Donald
1780 Ardachy, Kilmeny, 195
McIntyre, Donald
1799 Lower Kilinan, Kilmeny and
Kilarow, 208
McIntyre, Donald
1780 Neriby, Kilarow, 196
McIntyre, Donald
1773 Talent, Kilarow, 224, 226
McIntyre, Mrs Donald [widow]
1799 Talent, Kilarow, 213
McIntyre, Donald
1733 Tormiestell, Kilchoman, 18
McIntyre, Duncan
1780 Ardelister, Kildalton, 197
MacIntyre, Duncan
1798–99 Ardtalla, Kildalton, 206
MacIntyre, Duncan
1733 Avenlussa, Kilarow, 14
McIntyre, Duncan
1733 Gerrich, Kilchoman, 18
MacIntyre, Duncan
1733 Glenegedale, Kildalton, 12
McIntyre, Duncan
1741 Glenegedill, Kildalton, 39
MacIntyre, Duncan
1733 Moulindra, Kilarow, 13
McIntyre, Duncan
1741 Talent, Kilarow, 40
McIntyre, Duncan Bean
1741 Talent, Kilarow, 40
McIntyre, Finlay
1780 Balligrant, Kilmeny, 198
McIntyre, Finlay
1741 Gerrich, Kilchoman, 44
McIntyre, John [shoemaker]
1799 Bowmore, Kilarow, 211
McIntyre, John
1741 Kilcolmkill, Kilmeny, 41

McIntyre, John
1733 Octavoulin, Kilarow, 16
MacIntyre, John
1790 Park of Sunderland, Kilchoman,
205
McIntyre, Malcolm
1733 Octovoulin, Kilarow, 16
McIntyre, Neil
1780 Glassins, Kilchoman, 199
McIntyre, Peter
1799 Bowmore, Kilarow, 211
McInvin, Hugh
1780 Tormastil, Kilchoman, 195
McInvine, Colin
1780 Kinegary, Kilarow, 195
McIver, Archibald
1799 Gartintra, Kilarow, 211
McKay, Alexander
1799 Tacksman of Laggan, Duich, Kilarow, 207
McKay, Alexander
1733 Octavoulin, Kilarow, 16
MacKay, Ann
1733 Glenegedale, Kildalton, 12
MacKay, Florence
1733 Nerebie, Kilarow, 13
McKay, Hugh [son of Hugh]
1741 Ardlaroch and Cruach, Kilarow,
40
McKay, Hugh
1780 Tacksman for Laggan, Duich,
Strathnaboddach, Ardimersay, half
Grobolls, Kilarow and Kildalton,
197
MacKay, Hugh
1780 Neriby, Kilarow, 196
MacKay, Hugh
1799 Tirvagan, Kilmeny, 207
MacKay, John
1733 Ardlaroch, Kilarow, 13
McKay, John
1741 Ardlaroch and Cruach, Kilarow,
40
McKay, John
1733 town of Kilarow, 17
McKay, John
1774–80–99 Kippolsmore, Kilmeny,
109, 197, 208
McKay, Mrs
1799 Bowmore [Laggan Acres], Kilarow, 212

McKay, Robert
  1799 Bowmore, Kilarow, 211
McKecheran, Archibald
  1733 Gerrich, Kilchoman, 18
MacKecheren, Finlay
  1733–41 Carnbeg, Kilmeny, 15, 41
MacKeechan, Neil
  1799 Gortanilivory, Kilarow, 207
McKenzie, Alexander
  1780 Tormastil, Kilchoman, 195
MacKenzie, Archibald
  1733 Craïgfin, Kildalton, 9
MacKenzie, Dugald
  1733 Craigfin, Kildalton, 9
MacKerrell, Archibald
  1733 Lyrabus, the Oa, 11
McKerrell, John
  1733 Lyrabus, the Oa, 11
McKerrol, Duncan
  1804 Courloch, Kilarow, 227
McKerrol, Duncan [from Kintra]
  1779–80 Tighcarmagan, Kildalton, 196,
    232, 233, 234, 235, 238
McKerrol, Robert [from Torrodale]
  1779–80–98–99 Tighcarmogan, Kildal-
    ton, 196, 206, 232, 233, 238
McKiachan, John
  1799 part of Cruach, Kilarow, 210
MacKinnish [MacInnes], Angus
  1733 Kilbryde, Kildalton, 10
MacKinnish [MacInnes], Malcolm
  1733 Kilbryde, Kildalton, 10
McKoulikan, John
  1741 Changehouse of Kilnachtan, the
    Oa, 38
**McLACHLAN, MacLAUCHLAN, Mac-
  LAUCHLIN**
MacLachlan, Alexander
  1733 Upper Dunuvig, Kildalton, 10
MacLachlan, Archibald
  1733 Balulve, Kilmeny, 15
McLachlan, Archibald
  1733 town of Kilarow, 17
MacLachlan, Archibald
  1733 Neribie, Kilarow, 13
McLachlan, Duncan
  1733 Balymartin, Duisker, Kilmeny, 15
McLachlan, Duncan
  1733 town of Kilarow, 17
McLachlan, John
  1733 Nether Dunuvig, Kildalton, 10

MacLachlan, Lachlan
  1733 Balychillen, Kilmeny, 15
McLauchlan, Archibald
  1799 croft of Robolls, Kilarow, 210
McLauchlan, Archibald
  1780–99 Shengart, Kilmeny, 198, 209
McLauchlan, John
  1780 Shengart, Kilmeny, 198
McLauchlan, Neil
  1780 Shengart, Kilmeny, 198
McLauchlane, Alexander
  1741 Catadell, Kilmeny, 40
McLauchlane, Archibald
  1741 half Nether Stunsha, half Skerrols
    and Avenvogie, Balole, Kilarow,
    41
McLauchlane, Duncan
  1741 Ballegran, mill and changehouse,
    Ballemartin, Kilmeny, 41
McLauchlane, Mrs [Ballimartine] Bow-
    more, Kilarow, 132, 133, 212
McLauchlin, Alexander
  1774 Ballimartin, Kilmeny, 109
  1779–80 Ballimartin and Stoinsha, Kil-
    meny, 197
McLauchlin, Archibald
  1780 Ardmore, Ardmenoch, Kildalton,
    197
McLauchlin, Archibald
  1780 Ballimartine and Stoinsha, Kil-
    meny, 197
McLauchlin, Archibald
  1741 Nerebie, Kilarow, 40
McLauchlin, Duncan, heirs of
  1780 Portaskaig and Calumkill [Keils],
    Kilmeny, 123, 198
McLardy, Donald
  1733 Lagavulin, Kildalton, 12
McLargan, Archibald
  1799 Carndonachy, Kilchoman, 209
McLargan, Dugal
  1799 Carndonachy, Kilchoman, 209
McLean, A
  1799 Bowmore, Kilarow, 212
McLean, Alan
  1741 Carnglassansy and Olista, Kil-
    choman, 43
McLean, Archibald
  1733 town of Kilarow, 17
McLean, Archibald
  1733 Konigsbay, Kilchoman, 17

McNabb, Duncan
1741 Rosequern, Kilarow, 40
MacNabb, Duncan
1733 Upper Dunuvig, Kildalton, 10
McNabb, James
1741 Nerebie, Kilarow, 40
MacNabb, John
1733 Kilbryde, Kildalton, 10
MacNabb, John
1733 Knockcroch [Knocklerock], Kilmeny, 14
MacNabb, John
1733–41 Nether Glenastle, the Oa, 11, 39
McNabb, Patrick
1741 Naseberg, Kilarow, 40
MacNabb, Patrik
1733 Rosequeren, Kilarow, 13
McNakaird, Angus
1741 Rosequeren, Kilarow, 40
McNakaird, Archibald
1741 Nerebie, Kilarow, 40
McNakaird, Donald
1741 Rosequeren, Kilarow, 40
McNakard, John
1741 Kinegarie, Kilarow, 40
MacNaught, Alexander
1733 Balytarsen, Kilmeny, 13
MacNaught, Moses
1733 Balytarsen, Kilmeny, 13
McNeil, Alexander
1773–74 Corrary, Kilarow, 216
1780 Smaull, Kilchoman, 198
MacNeil, Archibald
1733 Kilcolumkill, Kildalton, 15
MacNeil, Donald
1733 Ariguary, Kilmeny, 14
McNeil, Donald
1780 Ballulive, Kilmeny, 194
MacNeil, Donald
1733 Kilcalumkill, Kildalton, 15
McNeil, Donald of Knocknohan [Campbeltown]
1741 Kentra, Machrie, Kildalton Grastill, Tockumill, the Oa, 39
McNeil, Donald
1780 Shengart, Kilmeny, 198
McNeil, Isobel
1733 Culabolls, Kilarow [later Kilchoman], 16
McNeil, Isobel

1733 Lyrobolls, Kilarow [later Kilchoman], 16
MacNeill, Malcolm of Ardtalla
1780 tacksman of Ardtalla, Claggan and Trudernish, Kildalton, 197
MacNeil, Malcolm
1733–41 Cornabus and Kilnachtan, Kildalton, 11, 38
MacNeil, Malcolm
1799 Craganinfinin, Kildalton, 207
MacNeil, Malcolm
1798–99 tacksman of Knockroanastle and Ardelistry, Kildalton, 206
MacNeil, Malcolm of Tarbert [Gigha]
1741 Ardtalla, Surnaig, Barr and Cragnagore, Kildalton, 9, 37
McNeil, Mary
1741 Duock, Strananbodauch, Kildalton, 39
McNeil, Neil of Ardnacroish
1741 Knock and Ardelister, Kildalton, 27
MacNeil, Neil
1733 Ariguary, Kilmeny, 14
McNeil, Neil
1799 Easter and Wester Ellister, Island Oversa, Kilchoman, half Dudilmore, Kilmeny, 209
MacNeil, Neil Oig
1733 Knock and Ardelister, Kildalton, 9
MacNeil, Torquil
1733 Cornabus and Kilnachtan, Kildalton, 11
MacNeill, Donald of Knocknahall [Campbeltown]
1733 Kentra, Kildalton, Grastell, the Oa, 11
McNeill, Godfrey
1780 tacksman Callumkill, Ardbeg, Arinabeist, Solam, Lergivreck, Ballynaughtonbeg, Kildalton, 197
1798–99 tacksman Collmkill, Ballinaughtonbeg, Miln of Lagavulin, 206
McNeill, Hector
1799 Arrichallich, Balimony, Balligally, Cladavill, Kilchoman, 210
McNeill, Mr
1760 tack of Kintraw, Kildalton and Grastil, the Oa, 110

McNicol, James
1799 Bowmore, Kilarow, 212
McNicol, Samuel
1780 Blackrock, Kilarow, 199
McNivan, Alexander
1779 Corsplan, Kilchoman, 108
MacNivan, Angus
1733 Arras and Kintour, Kildalton, 9
MacNiven, Archibald
1777–78–80 Conisby, Kilchoman, 195, 218
McNiven, Donald
1741 Mulendra, Kilarow, 40
McNiven, Donald
1780 Rosquern, Kilarow, 108, 198
McNiven, Dugal
1799 Allaly and Pendicle of Nosebridge, Kilarow, 207
McNiven, Duncan
1799 Bowmore, Kilarow, 212
McNiven, James
1799 Portnahaven, Kilchoman, 210
MacNiven, John
1779 Courlach, Kilarow, 207
MacNiven, John
1799 Corsapols, Kilchoman, 209
MacNokard, Angus
1733 Cattadill, Kilmeny, 14
MacNokard, Donald
1733 Cattadill, Kilmeny, 14
MacNokard, Donald
1733 Correry, Kilarow, 12
McNokard, Donald
1733 Gerrich, Kilchoman, 18
MacNokard, Duncan
1733 Upper Dunuvig, Kildalton, 10
MacNokard, Neil
1733 Avenlussa, Kilarow, 14
McNoquard, Donald
1741 Corrary, Kilarow, 39
McNougard, Donald
1741 Gerrich, Kilchoman, 44
MacPHAIDEN [McFADYEN]
MacPhadan, Finlay
1733 Clagangaroch, Kildalton, 9
McPhaden, Dug
1733 town of Kilarow, 17
MacPhaiden, Angus
1733 Kinegary, Kilarow, 14
McPhaiden, Archibald
1780 Kinegary, Kilarow, 195

McPhaiden, Donald
1780 Lossit in the Rhinns, Kilchoman, 196
McPhaiden, Finlay
1780 Kinegary, Kilarow, 195
McPhaiden, Hugh
1780 Kinegary, Kilarow, 195
McPhaiden, Malcolm
1780 Cattadale, Kilmeny, 198
McPhaill, Archibald
1799 Portnahaven, Kilchoman, 210
McPhaill, John
1799 Portnahaven, Kilchoman, 210
McPherson, Alexander
1780 Carabus, Kilarow, 194
McPherson, Alexander
1780 Kilneave, Kilchoman, 198
McPherson, Archibald
1733 Carabolls, Kilarow, 16
McPherson, Archibald
1741 Carabolls, Kilarow, 42
MacPhie, Alexander
1733 Knockcroch [Knockleroch], Kilmeny, 14
MacPhie, Alexander
1733 Neribie, Kilarow, 13
MacPhie, Ann
1733 Noseberg, Kilarow, 13
MacPhie, Archibald
1733 Nerebie, Kilarow, 13
McPhie, Dugald
1733 Octovulin, Kilarow, 16
MacPhie, Duncan
1733 Nerebie, Kilarow, 13
McPhie, John
1733 Gerrich, Kilchoman, 18
MacPhie, Malcolm
1733 Nether Stoinsha, Kilmeny, 15
McQuary, Donald
1741 Craigfad, Kilchoman, 43
MacQuary, Neil
1733 Keppolsmore, Kilmeny, 15
MacQueen, Allan
1799 Courlach, Kilarow, 207
MacQueen, Archibald
1780 Arriguary, Kilmeny, 197
McQueen, John [son of Neil]
1741 Areguirie, Kilmeny, 41
McQueen, John
1780–99 Ballygillin, Kilmeny, 196, 207

MacQueen, John
  1804 Courloch, Kilarow, 227
McQueen, Neil
  1741 Areguirie, Kilmeny, 41
MacQueen, Neil
  1733 Knockcroch [Knockleroch], Kilmeny, 14
McQueen, Patrick
  1780 Gartmain and Gartloist, Kilarow, 199
MacQueen Peter
  1780 Arriguiry, Kilmeny, 197
MacQueen, Peter
  1799 Rosquern, Kilarow, 207
McQuilkan, Alexander
  1804 Torodale, Kildalton, 228
McQuilkan, Duncan
  1804 Torodale, Kildalton, 228
McTaggart, Archibald
  1741 Killean, the Oa, 38
McTaggart, Duncan
  1741 Gill, the Oa, 39
McVastan, Malcolm [alias Malcolm Curry]
  1773 Lickoshnish, Kilchoman, 217, 218
MacVicar, Archibald
  1799 Gartachossan, Kilarow, 207
MacVicar, Duncan
  1733 Avenlussa, Kilarow, 14
McVicar, Duncan
  1733 Octofad, Kilchoman, 18
MacVicar, Rev. John
  1733–41 Ardinistle, Torrodale, half Tyndrom, Kildalton, 10, 38
McVORAN, MORRISON
McVoran, Gilbert
  1780 Stremnishmore, the Oa, 199
MacVoran, Malcolm
  1733–41 Stremnishmore, the Oa, 11, 38, 199
McVoren, John
  1741 Stromnishmore, the Oa, 38
McVoren, Neil
  1741 Killean, the Oa, 38
McVorran, Duncan
  1780 Stremnishmore, the Oa, 199
McVorran, John
  1799 Bowmore, Kilarow, 212
McVorran, John
  1774–80–99 Island, Kilarow, 109, 198, 207

McVourish, Archibald
  1733 Barr, Kilmeny, 14
McVourish, Dougald
  1733 Trudernish, Kildalton, 9
McVourish, John
  1733 Trudernish, Kildalton, 9
McVURRICH [CURRY]
MacVurich, Adam
  1733 Keppolsmore, Kilmeny, 15
McVurich, Gilbert
  1780 Losset in the Harris and Ballicrach, Kilmeny, 108, 197
McVurich, John
  1741 Kinegarie, Kilarow, 40
McVurrich, Archibald
  1780 Smaull, Kilchoman, 198
McVurrich, Donald
  1769–78–80 Losset in the Harris and Balicrach, Kilmeny, 108, 197
McVurrich, Donald
  1780 Balliclaugh, Kilmeny, 108, 197, 215
McVurrich, Donald Jr
  1780 Losset in the Harris and Balicrach, Kilmeny, 108, 197
McVurrich, Duncan
  1780 Leck Grunart, Kilchoman, 198
McVurrich, Duncan
  1780 Losset in the Harris and Balicrach, Kilmeny, 108, 197
McVurrich, James
  1780 Losset in the Harris and Balicrach, Kilmeny, 108, 197
McVurrich, John
  1780 Esknish, Kilmeny, 199
McVurrich, Lauchlan
  1780 Losset in the Harris and Balicrach, Kilmeny, 108
McVurrich, Mary
  1775–66–79–80 Barr, Kilmeny, 197, 230
McVurrich, Murdoch
  1769–78–80 Balliclaugh, Kilmeny, 197, 214, 215
McVurrich, Neil
  1780 Teorvagan, Kilmeny, 199
McVurrich, Ronald
  1773 Smail and Migrim, Kilchoman, 216
McVurrichs, etc
  1774–79 Lossit in Rines, Kilchoman, 109

McWilliam, Archibald
1780 Cattadale, Kilmeny, 198
McWilliam, Neil
1780 Carabus, Kilarow, 194, 198
McWilliam, Neil
1780 half Carabus, Kilarow, 198
Mitchel, William
1799 Bowmore, Kilarow, 211
Montgomery, Alexander
1733 Octovoulin, Kilarow, 16
Montgomery, John
1799 Gartfad and Lagintra, Kilchoman, 210
Montgomery, Robert
1733 Olista, Kilchoman, 18
Montgomery, Robert
1741 Torronich, Kilchoman, 43
MORRISON, McVORRAN
Morrison, John
1799 Bowmore, Kilarow, 212
Murdoch, John
1780 Minister of Bowmore [Kilarow] and Kilmeny, Gartbreck and Bunanuisk, Kilarow, 197
Murdoch, Mrs
1799 Gartbreck, Kilarow, 207
Murray, Sir Alexander, Bart.
1741 Torobolls, Kilmeny, 42

Niven − *see McNiven*

Ochiltree, Archibald
1741 Gartlosk, Kilarow, 40
Ochiltree, Archibald
1733 Keppolsmore, Kilmeny, 15
Oconocher, Kat
1733 Correry, Kilarow, 12
Odocherty, James
1733 Tormistell, Kilchoman, 18
Odocherty, William
1733 Tormistell, Kilchoman, 18
Ogilvie, William
1780 Glenegedale, Kildalton, 197
Ogilvy, Alexander
1799 Taynaknock, Pendicle of Leek Pendicle of Octovoulin, Kilarow, 208
Orr, John
1741 Nether Dunuvig, Kildalton, 38
Orr, John
1733 Nether Dunuvig, Kildalton, 10

Patterson, Robert
1780 Gartahossan, Kilarow, 199

Reid, Archibald
1780 Lower Killean, the Oa, 197
Reid, Duncan
1775−77−79−80 Barr, Kilmeny, 197, 230
Reid, Gilbert
1780 Lower Killean, the Oa, 197
Robertson, Alexander
1799 Ballitarsen, Kilmeny, 207
Robertson, Alexander
1733 Kenabolls, Kilarow, 16
Robertson, Archibald
1798−99 Achnacarnan, Kildalton, 206
Robertson, R
1741 Konigsbay, Kilchoman, 43
Robertson, William
1780 Ballitarsin, Kilmeny, 197
Ross, John
1780−99 Kelsay and half Olista, Kilchoman, 109, 199, 209

Semple, William
1799 Bowmore, Kilarow, 212
Schaw, Angus
1733−41 Port Askaig, Changehouse, ferry, maltkiln, changehouse of Balochroy, Persabolls, half Ariguary, Kilmeny, 15, 41
Schaw, Angus
1733 Persabolls, Kilmeny, 15
Schaw, John
1733 Persabolls, Kilmeny, 15
Schaw, Neil
1733 Lagavulin, Kildalton, 12
Shanks, George
1799 part Gartanloist, Kilarow, 210
Shaw, Donald
1799 Gartintra, Kilarow, 211
Shaw, Malcolm
1780 Kippolsmore, Kilmeny, 197
Simson, D
1799 Bowmore, Kilarow, 211
Simson, David
1780 Torrodale and Achnacarnan, Kilchoman, 199
1799 Gartmain, Kilchoman, 207
Simson, Hector
1799 Coultorsay, Kilchoman, 209

Stewart, John
  1741 Gartlosk, Kilarow, 40
Stewart, John
  1774–99 Gartloist, Kilarow, 109, 207
Stewart, S [Captain]
  1779 Bowmore, Kilarow, 211
Stewart, William
  1741 Arras and Keantour, Kildalton, 37
Sutherland, Angus
  1733 Glenegedale, Kildalton, 12
Sutherland, Angus
  1741 Glenegedill, Kildalton, 39
Sutherland, Ann
  1733 Tyndrom, Kildalton, 10
Sutherland, Hugh
  1733 Tyndrom, Kildalton, 10
Sutherland, John
  1733 Nerebolls, Kilarow, 18
Sutherland, Kat[herine]
  1733 Balychatrigan, the Oa, 11
Symson, Alexander
  1733 Lyrabolls and Culabolls, Kilarow
  [later Kilchoman], 16

Tayler, Dugald
  1733–41 Barr, Kilmeny, 14, 40
Taylor, Alexander
  1799 Skerrols walk miln and Lenimore,
  Kilarow, 210

Taylor, Angus
  1780 Balligrant, Kilmeny, 108, 198
Taylor, Duncan
  1799 Bowmore, Kilarow, 212
Taylor, Duncan
  1799 Kintra and Machary, Kildalton,
  207
Taylor, John
  1780 Skerrols and Waukmill, Kilarow,
  108, 198
Thomson, John
  1799 Bowmore, Kilarow, 212
Thomson, Marion
  1733 Arras and Keantour, Kildalton, 9
Torry, David
  1780 Ballitarsin, Kilmeny, 197

Watson, Samuell
  1741 Octavoulen, Kilarow, 42
Wilkieson, John
  1780 Knockroanistle, Kildalton, 194
Woodrow, Mr John, Minister of Kildalton
  1780 Ballyneal, Arrivolchallum, Kildalton, 199
Woodrow, Mrs
  1799 Ardlaroch, Kilarow, 207

Farms Listed in Rentals

Argyll Patent

Adair, William, 1740, 24, 33
Anderson, Anna [Mrs Alexander Hunter], 1739, 24
Anderson, Catherine [nee McLean] [Mrs Patrick Anderson], 1739, 23, 26
Anderson, Florence [Mrs Malcolm Martine], 1738, 22
Anderson, Mary, 1740, 24, 28
Anderson, Patrick, 1739, 23, 26

Beaton, Mary, 1738, 22, 28
Brady, Hugh, 1763, 34
Brady, John, 1740, 24, 34
Brown, Christian, 1740, 24, 34, 35
Brown, see Duncan McQuarrie [alias Brown], 1739, 23
Brown, Merran [Sara] [Mrs John Shaw], 1740, 24, 34, 35, 36

Calder, Janet [Mrs Duncan MacDougall], 1739, 23
Caldwell, Alexander, 1739, 23
Caldwell, James, 1739, 23
Caldwell, John, 1739, 23, 26
Caldwell, Mary [nee Nutt] [Mrs John Caldwell], 1739, 23
Cameron, James, 1739, 23
Campbell, Alexander, 1738–63, 22, 29, 34
Campbell, Alexander, 1740–63, 24, 28, 30
Campbell, Alexander of Landie, 1740–63, 24
Campbell, Angus, 1739, 24
Campbell, Ann, of Ballinaby [Mrs Duncan Campbell], 1740, 24, 30
Campbell, Anna, of Ballinaby [Mrs John Campbell], 1738, 22
Campbell, Anna [nee MacDougall] [Mrs James Campbell], 1738, 22, 25
Campbell, Anna [Mrs Alexander McDuffie] widow, 1739, 23

Campbell, Anna [Lenos] [Mrs Duncan Campbell], 1740, 24
Campbell, Anna, 1740, 24
Campbell, Archibald, 1738–63, 22, 25
Campbell, Archibald of Ardenton, 1740, 24, 30
Campbell, Archibald, of New York, 1763, 27
Campbell, Archibald, 1763, 28
Campbell, Catarine, 1740, 24
Campbell, Catherine, 1739, 23, 29
Campbell, Catherine, [Mrs Archibald McDuffie], 1739, 23
Campbell, Daniel, 1763, 33
Campbell, Donald, in Jamaica, 1738, 33
Campbell, Donald, 1738, 22, 26
Campbell, Dugald, dead, 1763, 27
Campbell, Duncan, 1739, 23, 26, 28
Campbell, Duncan, of Dunn, 1740, 24
Campbell, Duncan, of Duntroon, 1740, 24
Campbell, Duncan, of Lochnell, 1740, 24
Campbell, Duncan, 1740, 24, 30
Campbell, Duncan, 1740, 24, 25
Campbell, Duncan, 1763, 32
Campbell, of New York, 1763, 33
Campbell, Elizabeth, 1738, 22
Campbell, Elizabeth [Mrs John McNeil], 1738, 22
Campbell, George, 1742, 33
Campbell, George, 1763, 32
Campbell, Isabel, 1738, 22, 25
Campbell, Isabel, 1738, 22
Campbell, James, 1738, 22, 25
Campbell, James, 1738, 22
Campbell, Janet, 1738, 22
Campbell, John, 1739, 24, 25, 28
Campbell, John, of Balinabie, 1738, 22
Campbell, John, 1740, 24, 30
Campbell, Lachlan, Captain, 1738–39–40, 21, 22, 32

McArthur, Alexander, 1738, 22
McArthur, Alexander, 1739, 24, 28
McArthur, Anna [nee McQuinn] [Mrs Duncan McArthur], 1738, 22
McArthur, Anna, 1738, 22
McArthur, Ann, 1740, 24, 30
McArthur, Anne, 1740, 24, 30
McArthur, Catherine, 1738, 22
McArthur, Catherine [nee Gillies] [Mrs Alexander MacArthur], 1739, 24
McArthur, Charles, 1738, 22, 32
McArthur, Charles, 1738, 22
McArthur, Christian, 1738, 22
McArthur, Christian, 1740, 24
McArthur, Colin, 1738, 22
McArthur, Donald, 1738, 22
McArthur, Duncan, 1738, 22, 26
McArthur, Duncan, 1738, 22
McArthur, Duncan, 1739, 24
McArthur, Flora, 1739, 24
McArthur, Florence, 1738, 22
McArthur, Isabel [Mrs John Christy], 1740, 24
McArthur, Janet, 1738, 22
McArthur, John, 1738, 22, 26
McArthur, John, 1738, 22, 28
McArthur, John, 1740, 24
McArthur, John, 1738, 22
McArthur, Margaret, 1738, 22
McArthur, Margaret [Mrs Archibald McCollum] [New York], 1740, 24
McArthur, Mary [nee MacDougall] [Mrs Patrick MacArthur], 1738, 22
McArthur, Mary [nee Campbell] [Mrs Neil MacArthur], 1738, 22
McArthur, Mary [Mrs John McNiven], 1738, 22
McArthur, Mary, 1738, 22
McArthur, Neil, 1738, 22, 25
McArthur, Neil, 1740, 24
McArthur, Patrick, 1738, 22, 26
McAulla, Christain, 1739, 23
McChristen, Alexander, 1739, 23
McCloud, Catharine [nee Graham] [Mrs Donald McCloud], 1738, 22
McCloud, Donald, 1738, 22, 25
McCloud, Duncan, 1738, 22
McCloud, John, 1738, 22
McColl, John, 1738, 23
McCollum, Allan, 1739, 24
McCollum, Anna, 1740, 24
McCollum, Archibald, 1739, 24, 27

McCollum, Archibald, 1740, 24, 28
McCollum, Archibald, in New York, 1740, 24
McCollum, Donald, 1739, 24
McCollum, Duncan, 1740, 24, 33
McCollum, Duncan, 1740, 24, 33
McCollum, Flory [nee McEacheon] [Mrs Archibald McCollum], 1740, 24
McCollum, Flory [Mrs Duncan McPhadden], 1740, 24
McCollum, Hugh, 1740, 24
McCollum, John, 1739, 24
McCollum, Margaret, 1739, 24
MacCollum, Margaret [nee MacArthur] [Mrs Archibald MacCollum in New York], 1740, 24
McCollum, Marian [Mrs Duncan McKinven], 1740, 24, 28
McCollum, Mary, 1739, 24
McCollum, Mary, in New York, 1740, 24
McCollum, Mary [Mrs Angus Clark], 1740, 24
McCollum, Merran [nee McLean] [Mrs Archibald MacCollum], 1739, 24
McCoy, Archibald, 1739, 32
McCore, John, 1739, 32
McCore, Cormick, 1763, 25, 26
McCuarg, Anna [Mrs John McGown], 1739, 23
McCuarg, Isabel [Mrs Donald Livingston], 1739, 23
McDearmid, Mary [Mrs Neil McPhaden], 1739, 23
McDonald, Alexander [son of Janet McDonald], 1738, 22, 33
McDonald, Allan, 1763, 27
McDonald, Allan, in New York, 1763, 32, 33
McDonald, Allan, 1763, 33
McDonald, Anna [Mrs Donald McEachern], 1738, 22
McDonald, Anna [nee McDuffie] [Mrs Neil McDonald], 1738, 22
McDonald, Archibald, 1738, 22
McDonald, Catarine [Mrs John McGilvrey], 1740, 24
McDonald, Catherine [Mrs Neil McInnish], 1739, 23
McDonald, Catherine, 1738, 22
McDonald, Donald, 1738, 22
McDonald, Jean [Mrs Archibald McEchern], 1738, 22, 33

McKinven, Duncan, 1740, 24, 28
McKinven, Marian [nee McCollum] [Mrs Duncan McKinven], 1740, 24
McKinven, Mary, 1740, 24
McKinzie, Archibald, 1738, 22
McKinzie, Florence, 1738, 22
McKinzie, John, 1738, 22, 26
McKinzie, Mary [nee McVurrich] [Mrs John McKinzie], 1738, 22
McKnight, Alexander, 1771, 35
McLachlin, Florence [Mrs Neil Shaw], 1739, 23
McLean, Alexander, 1738, 22
McLean, Alexander, 1763, 34
McLean, Catherine [Mrs Patrick Anderson], 1739, 23
McLean, Catherine, 1763, 29
McLean, John, 1738, 22, 29, 34
McLean, Lauchlin, 1740, 24, 29
MacLean, Marry [Mrs Robert Fraser], 1739, 23
MacLean, Mary [nee Ross] [Mrs Lauchlin MacLean], 1738, 23, 29
McLean, Merran [Mrs Archibald McCollum], 1739, 24
McMillan, Alexander, 1739, 23
McMillan, Donald, 1738, 22, 25, 32
McMillan, Donald, 1739, 23, 27
McMillan, Janet [nee Gillies] [Mrs Donald McMillan], 1739, 23
McMillan, Mary [nee McEachern] [Mrs Donald McMillan], 1738, 23
McNaught[on], Alexander, 1738, 22, 25
McNaught[on], Alexander, 1763, 32, 33
McNaught[on], Eleanor, 1738, 22
McNaught[on], James, 1740, 32
McNaught[on], Janet, 1738, 22
McNaught[on], John, 1738, 22
McNaughton, John, 1763, 32
McNaught[on], Mary [nee McDonald] [Mrs Alexander MacNaughton], 1738, 22
McNaught[on], Moses, 1738, 22
McNeil, Anne [widow of Hugh MacEwan], 1740, 24, 28
McNeil, Barbra, 1738, 22
McNeil, Betty, 1738, 22
McNeil, Catharine, 1738, 22
McNeil, Elizabeth [nee Campbell] [Mrs John McNeil], 1738, 22
McNeil, Jane, 1763, 25

McNeil, John, 1738, 22, 25
McNeil, Margaret, 1738, 22, 29
MacNeil, Mary [Mrs John Shaw], 1739, 23
McNeil, Neil, 1738, 22
McNeil, Peggie, 1738, 22
McNeil, Roger, 1740, 24, 30
McNiven, Catherine [Mrs George McKenzie], 1738, 22
McNiven, Elizabeth, 1738, 22
McNiven, John, 1738, 22, 25
McNiven, Mary [nee McArthur] [Mrs John McNiven], 1738, 22
McNiven, Mary, 1738, 22
McNiven, Merran, 1738, 22, 29
McNiven, Rachel Mrs, 1738, 22, 29
McPhaden, Dirvorgill, 1739, 23
McPhaden, Donald, 1739, 23
McPhaden, Margaret, 1739, 23, 26
McPhaden, Mary [Mrs Dugald McAlpine], 1738, 22
McPhaden, Mary [nee McDearmid] [Mrs Neil McPhaden], 1739, 23, 26
McPhaden, Neil, 1739, 23, 26
McPhadden, Duncan, 1740, 24, 28
McPhadden, Duncan, 1740, 24, 28
McPhadden, Flory [nee McCollum] [Mrs Duncan McPhadden], 1740, 24
McPhadden, John, 1740, 24, 28
McPhail, Christy [nee Clark] [Mrs John McPhail], 1739, 24
McPhail, John, 1739, 24, 27
McQuarrie, Christian, 1739, 23
McQuarrie, Donald, 1739, 23
McQuarrie, Duncan [alias Brown], 1739, 23, 27
McQuarrie, Effie [nee McIlpheder] [Mrs Duncan McQuarrie], 1739, 23
McQuarrie, Gilbert, 23
McQuarrie, John, 1739, 23, 26
McQuarrie, Mary [Mrs Donald Lindsey], 1739, 23
McQuarrie, Mary [Mrs Patric McEachern], 1739, 23
McQuary, Anna [nee Quary] [Mrs John McQuary], 1739, 23
McQuary, John, 1739, 23
McQuin, Anna [Mrs Duncan McArthur], 1738, 22
McVuirich, Lauchlin, 1738, 22
McVurich, Archibald, 1739, 23, 26
McVurich, Florence, 1739, 23

McVurich, Lauchlin, 1739, 23
McVurich, Merran [nee Shaw] [Mrs Archibald McVurich], 1739, 23
McVurrich, Mary [Mrs John McKenzie], 1738, 22
Martine, Florence [nee Anderson] [Mrs Malcolm Martine], 1738, 22
Martine, Malcolm, 1738, 22, 26
Montgomery, Alexander, 1738, 22, 25
Montgomery, Alexander, 1763, 32
Montgomery, Anna [nee Sutherland] [Mrs Alexander Montgomery], 1738, 22
Montgomery, Catherine, 1763, 34
Montgomery, Hugh, 1738, 22, 28
Murphy, Anthony, 1740, 24

Nutt, Elizabeth, 1739, 23
Nutt, James, 1739, 23
Nutt, John, 1739, 23, 26
Nutt, Mary [Mrs John Caldwell], 1739, 23
Nutt, Rebecca [nee Creighton] [Mrs James Nutt], 1739, 23
Nutt, Robert, 1739, 23

Paterson, Christain, 1738, 22
Peterson, Margaret [Mrs Nicholas McIntyre], 1739, 24

Quary, Anna [Mrs John McQuarry], 1739, 23

Reade, Duncan, 1771, 36
Reed, Jannet [Mrs Archibald McKellar], 1738, 22
Reid, Alexander, 1739, 23
Reid, Angus, 1739, 23
Reid, Donald, 1739, 23
Reid, Duncan, 1763, 27, 32
Reid, Duncan [N.Y.], 1763, 32, 34
Reid, Duncan [New York], 1763, 33
Reid, Duncan, 1739, 1763, 23, 34
Reid, Jennie, 1739, 23, 34
Reid, John, 1739, 23, 27
Reid, John 1740, 24, 33
Reid, Margaret [nee Hyman] [Mrs John Reid], 1739, 23
Reid, Mary [nee Semple] [Mrs Duncan Reid], 1739, 23
Reid, Nicholas, 1739, 23
Reid, Peter, 1763, 33
Reid, Roger, 1739, 23, 29

Robertson, Patrick, 1739, 23
Robertson, Peter, 1739, 32
Ross, Jean, 1738, 23, 33
Ross, Mary, 1738, 23, 29
Semple, Mary [Mrs Duncan Reid], 1739, 23
Shaw, Catherine, 1739, 23, 29
Shaw, Daniel, 1771, 34, 35
Shaw, David, 1739, 23, 29
Shaw, Donald, 1738, 22, 25
Shaw, Donald, 1740, 24
Shaw, Duncan, 1739, 23
Shaw, Florence [nee McLachlin] [Mrs Neil Shaw], 1739, 23
Shaw, Flory [Mrs Donald Ferguson], 1739, 23
Shaw, Gustavus, 1739, 23, 24
Shaw, John, 1739, 23, 27, 34
Shaw, John [New York], 1740, 24, 28, 34, 35, 36
Shaw, Margaret [Mrs McDougall], 1740, 34, 35
Shaw, Margaret [infant born at sea], 24
Shaw, Mary [nee McNeil] [Mrs John Shaw], 1739, 23
Shaw, Mary, 1740, 24
Shaw, Merram [nee McInish] [Mrs Donald Shaw], 1738, 22
Shaw, Merran [Mrs Archibald Mac-Vurich], 1739, 23
Shaw, Merram [Sarah] [nee Brown] [Mrs John Shaw], 1740, 24, 34, 36
Shaw, Neal [New York], 1763, 34
Shaw, Neal, [ropemaker, New York], 1763, 34
Shaw, Neil, 1739, 23, 27, 34
Shaw, Neil, 1739, 23, 34
Shaw, Neil, 1739, 23, 34
Shaw, Sarah [Merram] [nee Brown] [Mrs John Shaw], 1740, 24, 34, 35
Smith, Donald, 1763, 33
Smith, Duncan, 1738, 22
Stevenson, Catherine, 1763, 34
Stewart, James, 1738, 22
Sutherland, Anna [Mrs Alexander Montgomery], 1738, 22
Sutherland, Elisbie [Mrs Gillies], 1738, 22, 25

Taylor, Alexander, 1763, 33
Taylor, Duncan, 1738, 22, 25

Taylor, Mary [nee Gillies] [Mrs Duncan Taylor], 1738, 22
Taylor, Mary, 1738, 22
Thompson, Allen, 1738, 22
Thompson, Elisbie, of Dunardrie, 1738, 22
Thompson, Mary, 1739, 23, 29, 32
Thompson, Roger, 1740, 24, 30, 33
Thomson, Archibald, 1739, 23
Thomson, Christie, 1739, 23
Thomson, Dugald, 1739, 23, 26
Thomson, Duncan, 1739, 23
Thomson, Margaret [nee McDuffie] [Mrs Duncan Thomson], 1739, 23
Torry, Catharine, 1739, 24
Torry, Florence [nee McKay] [Mrs James Torrie], 1739, 24

Torry, George, 1739, 24, 29
Torry, James, 1739, 24, 27
Torry, John, 1740, 24, 30, 33
Torry, Mary, 1739, 24
Tyron, William, the Honourable, 1771, 34, 36

Vandle, Jacob [New York], 1763, 32
Vandle, Mrs Jacob [New York], 1763, 32
Van Vleck, Jean [nee Cargill] [Mrs Van Vleck of New York], 1739, 29
Van Vleck, Mr [New York Merchant], 1763, 29

Widrow, Jean Mrs [?], 1740, 24, 30

Campbells of Cawdor and Islay
showing the Progenitors of many Islay Tacksmen

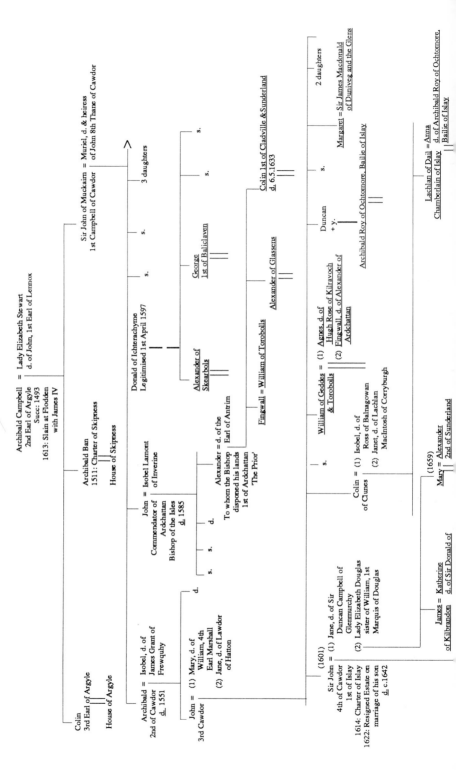

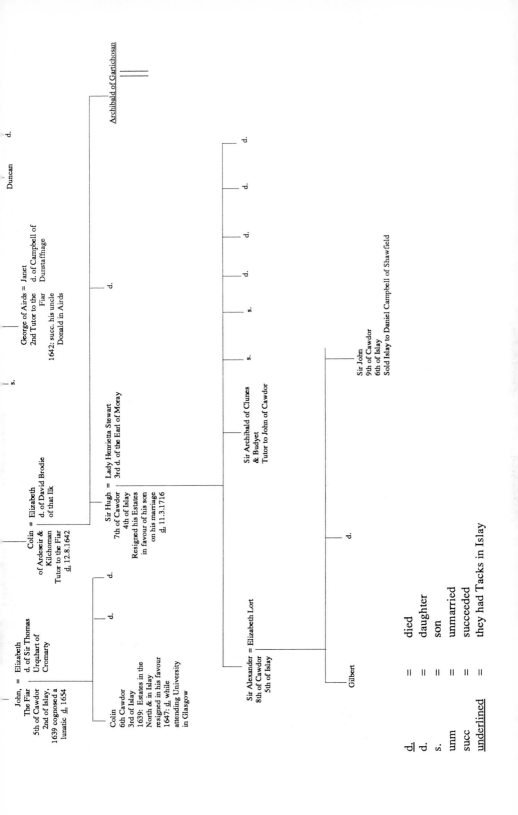

Duncan
d.

Archibald of Gartichosan

John, = Elizabeth
The Fiar   d. of Sir Thomas
5th of Cawdor   Urquhart of
2nd of Islay,   Cromarty
1639 cognosed a
lunatic d. 1654

Colin = Elizabeth
of Ardersir &   d. of David Brodie
Kilchoman   of that Ilk
Tutor to the Fiar
d. 12.8.1642

George of Airds = Janet
2nd Tutor to the   d. of Campbell of
Fiar   Dunstaffnage
1642: succ. his uncle
Donald in Airds

d.

s.

Colin
6th Cawdor
3rd of Islay
1639: Estates in the
North & in Islay
resigned in his favour
1647: d. while
attending University
in Glasgow

d.

Sir Hugh = Lady Henrietta Stewart
7th of Cawdor   3rd d. of the Earl of Moray
4th of Islay
Resigned his Estates
in favour of his son
on his marriage
d. 11.3.1716

Sir Archibald of Clunes
& Budyet
Tutor to John of Cawdor

s.   s.   s.   d.   d.   d.   d.

Sir Alexander = Elizabeth Lort
8th of Cawdor
5th of Islay

d.

Sir John
9th of Cawdor
6th of Islay
Sold Islay to Daniel Campbell of Shawfield

Gilbert

d   =   died
d.   =   daughter
s.   =   son
unm   =   unmarried
succ   =   succeeded
underlined   =   they had Tacks in Islay

Campbells of Skipness, Shawfield and Islay

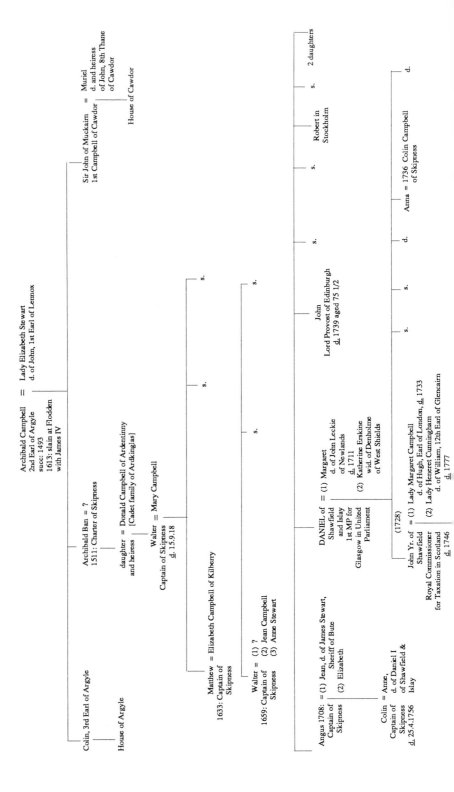

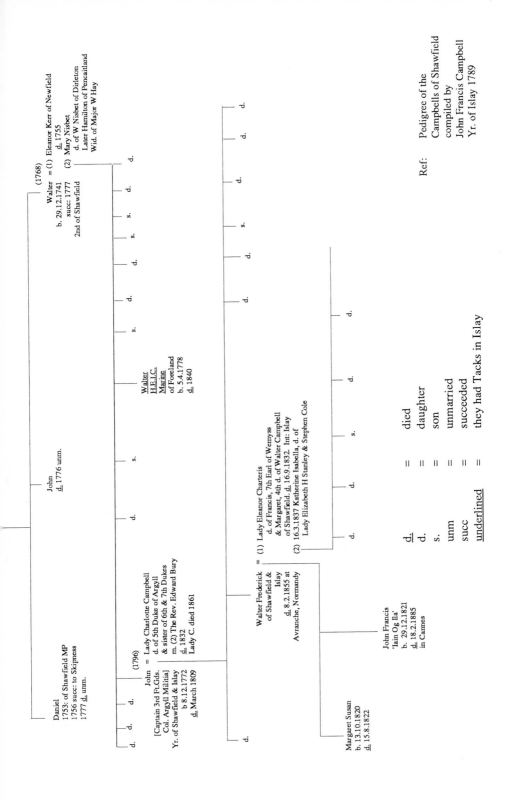

Walter = (1) Eleanor Kerr of Newfield
b. 29.12.1741   d. 1755
succ: 1777   (2) Mary Nisbet
2nd of Shawfield   d. of W Nisbet of Dirleton
        Later Hamilton of Pencaitland
        Wid. of Major W Hay

(1768)

John
d. 1776 unm.

Daniel
1753: of Shawfield MP
1756 succ: to Skipness
1777 d. unm.

John = Lady Charlotte Campbell
[Captain 3rd Ft.Gds.
Col. Argyll Militia]
Yr. of Shawfield & Islay
b 8.12.1772
d. March 1809
    d. of 5th Duke of Argyll
    & sister of 6th & 7th Dukes
    m. (2) The Rev. Edward Bury
    d. 1832
    Lady C. died 1861

(1796)

Walter
H.E.I.C.
Marine
of Foreland
b. 5.4.1778
d. 1840

Walter Frederick
of Shawfield &
Islay
d. 8.2.1855 at
Avranche, Normandy
= (1) Lady Eleanor Charteris
d. of Francis, 7th Earl of Wemyss
& Margaret, 4th d. of Walter Campbell
of Shawfield. d. 16.9.1832. Int: Islay
(2) 16.3.1837 Katherine Isabella, d. of
Lady Elizabeth H Stanley & Stephen Cole

John Francis
'Iain Og Ila'
b. 29.12.1821
d. 18.2.1885
in Cannes

Margaret Susan
b. 13.10.1820
d. 15.8.1822

d. = died
d. = daughter
s. = son
unm = unmarried
succ = succeeded
underlined = they had Tacks in Islay

Ref: Pedigree of the
        Campbells of Shawfield
        compiled by
        John Francis Campbell
        Yr. of Islay 1789

... ... by John Bearhor
... Kirkmenn, Hugh Lesley at Coltown
Donald MacLellan at Ballinaby
Archibald and Neil Smiths at ...
and Rogan MacIntyre at Sunderlow
£50 ——— The Marches between Ban
and Storgaig to be settled ——— Enquire of
... MacGibbon if the Offer Mann Campbell ...
Barichlay kept any promise from my Brother
of a House or farm ——— The Marches between
... and Trachkelts to be settled — also
... of Kinnoakleroch ——— is any ...
of Ballakotregin not let; Donald McGowan
... possessor wants a two pence land
of it ——— James Campbell widow of Alex
... in Ballachroach went to a farm
... Tennants in the whole Estate to be ...
... duely warned, they in Ballavan
be warned directly ——— Neil Anderson
... three others in Tormaxatte want a
... in hand of ...